Magic Guidebooks
Walt Disney World
2020

Insider Secrets, FastPass+ Hacks, Disney Dining Guide,
Tips for the Magic Kingdom, Epcot, Disney's Hollywood Studios,
Disney's Animal Planet, Disney Springs,
Hidden Mickeys, Universal Studios Orlando & More!

Magic Guidebooks
Walt Disney World 2020

- Covers the entire Walt Disney World Resort including the Magic Kingdom, Epcot, Disney's Hollywood Studios, Disney's Animal Kingdom, Disney Springs, and more!

- A complete Star Wars: Galaxy's Edge guide with reviews and tips for visiting Disney's largest expansion

- Easy FastPass+ strategies and line-skipping hacks

- Discover the BEST food with unbiased restaurant coverage, delicious fan-favorite menu choices, and a review of the Disney Dining Plan

- Must-know tips for visiting with kids, tweens, teens, and even Disney World fun just for adults!

- Event recommendations and tips for Disney After Hours, Early Morning Magic, Halloween, Holiday, Epcot's Food & Wine, & more!

- Money and time-saving tactics for worry-free planning

- Explore secrets, histories, and magical details found around the Walt Disney World Resort—including lists of Hidden Mickeys!

- BONUS: Guide to Universal Studios Orlando!

Table of Contents

CHAPTER TWELVE

CHAPTER THIRTEEN

CHAPTER FOURTEEN

CHAPTER FIFTEEN

GET UPDATES!

Sign up for our FREE e-mail list!

www.magicguidebooks.com/signup
(We promise no spam!)

Wishing you a magical vacation!
Magic Guidebooks

INTRODUCTION

ABOUT THIS GUIDE

When writing and designing this book, we had *you* in mind. Maybe you're a first-time visitor to the Walt Disney World Resort, or perhaps you've frequented it for many years. Wherever you come from and whatever your experience, we wanted to provide a complete guide from start to finish, while giving a critique of the attractions and restaurants in the resort. In fact, the entire purpose of this guide is to give real advice covering the many attractions, restaurants, and hotels from the Disney World Resort and beyond.

Who are we? Well, we're theme park enthusiasts who spend a lot of time gathering first-hand knowledge and experiences from all around the world. In fact, we've visited every single Disney Resort, including the new Shanghai Disneyland, because we love them so much. In other words, advice in this guide is crafted from trial and error—and we're passing the fruits of our hard work onto you!

The Walt Disney World Resort is a constantly changing place. From exciting themed dining to limited-time thrilling attractions, sometimes we can never imagine what might be coming next! Since experiences come and go, we also invite you to subscribe to our free e-mail list for up-to-date travel information.

Keep in mind that this guide is an "unofficial edition," meaning that we are not sponsored or employees of the Walt Disney Company, the Disneyland Resort, or the Walt Disney World Resort, and nor have we ever been. We are simply fans of the Walt Disney World Resort who are giving an honest opinion on what it has to offer!

FOR DISNEY WORLD NEWBIES

If you've never been to the Walt Disney World Resort (WDW) before, this book is perfect for you! We've crammed our guide with tidbits about the best food, attraction recommendations, hotel pros/cons, and so much more. We'll fill you in on WDW lingo and history to what's coming next. In the end, you'll have the knowledge of a pro!

FOR RETURN VISITORS

The Walt Disney World Resort is a constantly changing place. From exciting themed dining to limited-time attractions, we can never imagine what might be coming next! If you haven't been to WDW in ten years, this guide is a great fit.

However, If you go every week, you probably won't learn much. That, of course, doesn't mean that you won't learn *anything*, but you're likely already a pro and a guide to a park that's basically your second home won't be much use. Still, if you're curious, we welcome you along for the ride!

A WORD FOR ALL

Since WDW updates so frequently that some of the items in this guide will change even weeks after its publication. Restaurants in Disney Springs might close, attractions may be re-themed, popular food items could become discontinued... To patch this, we send updates via our free e-mail newsletter to our readers. If you'd like to be updated, visit our website and sign up today: **www.magicguidebooks.com/list** (don't worry, we won't spam you). On our website, we also keep a list of ride and attraction refurbishments, so you'll learn which experiences might be unavailable during your vacation—check it out!

THE HISTORY

Four years after opening his iconic Disneyland Resort in Southern California, Walt Disney started a new dream: to create something bigger to enchant the globe. In essence, he wanted to build more than a *land*—Walt wanted a *world*!

In 1964, that dream was planted like a seed which would eventually grow into the massive, enchanting tree of reality. Originally nicknamed the covert "Florida Project," Disney secretively bought nearly 30,000 acres of marsh, swamps, and groves in central Florida. Unfortunately, the next year, Walt Disney passed away. Luckily for all of us, his brother, Roy, kept Walt's dream alive.

By 1969, the secret was out, and construction began on the Magic Kingdom, Florida's version of Disneyland. Orlando's massive 189-foot (56 meters) Cinderella Castle towers far beyond Disneyland's Sleeping Beauty Castle—which is only 77 feet (23 meters). In October of 1971, Walt Disney World opened its gates to visitors, bringing classic attractions like Peter Pan's Flight, "it's a small world," and the Jungle Cruise!

The flat, Floridian lands just outside of Orlando now had a center of magic for all to behold. It wouldn't be long before thousands of visitors turned into millions, making it the most successful theme park resort in history (and it still is today). Nearly 20 million people visit the Walt Disney World Resort annually to live the stories from classics like *Snow White and the Seven Dwarfs*, experience the frosty magic of *Frozen*, and to meet Mickey Mouse himself.

Disneyland fans will notice the wider streets of the Magic Kingdom and the spacious, interactive queues. Since it rains in Orlando more than Southern California, many of the queues are indoor and some of the classic rides have covers, like the Mad Tea Party. Florida makes an ideal spot for the Walt Disney World Resort as there is plenty of space for dozens of Disney hotels, four world-class theme parks, a shopping center, water parks, golf courses — the list goes on seemingly forever! With warm weather nearly year-round, it's the ideal destination for vacationers of all ages to experience the massive, endless magic that Walt Disney has brought to the world.

Soon after the construction of The Magic Kingdom, Walt Disney World continued its mission to become the massive theme park resort that it is today by adding the futuristic Epcot (which stands for Experimental Prototype Community of Tomorrow) in 1982, followed by MGM Studios (now called Disney's Hollywood Studios) in 1989, and Disney's Animal Kingdom in 1998. Walt Disney World also has two themed water parks, Disney's Typhoon Lagoon (opened in 1989) and Disney's Blizzard Beach (opened in 1995). There is also a downtown shopping area known as Disney Springs, a boardwalk, the ESPN Wide World of Sports Complex, and an NBA Experience.

THEME PARK BREAKDOWN

Magic Kingdom
This is Walt Disney World's most crowded theme park. During the holidays and weekends, this park is a crowd favorite and draws the most visitors. In fact, the Magic Kingdom pulls in roughly 20 million visitors a year, doubling the number of guests for Disney's Animal Kingdom.

Epcot
Built over a decade after the Magic Kingdom in 1982, Epcot is one of Walt Disney World's most iconic parks. With a world travel theme and a massive, golf ball-looking centerpiece, Epcot brings in over 11 million visitors annually. Epcot is popular for its food and unique attractions like Soarin' Around the World and the new Frozen Ever After ride. Epcot picks up at night with locals looking to drink along its beautiful lake.

Disney's Hollywood Studios
WDW never quite hit its expectations with its movie-themed park, Hollywood Studios. The new additions of Toy Story Land (2018) and Star Wars: Galaxy's Edge (2019) should see this park's attendance drastically increase. Hollywood Studios is home to thrilling attractions like the Twilight Zone Tower of Terror and the Rock 'n' Roller Coaster Starring Aerosmith! Hollywood Studios is a favorite of those looking for rides that make you scream!

Disney's Animal Kingdom
With popular rides like Expedition Everest, stunning shows, and beautiful exotic animals, Animal Kingdom is the third most popular destination (but nearly tied with Hollywood Studios). The newest expansion, Pandora—The World of Avatar, cost $400 million to build and is one of the most popular areas in all of WDW! Animal Kingdom is perfect all ages—especially animal lovers!

The Waterparks

Disney also offers two world-class water parks at its Walt Disney World Resort. Typhoon Lagoon is a thrilling shipwreck-themed oasis where islands filled with waterslides bring the fun! Meanwhile, Blizzard Beach brings a frosty look to Florida's warm weather. Built like a ski lodge, Blizzard Beach offers loads of fun down slopes of waterslides and wave pools.

Universal Orlando
Separate from Disney World are 3 stunning theme parks in the heart of Orlando. Universal Studios, Islands of Adventure, and Volcano Bay are theme parks based around the cinema magic from Harry Potter and Despicable Me to Transformers and Jurassic Park. We cover these parks with tips, tricks, and travel plans near the end of this guide.

THE DISNEY WAY

The Walt Disney World Resort prides itself for being "show ready"—meaning that the attractions and experiences are all part of a believable, functioning show. Every piece of Disney World is treated like an on-going theatrical production and run like a well-oiled machine. The idea is that the storytelling is convincing and surprising to all guests. After all, you're paying a ticket price to visit a place that feels like magic.

Another facet of Disney's "show ready" concept is a spotless stage. The Walt Disney World Resort is immaculately clean. This means that you're never too far from a trash or recycle bin (they're practically everywhere). These receptacles are decorated to fit within the lands and are frequently emptied by custodial staff. The janitors in the theme parks are also part of the show. You might catch them greeting guests and painting Disney characters on sidewalks with their brooms and a bucket of water!

In the event that an attraction doesn't feel show ready, Disney will pull the plug. A single, flickering lightbulb on a ride could force the attraction to close until it's show ready again. If you've ever visited another theme park and spotted dirty restrooms, piles of trash, and graffiti, Walt Disney World will feel like a breath of fresh air.

WHY DO I NEED A GUIDE?

While you can visit the Walt Disney World Resort any time and attempt to experience it on your own, having invaluable tips from insiders will make all the difference. This guide will save you time waiting in lines, money, and give you the best options to fit your mood.

Truthfully, you'd need to stay an entire month (or more) to do everything in Walt Disney World—it's *that* massive. Think of it as a playground for the whole family, where you'll feel safe, accommodated, and in awe as you make your adventure through the Magic Kingdom and beyond. As there is so much to do in Disney World, people often wonder: where do I start? Where should I stay? How long should I stay? Is this going to cost me an arm and a leg? That's where we come in! At Magic Guidebooks, we absolutely love the Disney theme parks. We visit all of the time and know the ins and outs of theme park travel. Not only can our insider know-how help make your vacation more enjoyable, but we can also save you time waiting in lines and money on travel, tickets, and hotels. We also recommend the best of where to eat, how to get from place to place, and where to stay.

So, how do we do it? Why is this guide important? We're glad that you asked! As you read this guidebook, we'll show you all of the tips, tricks, and secrets to maximize your vacation! We've done Disney World on the cheap and never felt like we were uncomfortably frugal. With careful planning and our help, you can have the time of your life with your family and build everlasting memories!

WHAT TO EXPECT

Orlando, Florida is an ideal location for the Walt Disney World Resort because of its year-long sunshine. Likely, as your plane lands or car or bus arrives, you'll see the sun shining with white tufts of cottony clouds. Many times, especially in the late afternoon, it'll be cloudy and gray for an hour or so. Thunderstorms, especially in the summer months, will sweep by and leave as quickly as they came. It's not uncommon for it to rain each day at the WDW Resort, but, fortunately, it doesn't last for long. Meanwhile, half of the year in Florida, the humidity is high, sometimes 100% saturating the air. It can feel a bit stifling, but the Resorts and Parks know this. Air conditioning pumps in every car, Hotel, and indoor ride to help you enjoy your stay.

If you're flying into Orlando International Airport and staying at the Disney World Resort, you'll arrive at your hotel via Disney's Magical Express. This is a complimentary Disney charter bus with comfortable seats, air conditioning, and cartoons playing on several television screens. After a stop or two at other hotels, you'll be at your new home.

The MagicBands feel like gifts that Disney provides to its guests staying at the Resort. These are light, waterproof bracelets that you customize on the internet before your stay. These special bands are your room key, your ticket into the Parks, and a payment method. If you've checked in ahead of time, you can continue directly to your room without stopping at the front desk. Disney delivers your bags from the luggage pickup at the airport within an hour after your arrival. Soon you'll be at the Parks or the pool, enjoying your stay.

The Parks are massive and filled with people ready to enjoy Walt Disney World. You'll see visitors from all over the world. The magic of Disney overtakes them, and they instantly act happier. Walt Disney World is a different place, and while it's not cheap, it gives you countless memories for your dollar!

The employees of Walt Disney World are also generally friendly and have been properly coached to show you a good time. They keep the Parks and Hotels especially clean, setting the WDW Resort apart from the typical feel of a carnival or other theme parks. You and your family or group will feel safe and welcome everywhere you go. There are several delicious items to eat throughout the Resort, as well as picturesque scenes that come to life before your eyes.

WHY IS DISNEY WORLD SO EXPENSIVE?

It's no secret that Walt Disney World tickets, hotel rooms, dining, and merchandise cost a pretty penny. Alright, it's more than a pretty penny; Disney World is expensive! A bottle of soda costs around $4-$5 and one meal for a family of four can easily exceed $100. Disney claims that it raises prices to help with guest flow. Popular dates, like weekends, have higher prices than a Tuesday or Wednesday. We've been a little skeptical of this claim in the past (is Disney just being greedy?), but recently the crowds have thinned on typically popular days. Even traditionally busy summer months like June, July, and August have dwindled in attendance. Instead, guests are visiting during the fall and spring to save money on vacation. Families can often save *hundreds* of dollars just by booking on a less expensive date versus a holiday weekend.

Parents who want to experience Disney magic with their kids often save for years before booking. We understand the worry that your trip could break the bank—or become a total bust with a high price tag. Thus, we've created this guide to plan your Disney World trip with ease—and save some money along the way. Keep in mind that Walt Disney World isn't just any set of amusement parks. This is a world-class, premium resort. Yet, there are several tricks, discounts, and tips you'll want to pick up from this guide before you go.

DISNEY WORLD LINGO

If you are new to the Disney theme parks or just haven't been in some time, you'll instantly notice the vibrant lingo that arises at the resort. Most of the time these come from well-seasoned guests and Disney employees—known as Cast Members. Sometimes they will say something like "Snow White is a classic dark ride" and if you're not up on the knowledge, you might feel lost at the start. Whether you're talking to a fellow guest, Cast Member, or reading signs by the rides, it helps to know the terms first.

We also have our own terms that we frequently use throughout this book. They are fairly intuitive, but just so that we are all on the same page (yay book puns!), we invite you to familiarize yourself with this section to help with reading this guide.

THE LINGO

The Walt Disney World Resort
The area that encompasses all of Disney's theme parks (Magic Kingdom, Epcot, Disney's Hollywood Studios, Disney's Animal Kingdom, and the water parks), the Walt Disney World hotels, the Disney Springs shopping area, parking lots, and more. We may also abbreviate Walt Disney World to, simply, WDW.

Cast Member
A term for all Disney employees. They often wear themed costumes when they work in the Resort, but the behind-the-scenes employees will typically wear business casual clothing or engineering jumpers.

MagicBand
This amazing (and stylish) piece of technology allows WDW hotel guests to do it all with a simple bracelet. The MagicBand allows you to unlock the door of your hotel room, it's your ticket into the theme parks, your FastPass+ authorization, and you can make purchases with it!

Park Hopper

A ticket that allows you to visit multiple parks, as many times as you'd like during that day. You can purchase Park Hopper tickets for WDW that will allow you to hop between the four theme parks, while others allow you to visit the water parks in addition to the theme parks.

FastPass+

Said "Fast Pass Plus", it's an easy and free way to cut the lines! FastPass is your way to pre-reserving your tickets online up to 60 days before your vacation begins. The "Plus" comes from the adopted system of being able to swipe your MagicBand to activate your FastPass. It's *very* cool!

Single Rider Line

A fast way to get on the rides as long as you don't mind riding by yourself.

Passholders

A nickname for those who purchased Annual Passes.

3D

The use of 3D glasses during the ride or attraction.

4D

The use of 3D glasses with added effects like splashing water and rumbling seats.

PhotoPass and Memory Maker

A paid Disney service to have professional photographers take your picture around the WDW Resort. We *highly* recommend adding this feature so that you can download quality photos on your mobile device or home computer!

My Disney Experience

WDW's stunning app that works with your phone or tablet. You can change FastPass+ reservation times, schedule and check dining reservations, see line wait times, and much more!

Extra Magic Hours

Special extended hours for WDW Resort Hotel guests. These either grant entry the parks early or for staying after they are closed to continue enjoying the attractions. These hours change daily, so check the WDW website to view the times.

"Dark Ride"

An indoor ride where the vehicle is guided along a track. Typically, these are family-friendly rides like "it's a small world," and they also have air conditioning to escape the heat on hot days!

Disney Dining Plan

Pre-purchased meal plans to select eateries around the Walt Disney World Resort.

Animatronic

Robotics brought to life for music and narration, typically used in stage shows and rides.

Closed for Refurbishment

No one likes seeing this sign as it means that the ride is closed for restoration. Some refurbishments can last a couple of days, while others have lasted years. Refurbishment scheduling occurs most in the off-season months like January through March.

We keep an updated list of closed attraction and their opening dates on our website. Check it out:

www.magicguidebooks.com/waltdisneyworld

LINGO FOR THIS GUIDEBOOK

Magic Tips

These are special tips and secrets to enhance your vacation! Magic Tips are designed to:

- Save time waiting in lines
- Get the best viewing areas for shows and parades
- Save money booking and *a lot* more!

RIDE LEVELS

Everyone

Perfect for anyone of all ages.

Family

Suited for anyone of all ages, both kids and adults. However, these rides may not interest Thrill Riders.

Young Kids
Children 2-5.

Kids
Children ages 6-9.

Tweens
Children ages 10-12.

Teens
Young people ages 13-17.

Adults
People ages 18 and older.

Thrill Riders
Those looking for the maximum thrill from attractions. Whether it's a ride with loops like the Rock 'n' Rollercoaster or the high-dropping Tower of Terror, we guide you to the biggest thrills of the WDW Resort!

RESOURCES

DISCOUNT BOOKING WEBSITES

DisneyRewards.com
If you have a Disney Visa® Card, earn points and claim special rewards.

Orbitz.com/deals
For special promotions (look for codes up to 15% Off hotels).

Bookit.com/coupon-codes
Search here for discounts on flights, hotels, and ticket bundles.

Amextravel.com
If you have an American Express Card, this can save you, plus earn more rewards.

CONTACT INFORMATION

The following are official contact channels for the Walt Disney World Resort. We recommend booking online instead of calling because wait times can be long with WDW (and often the automated phone line doesn't tell you how long the wait will be). Also, while Cast Members are very friendly, courteous, and knowledgeable, they sometimes are pushy with sales over the phone!

General
Visit for booking and reservations.
www.WaltDisneyWorld.com

Hotel Reservations (407) 939-1936
https://disneyworld.disney.go.com/resorts

Disney Dining (714) 781-DINE
Book your restaurant reservations in advance.
https://disneyworld.disney.go.com/dining

Ticket Booking (407) 939-7679
Book your tickets in advance.
https://disneyworld.disney.go.com/tickets
Existing Tickets: (407) 939-7523

Group Reservations (407) 939-1942
For 10 or more guests.
https://disneyworld.disney.go.com/tickets

Annual Passholders (407) 560-7277
https://disneyworld.disney.go.com/passes

Help
with My Disney Experience, MagicBands, and FastPass+
(407) 939-4357

CHAPTER ONE

WHAT'S NEW IN 2020

INTRODUCTION

After the highly anticipated opening of Star Wars: Galaxy's Edge in 2019, the Walt Disney World Resort isn't stopping with its world class entertainment offerings. Several attractions are opening at Epcot and Hollywood Studios in 2020, making this an exciting time to visit!

NEW ATTRACTIONS

EPCOT UPDATES
Epcot
Opening Date: January 2020
Several new shows are opening in Epcot at the start of the year. A "Beauty and the Beast Sing-Along" film will open in the France pavilion, rotating throughout the day with *Impressions de France*. Canada Far and Wide is a new Circle-Vision 360 show in the Canada pavilion and Wondrous China will also open in the China pavilion.

REMY'S RATATOUILLE ADVENTURE
Epcot
Opening Date: Summer 2020
The France pavilion will host an amazing Disney dark ride styled after Pixar's *Ratatouille*. Based on the ride originally opened in Disneyland Paris, guests will

23

shrink down to the size of a rat and dash through a kitchen!

HARMONIOUS
Epcot
Opening Date: Likely Fall 2020
A new nighttime spectacular taking place in the World Showcase Lagoon. This will be a permanent replacement for Epcot Forever. Expect water features with projections, special effects, a beautiful soundtrack, and plenty of Disney characters.

MICKEY AND MINNIE'S RUNAWAY RAILWAY
Disney's Hollywood Studios
Opening Date: Likely Spring 2020
This attraction was originally set to open in 2019, but production delays (and likely the construction of Star Wars: Galaxy's Edge) pushed the opening date back to 2020. Using advanced projection mapping, silly animation, and 2 1/2-D effects, this is the first ride based around Mickey and Minnie Mouse!

MORE EXPERIENCES

RUNDISNEY
Every year, Disney organizes marathon events at their theme park resorts around the world. With over 150,000 runners in more than two dozen running events, runDisney has quickly become a phenomenon. Throughout 2020, Walt Disney World will host several runDisney events. For more information and to sign up, visit: www.rundisney.com.

New dining spots, shows, and other attractions will debut in 2020 at the Walt Disney World Resort! We detail these in the coming chapters.

PLANNING YOUR WALT DISNEY WORLD VACATION

PLANNING WHEN TO VISIT

Wanting to go to Walt Disney World is easy—planning *when* to go can be a whole other animal! As we've said before, there's *so* much to do at WDW that it can feel impossible to wrap your mind around the seemingly limitless possibilities. We completely understand your headache! Depending on the dates you choose, whether it's the Awaken Your Summer events, the Halloween themes in the fall, the Food and Wine Festival at Epcot, or Disney's holiday events, there are several unique attractions in store. In short, whether you have a set of dates in mind or you're looking for the best times to go—we're here to help.

We've picked up TONS of useful tips for you during our vacations, our friends' vacations, and by talking to the Cast Members. In this chapter, we will walk you through the choices of travel and our recommendations for saving time and money. Choosing a time for your vacation may not be entirely up to you. It could depend on your work schedule, your travel schedule, or your children's vacation days from school. Whether you have flexible travel days or not, we have laid out a month-by-month breakdown of what to expect when you visit WDW. We also give you tips on how to avoid the long lines and save time to make your stay a magical one!

MOST-RECOMMENDED MONTHS

1. September

Summer continues throughout September in Central Florida. Expect hot days and far less crowds than in June, July, and August. Halloween decorations will spread throughout the Magic Kingdom most of the month. Mickey's Not-So-Scary Halloween Party also premieres. While the weekends can get a bit packed, the weekdays have the thinnest crowds.

2. February

The WDW Resort typically has fewer crowds at this time, though weekends can be busier. Still, we find that this is one of the better months if you are looking for cooler weather and thinner crowds.

3. October

Though Halloween has become one of the busier times to visit, the experiences and weather still make it a great bet. The WDW parks continue to come alive during Halloween with typically perfect weather. Decorations, desserts, special rides, and Mickey's Not-So-Scary Halloween Party await you! Like in September, the weekdays are the best time to book your reservations to avoid the local crowds who come for the Halloween décor (especially at the Magic Kingdom). Expect warm, humid weather for most of the month.

LEAST-RECOMMENDED MONTHS

1. December

While park guests are treated to the holiday decorations, treats, and special rides, the crowds are some of the most massive. If you must go in December, we recommend the first week.

2. **July**

   Massive crowds from all over the world flood the Walt Disney World Resort. Expect long lines, and the hottest, most humid weather of the year.

3. **August**

   Similar to July, summer crowds and hot weather make this month one of the most miserable times to visit. August crowds die down in the last two weeks of the month when children go back to school.

Note: Are you planning your visit during one of our least recommended travel dates? Don't worry! This guide will help you avoid those long lines. Be sure to follow one of our pre-planned attraction lists—we use them ourselves and they can save you hours of time waiting in lines—or avoid them altogether. Tips for beating the crowds are at the end of this chapter.

MORE DATES TO CONSIDER

Holidays

Holidays can feel quite bustling when throngs of people escape the cold and head to the warmth of Florida. Here are a list of days you might want to consider avoiding:

- Christmas (all week)
- New Year's (all week)
- Thanksgiving (all week)
- Easter (all week)
- The 4th of July (all week)
- Memorial Day weekend
- Labor Day weekend
- Martin Luther King Jr. weekend
- Presidents' Day weekend
- Columbus Day
- Veterans Day weekend
- Mother's Day
- Father's Day (even more crowed than Mother's Day)

Weekdays

This might not seem like much of a secret, but weekdays are the best times to plan trips to the more popular parks like the Magic

Kingdom and Disney's Animal Kingdom. If you must go on a weekend date, we would recommend saving Hollywood Studios and Epcot for those dates, since those parks don't attract as many visitors.

Marathons
Many vacation planners wouldn't normally consider running a marathons as part of their vacation. However, *run*Disney is an awesome event (with an extra fee) for runners to marathon around the resort. Though these take place in the early hours on the weekend, the crowds flock to the parks afterward. Sometimes guests will stay for a few days after the run, making it extra crowded on dates you might not otherwise think would be packed.

RunDisney.com has released the dates:
- Jan 8-12, 2020: Walt Disney World Marathon Weekend
- Feb 20-23, 2020: Disney Princess Half Marathon Weekend
- Apr 16-19, 2020: Star Wars Rival Run Half Marathon
- TBA November 2020: Wine & Dine Half Marathon

Considering running?
Visit www.runDisney.com for more details.

DAILY CROWDS

Monday
Often these can be just as crowded as Sundays because people take off extra days to avoid weekend traffic. On Monday holidays, expect very larger crowds.

Tuesday
Typically has the fewest crowds during the week.

Wednesday
Typically has second fewest crowds.

Thursday
Third most recommended day for thinner crowds.

Friday
Less busy in the morning, but busiest in the evening after school is out for the Annual Passholders.

Saturday
The busiest day at the resort.

Sunday
Weekend crowds, but far less than Saturday. Sundays are especially busy on holiday weekends.

Holidays
It's best to avoid the busy holidays and three-day weekends (Friday through Tuesday) as they get very busy.

MOST CROWDED DAYS

1.   Christmas Day (and week)
2.   New Year's Eve/Day
3.   Thanksgiving week
4.   Veterans Day
5.   Memorial Day weekend
6.   Fourth of July
7.   Labor Day weekend

· **Magic Tips** ·

We gathered our crowd information from inside sources and our own observations and calculations. Some crowd measurements can be seen via the Walt Disney World mobile app when looking at ride wait times. Keep in mind that this data can be faulty as the app isn't always accurate and hourly ride capacity can change depending on how many vehicles Disney runs at a time.

A better way to check for crowds is via Walt Disney World's pricing calendar. Daily ticket costs will be higher on more crowded days and lower on less crowded days. Visit the Disney World ticketing website to see for yourself: **disneyworld.com/tickets**

MONTH BREAKDOWN

JANUARY

Overview: January is busy in the first week, and generally less busy after that. This week will be crowded from and filled with holiday rides, treats, music, and decorations lighting the resort. Holiday rides continue through the first week of January.

Weather: Mid-70°F (mid-20°C) during the day and chilly at night (sometimes in the 40°'s F / 4-9° C). The humidity is low.

Least Crowded Days: The last week in January

Most Crowded: The first two weeks (especially around New Year's) and Martin Luther King Jr. Weekend (Friday through Monday). January 8-12, 2020 for the Walt Disney World Marathon Weekend.

SPECIAL EVENT: NEW YEARS EVE

December 31st

New Years is a popular—and crowded—event widely celebrated around Walt Disney World. The Magic Kingdom and Epcot display fireworks at midnight. Hollywood Studios keeps a dance party going until 1AM. Due to sleeping creatures, Animal Kingdom does not organize a New Years Eve celebration and will close earlier than midnight. If you wish to escape the crowds, head to the Beach Club Resort or Polynesian Resort and watch the fireworks from the beach area. These spots become crowded, but getting in and out of the hotels is much easier there than at the theme parks.

      For those looking for an upscale event, Disney's Contemporary Resort hosts an annual New Years Eve party in their Fantasia ballroom. There's live music, gourmet food, and champagne. Just before midnight, guests head outside to watch the fireworks from The Magic Kingdom. Tickets are about $275 each and adults must be 21 years or older to drink with a valid ID. While adults attend the party, kids can enjoy the Pixar Play Zone on NYE. Reservations should be made in advance for both. Book online at **www.waltdisneyworld.com**.

FEBRUARY

Overview: Possibly the least crowded month to visit WDW. Like January, the weather is cooler, and some of the rides may be closed for refurbishment.

Weather: Mid-70°F (mid-20°C) during the day and chilly at night (low 50°'s F / 10-12°C). Also expect far less humidity than in the summer and fall. The humidity is low.

Least Crowded Days: Any week except near Presidents' Day Weekend (Friday through Monday)

Most Crowded: President's Day Weekend (Friday through Monday). February 20-23, 2020: Disney Princess Half Marathon.

Mardi Gras: WDW will hold a Mardi Gras event on February 13th, 2018. Expect to see celebrations and delicious New Orleans food at the Magic Kingdom, Disney Springs, and Disney's Port Orleans Hotel.

SPECIAL EVENT:
EPCOT INTERNATIONAL FESTIVAL OF THE ARTS
January 17 - February 24, 2020
From music to specialty dishes, Epcot's Festival of the Arts takes you on a virtual journey around the world to celebrate a variety of cultures. Look for fantastic chalk drawings on the streets, living statues (street performers dressed as metal statues), nighttime concerts, delicious treats, and more! Festival of the Arts is highly rated by guests and we recommend checking it out!

· Magic Tips ·
For parts of January through March, Typhoon Lagoon and/ or Blizzard Beach may be closed for refurbishment. Park hours may also be shorter after the holidays, so we recommend an early arrival to get everything done.

MARCH

Overview: March's popularity has increased recently as spring breaks spread throughout the month. If you visit in March, be sure to do so during the week, Tuesday through Thursday.

Weather: mid-70°F (21°C) during the day and chilly at night. March has been known to have occasional heatwaves, bringing the weather above 90°F (32°C). The humidity is medium.

Least Crowded Days: the first Tuesday, Wednesday, and Thursday of March.

Most Crowded: Last two weeks of the month.

ST. PATRICK'S DAY

On March 17th, come in green to the WDW resort for some fun, Irish treats:

1. Green beer cider at the United Kingdom Pavilion in Epcot.
2. Chocolate Mint Cupcakes, apparel, and other treats sold at various carts throughout the Resort theme parks.
3. Head to the Irish pub, Raglan Road in Disney Springs, for some live music, beer, and traditional food.

SPECIAL EVENT:
EPCOT FLOWER AND GARDEN FESTIVAL
March 4 - June 1, 2020
Every spring, Epcot hosts the unforgettable International Flower and Garden Festival. Sample delicious treats from around the world while you walk the park and spot floral topiaries made into classic and new Disney characters. Also feed butterflies, walk fields of flowers, and break near pop-up play areas for the kids! This festival comes with your Epcot ticket cost, however, sampling most of the food and drink costs extra.

APRIL

Overview: With spring breaks continuing through April, the end of the month tends to be the least crowded. We love visiting in April because the weather feels a lot more manageable (though it may not be very ideal for the water parks). Also there usually isn't very much humidity in the air. Lately, WDW has been more crowded in April. We believe that this is because of schools changing their spring break schedules.

Weather: Low-80°F (25-28°C) during the day and cooler at night (mid-60°F / 15-19°C). The humidity is medium.

Least Crowded Days: The last two weeks of the month.

Most Crowded: First two weeks of the month. April 16-19, 2020 for the Star Wars Rival Run Weekend.

SPECIAL EVENT: EASTER
Sunday, April 12, 2020
See a special Easter parade at the Magic Kingdom. Rare characters and the Easter bunny make appearances in this color daytime parade.

MAY

Overview: Spring at WDW is beautiful and it will feel like the Floridian summer has begun. Storms tend to pick up during this time and it might rain during the day for an hour or so. The rain consists of short showers, so it shouldn't put a damper on your vacation.
Weather: Mid-70°F (21°C) during the day and sometimes chilly at night. The humidity is medium/high.
Least Crowded Days: The first two weeks of the month.
Most crowded: Memorial Day weekend (Friday through Tuesday).

JUNE

Overview: The warm June weather perfectly suits the Walt Disney World Resort. The first two weeks of June are the least crowded until schools release mid-June and the summer crowds begin.
Weather: Mid-80°F (27°C) during the day. Typically keeps warm at night. The humidity is medium/high.
Least crowded days: Tuesday, Wednesdays, and Thursdays and the first week of the month.
Most crowded: The last week of the month.

Events: *Sounds Like Summer Concert Series* – Bands and musicians take over Epcot's World Showcase as they perform covers of your favorite songs and tributes to your favorite artists.

JULY

Overview: The weather heats up (often, unbearably so) and crowds from all over the world venture into the WDW Resort during July. Though July is crowded, it does make a great opportunity to visit the water parks and ride the many water-themed attractions, like Splash Mountain, throughout the parks.

Weather: Low-90°F (32-34 °C) during the day, but the humidity can make July feel even warmer. The weather typically stays warm and humid at night. The humidity is high.

Least Crowded Days: Tuesday, Wednesdays, and Thursdays (unless one is July 4th).

Most Crowded: July 4th

Events:

• *Sounds Like Summer Concert Series* – Bands and musicians take over Epcot's World Showcase through the middle of July. See June for more details.

• *Fourth of July "Concert in the Sky"* – Stunning nighttime fireworks all around the Magic Kingdom.

AUGUST

Overview: Just when you think Florida couldn't get any hotter than in July, August comes around. This is most likely the hottest month all year round. The weather continues to blaze in August as crowds continue to pour in until school begins around the middle of the month. August rarely feels as crowded to us as July does, so if you want to get away during the summer, this is the month to pick.

Weather: Mid-90°F (32°C) during the day with usually near 100% humidity. Nights are sometimes just as warm and balmy. Showers typically occur once a day for an hour or two, but the queues for most rides have coverings. The humidity is very high.

Least Crowded Days: Tuesday, Wednesdays, and Thursdays and the last two weeks of the month.

Most Crowded: The first 2 weeks of the month.

SPECIAL EVENT:
EPCOT INTERNATIONAL FOOD AND WINE FESTIVAL
End of August through Mid-November
Every fall, Epcot hosts the wildly popular International Food and Wine Festival. Taste foreign delights from around the world while you walk the park. With 30 kiosks of food and drink to fill your curiosity, adults will especially love Epcot's Food & Wine!

Eat to the Beat is another great seasonal attraction that takes place during Epcot's Food & Wine. See popular singers and bands perform their hits in World Showcase. Best of all, these concerts are free! Concert lineups are usually announced in the spring. For the best seats, book an Eat to the Beat dining package at select restaurants.
More information and booking: www.epcotfoodandwine.com

SEPTEMBER

Overview: More hot weather typically all month long with Halloween rides and treats beginning mid-September. See October for Halloween details

Weather: High-90°F (32°C) during the day. Typically keeps very warm at night. The humidity is very high.

Least Crowded Days: Tuesday, Wednesdays, Thursdays, and Fridays (except for Mickey's Halloween Party nights)

Most Crowded: Labor Day weekend.

OCTOBER

Overview: October is a favorite time of ours at the WDW Resort! The weather cools down (though it can still feel like summer) as the Halloween party kicks into full gear.

Weather: High-80°F (29-31°C) during the day, cools a bit at night. The later you go in October, the more likely tropical storms can come into play. If you are planning a visit, we recommend somewhere in the first couple of weeks. The humidity is very high.

Least Crowded Days: Tuesday, Wednesdays, and Thursdays

Most Crowded: Halloween and Mickey's Not-So-Scary Halloween Party on select dates.

SPECIAL EVENT:
HALLOWEEN AT THE MAGIC KINGDOM
End of August - October 31, 2020

Mickey's Halloween party begins in the Magic Kingdom! A perfect time to dress in costume (all ages) and snag some treats. Many adults love visiting as much as the kids because they can finally wear their costumes into the park (Disney has a ban on anyone over 13 from entering the park dressed as a character for safety reasons). You must purchase a separate ticket for this event (usually starting around $80 each). See WaltDisneyWorld.com for dates as they are usually not released until Spring.

MICKEY'S NOT-SO-SCARY HALLOWEEN PARTY REVIEW

Join Mickey, Minnie, Donald, Goofy, and the rest of their friends as you trick or treat around the park, see a Halloween parade, meet rare costumed characters, and end it all with a nighttime fireworks display starring Jack Skellington from *The Nightmare Before Christmas*. This Halloween party isn't necessarily scary, but there is a fun spookiness to it. Villains like Maleficent and Gaston appear to relish in the wicked affair. We love Mickey's Not-So-Scary Halloween Party because it's a time when guest of all ages can dress in costume and see some unique lighting around the Magic Kingdom.

The event is a lot of fun—and *very* popular. Expect tickets to sellout for dates around Halloween. Whether or not the event reaches capacity, you'll likely face heavy crowds for the Halloween parade and fireworks (though attraction wait times tend to remain low). Buy in advance because Disney limits the tickets—hence the extra cost of $80+ per person.

> **· Magic Tips ·**
> Most families opt to see the early parades and other shows. To avoid these crowds, start your night with the fireworks and then see the later parade and other nighttime shows!

NOT-SO-SCARY HALLOWEEN ATTRACTIONS

- **Hocus Pocus, Parade, and Fireworks –** During Mickey's Not-So-Scary Halloween Party, Disney Villains take over the Magic Kingdom from Maleficent to the Sanderson Sisters. You'll also see Mickey's Boo-to-You Halloween Parade led by the Headless

Horseman! The night concludes with stunning Halloween-themed, Not-So-Spooky Spectacular fireworks!

- **Halloween Décor** – See Mickey-shaped pumpkins, try delicious treats, and see your favorite characters dressed in their Halloween costumes!
- **Halloween Dining** – The Be Our Guest restaurant, Cinderella's Royal Table, and Crystal Palace host special dining events for Halloween. Enter one of these dining areas for a Halloween-themed dining experience.
- **Halloween Attraction Overlays** – During the Halloween Party, ride Space Mountain in complete darkness, see live actors on Pirates of the Caribbean, and hear an eerie new tune on the Mad Tea Party.
- **Cruella's Hide-a-Way** – An extra-paid event at Tony's Town Square Restaurant with treats, wine and beer (for guests 21+), and the chance to hang with Cruella De Vil! You'll also have exclusive viewing of Mickey's Boo-to-You Halloween Parade and the fireworks.

NOVEMBER

Overview: The holidays begin mid-November at the WDW Resort. Expect larger crowds beginning Veterans Day and onward.
See December for WDW Holiday details.
Weather: High-70°F during the day, cools at night to High-50°F. The humidity is medium.
Least Crowded Days: The first week of the month.
Most Crowded: Veteran's Day weekend and Thanksgiving week. The first weekend of the month for the marathon.

SPECIAL EVENT: THANKSGIVING AT WALT DISNEY WORLD
November 26, 2020
Thanksgiving is a busy day at WDW, but there are plenty of places to enjoy a delicious turkey dinner—and many other Thanksgiving favorites! Restaurants all over WDW offer fine meals, including:

> **Magic Kingdom** – Liberty Tree Tavern.
> **Epcot** – Akershus Royal Banquet Hall, Biergarten, Coral Reef, Le Cellier Steakhouse, Restaurant Marrakesh, Rose & Crown, Sunshine Seasons.
> **Disney's Hollywood Studios** – 50's Prime Time Café
> **Disney's Animal Kingdom** – Tusker House

Disney Springs – Raglan Road, Fulton's Crab House, Planet Hollywood, Portobello

Resort Hotel Dining:

- Disney's All-Star Sports – End Zone Food Court
- Disney's Animal Kingdom Lodge – Jiko, Sanaa
- Disney's Beach Club – Cape May Café
- Disney's Boardwalk Resort – Flying Fish Café, Trattoria al Forno
- Disney's Caribbean Beach Resort – Sebastian's Bistro
- Disney's Contemporary Resort – California Grill, Chef Mickey's, The Wave
- Disney's Fort Wilderness Resort – Mickey's Backyard Thanksgiving Feast, Trail's End Restaurant
- Disney's Grand Floridian – Citricos, Grand Floridian Café, Narcoossee's, Victoria and Albert's
- Disney's Old Key West Resort – Olivia's
- Disney's Polynesian Resort – Kona Café
- Disney's Port Orleans Resort – Boatwright's Dining Hall (Riverside)
- Disney's Saratoga Springs Resort – The Turf Club Bar & Grill
- Walt Disney World Dolphin and Swan Hotels – Garden Grove, Fresh Mediterranean Market, Il Mulino, Todd English's Bluezoo
- Disney's Wilderness Lodge – Artist Point, Whispering Canyon Café
- • Disney's Yacht Club – Yachtsman Steakhouse

DECEMBER

Overview: The holidays are in full gear at the WDW Resort. See decorations all around with special treats, fun holiday-themed rides, and a chance to meet Santa Claus!

Weather: Low-70°F (21-23 °C) during the day, cools at night to Low-50°F (10-12°C). The humidity is low.

Least Crowded Days: The first week of the month.

Most Crowded: The last two weeks, especially Christmas Day and New Year's Eve.

HOLIDAY

Holiday attractions at Walt Disney World mostly focus on the Christmas holiday. See glittering lights dazzling Cinderella Castle, Toy Story Land, and the Hollywood Tower Hotel! From magnificent Christmas trees to endless strings of ornaments, you'll be in awe of the holiday transformation around the resort.

Note: The holiday events at Walt Disney World run from mid-November through the first week of January.

MICKEY'S VERY MERRY CHRISTMAS PARTY

Select Dates in November and December

Mickey and his friends (including Santa!) bring their Christmas spirit to the Magic Kingdom park with special costumes, shows, fireworks, and even snow! Like Mickey's Halloween event, this is a night with a separate admission cost. Though Disney specifically uses the word "holiday" to describe many of its attractions, this event is mostly centered on Christmas traditions. Upon arriving, you'll receive an event map with character spots, locations for complimentary sweets, and special attraction times.

Several exclusive holiday-themed attractions are designated for this event. The Once Upon a Christmastime Parade, Minnie's Wonderful Christmastime Fireworks Show, and A Frozen Holiday Wish dazzle the night with winter magic. Best of all, you only need to show up 5-10 minutes early for a great spot. Other attractions including Space Mountain, the Mad Tea Party, and the Tomorrowland Speedway may also have Christmas overlays with music and added lighting. These attraction overlays cannot be experienced during normal park hours.

> **· Magic Tips ·**
>
> There are fewer crowds during Mickey's Very Merry Christmas Party in contrast with the daytime. If you're visiting during the busier dates closer to Thanksgiving or Christmas, you may want to purchase a ticket to this party to save on wait times. Unfortunately, FastPass+ selections aren't available, but they are rarely needed. We don't recommend using this time for very popular rides like Peter

Pan and the Seven Dwarfs Mine Train as these attraction tend to have long lines during the event.

TONY'S MERRIEST TOWN SQUARE PARTY

This event is an add-on ticket for Mickey's Very Merry Christmas Party. Tony's Town Square Restaurant serves appetizers, sweets, and drinks for all guests (including alcoholic beverages for adults 21 and older). These are gourmet treats including meat and cheese boards and hand-decorated Christmas sweets. Guests also have premium views of the parade. However, at about $100 a ticket (on top of your Christmas Party admission), you'd have to eat a lot of cheese to make up for the cost.

HOLIDAYS IN THE THEME PARKS

MAGIC KINGDOM

The Magic Kingdom has the most celebrations and decorations for the holiday season. Nightly, Cinderella Castle dazzles with white and blue holiday lights! There are also themed attractions, shows, and plenty of holiday treats to enjoy around the park.

- **Jingle Cruise** – The Jungle Cruise gets a Christmas makeover with holiday humor and decorations around the riverboat ride.
- **A Christmas Fantasy Parade** – Mickey, Santa, and Disney Princesses celebrate Christmas aboard stunning floats.
- **Meet Santa Claus** – and greet Mickey and his friends in their holiday clothing!

· **Magic Tips** ·
Santa Claus also shows up at Disney Springs for photo opportunities with guests!

EPCOT

From stunning fireworks displays at night to the holiday traditions of Epcot's 11 countries, you'll feel the magic of the holidays! There is also a Candlelight Processional with a massive orchestra and choir. Holidays Around the World celebrates global winter traditions at each of the World Showcase pavilions. Tour around to taste the delicious holiday cuisine of nearly a dozen countries!

HOLLYWOOD STUDIOS

If you're visiting WDW during the holiday season, you'll want to add a night at Hollywood Studios to your list! With a nighttime show, "Jingle Bell, Jingle BAM!" and the new "Sunset Seasons Greetings" there is plenty of Christmas spirit at the park! Toy Story Land also lights up with special decorations and picturesque moments that look fantastic at night.

- **Jingle Bell, Jingle BAM!** (Hollywood Studios) – See a stunning Christmas fireworks and projection show on the Chinese Theatre. Show times are usually around 8PM, so get there 20-30 minutes early for a better spot!
- **Sunset Seasons Greetings** (Hollywood Studios) – Mickey, Minnie, Olaf, and their friends celebrate Christmas on Sunset Blvd. See a wonderland of decorations and holiday projects on the Tower of Terror!
- **Toy Story Land Holiday** (Hollywood Studios) – Andy's toys come to life to bring Christmas cheer! Expect unique decorations and a jolly song on Alien Swirling Saucers.

ANIMAL KINGDOM

Animal Kingdom celebrates holidays from around the world with artisan crafts on Discovery Isle. At night, the lanterns around the park glow with festive colors. Projections on the Tree of Life also star illuminated animals with wintery magic. In Pandora, the humans have lightly decorated spots with tinsel and small ordainments from their worldly celebrations.

- **UP! A Great Bird Holiday** – Holiday cheer comes to Animal Kingdom in this unique and charming stage show starring Pixar's UP! characters and real-life birds!

HOLIDAY DINING EVENTS

Nearly every Resort Hotel dining features holiday treats from Mickey caramel apples to holiday macaroons. With Christmas décor all around, the holidays are a treat for your sights and your taste! Epcot's Promenade Refreshments hosts annual Christmas quick-service savory treats like a turkey sweet potato waffle, holiday teas, hot chocolates, and ciders.

TIPS TO BEAT CROWDS

1. **Use FastPass+** – Book your FastPass+ selections As early as possible (beginning 60 days ahead of your reservation), get passes to the rides that you want to experience.

2. **Be Early** – Get to the park at opening before the crowds. If you are staying at a Walt Disney World Resort hotel you can get "Extra Magic Hours" which allow you to arrive early (or stay late) on selected days. Check the WDW website for hours: https://disneyworld.disney.go.com/calendars

3. **Plan Your Day** – Follow one of our pre-set day plans (or make your own). We use these planners ourselves and it will save you hours of time waiting in lines (many times you'll miss the long lines altogether).

4. **Book Dining Reservations Early** – We can't stress this enough. Many of the more popular restaurants will be booked full, like the Beauty and the Beast Be Our Guest dining experience in the Magic Kingdom. Luckily, WDW allows you to book your reservations 180 days in advance!
    Book Early: https://disneyworld.disney.go.com/dining or call (407) 939-3463

5. **Avoid Typical Meal Times** – If you don't have a restaurant reservation, the times to avoid would be:
    Lunch: Dine before 11.30am and after 2.30pm
    Dinner: Dine before 5.00pm and after 7.30pm

6. **Plan Your Parks** – We recommend avoiding the Magic Kingdom and Epcot on the weekends as they often pull the most crowds. Instead, head over to Animal Kingdom or Hollywood Studios. If you can, it's best to save the Magic Kingdom and Epcot for the weekdays. Watch out for Mondays at the Magic Kingdom as these can often be busier than the weekends. Since so many people know to avoid the weekends at this park, they tend to save it for a weekday when it's believed that no one will be there. Magic Kingdom is less busy usually Tuesday through Thursday.

7. **Book a Night Party** – Mickey's Not-So-Scary Halloween Party, Mickey's Very Merry Christmas Party, and Disney's After Hours parties are great ways to enjoy the parks with far less crowds. These evening, extra-paid events cost a little less than a typical daytime ticket and have limited late-night hours. However, the sparse crowds, unique entertainment, and sometimes complimentary snacks are well worth the cost!

8. **You Might Have to Wait** – Waiting in line isn't the end of the world. Sometimes we all have to do it for the best attractions. The trick is to wait the *shortest* amount of time for the *fewest* rides possible. You can avoid the longest lines by following our planned out ride lists.

9. **Avoid Extra Magic Hours** – Extra Magic Hours attract huge crowds of guests staying at Walt Disney World Resorts. If you are not staying at a resort hotel, you might want to avoid the park with Extra Magic Hours, as you won't be able to experience the attractions until the regular park hours begin.

· **Magic Tips** ·
Guests staying on hotel property should take advantage of Extra Magic Hours and then park hop for another destination. This way you avoid the influx of guests after regular park hours become available. Parks without Extra Magic Hours also tend to be less crowded.

10. **Take a Break** – If you are feeling worn out, take a break at your hotel or visit Disney Springs for some shopping. If you're not near your resort hotel, head to the nearest one for dinner or to look around. The WDW Resort offers so many surprises that you might have a blast drinking a cup of coffee while you listen to music near Starbucks rather than surrounded by a swarm of people. After you and your group have recharged, take a free bus back into the parks.

DISNEY MOBILE APPS

WALT DISNEY WORLD APP

We highly recommend downloading the Walt Disney World application on your phone or tablet (also known as My Disney Experience). Walt Disney World's official mobile application works on most Apple and Android devices and can save you a lot of hassle while planning your visit.

You can do the following with the application:

1. Purchase park tickets and use them while at the Resort.
2. View wait times for attractions at every park.
3. Book and manage your FastPass+ selections for your entire group.
4. Reserve Disney Dining around the Resort.
5. Mobile Order food at several locations.
6. Resort hotel details and check-in.
7. View park hours, schedules, and your pre-selected vacation plans.
8. View and download PhotoPass images
9. Buy or upgrade to an Annual Passport.

Disney is always adding features to improve its application. Keep in mind that this app may drain your battery and does need a cellular or Wi-Fi connection to work. We recommend bringing a pocket phone charger and having a data plan to support your needs. Disney also offers free Wi-Fi throughout the theme parks and Resort hotels. You can access the Wi-Fi widely in the Resort.

PLAY DISNEY APP

Play Disney is a free mobile application to play games around the theme park. This app is available to download on the Apple and Android mobile market places as a complimentary entertainment piece. Simply download, create an account, and start playing! The app works especially well with features in Star Wars: Galaxy's Edge.

    It was inevitable that guests would stare at their phones while waiting in lines, so Disney designed a free mobile app to use for this specific purpose. Play Disney immerses visitors in games and other added magic designed for all ages. Some of these fun experiences include trivia, music, and collectables!

Overall, Play Disney will score better with kids and tweens as the cartoonish appearance of the app seems catered to them. Teens and adults might enjoy the trivia which can be challenging at times. Play Disney is also better in small groups as the competition can heat up to see who scores the highest.

If you're planning on trying Play Disney, we recommend downloading the app before you leave home, that way you don't have to worry about poor connectivity or waiting to download a large file. The application is also a bit of a battery drainer, so make sure to pack a portable charger!

Some of the experiences can only be played while physically in the queue for a ride. For example, Space Mountain Rocket Race is a competitive mini game designed for 2-5 players, and will only open once your phone recognizes that you are near Space Mountain in Tomorrowland. However, some other experiences, like listening to music from around the park and Disney Parks Trivia, can be played anywhere—including home! Getting acquainted with the application and its features before you arrive will help with the fun of using it at the theme parks.

· **Magic Tips** ·

The Play Disney app also accesses attractions at Disney's Art of Animation Resort. If you're interested in the experiences there, you'll need to be on site. We recommend taking a Disney Skyliner Gondola to Art of Animation before playing!

BOOKING YOUR TRIP

INTRODUCTION

If you've never been to Walt Disney World, booking a vacation to the Resort can feel overwhelming. While booking websites are extremely helpful, they don't give you a feel of what it's like to stay there or visit the parks firsthand. There are dozens of choices in and out of the Resort, and they all seem to be fun and full of magic. The earlier you can begin planning your Walt Disney World vacation, the better. We recommend at least 6-8 months ahead of your trip in order to book the hotel and dining reservations. Keep in mind that dining can be booked up to 180 days in advance and FastPass+ reservations can be booked 60 days ahead if you're staying at a Walt Disney World resort property (30 days if you are not).

If you're planning last-minute, there are several ways that you can save on booking a hotel. Depending on your plans, personality, and needs, some of the Resort Hotels will fit you better than others—that's where this chapter comes into play. Here, we outline how to save yourself money when booking so that you can pick your favorite hotel with ease (Chapter 13 covers hotels). You also might be wondering which park to check out and which ones you could afford to skip. If you are planning a week-long visit, we highly recommend getting a park hopper ticket so that you can visit any location when you want (more on that later).

Here is a breakdown of the Theme Parks we recommend, in order:

1. **The Magic Kingdom** – It's very similar to Disneyland in California, but it's the world's most visited theme park for a reason. With more attractions than anyone can experience in a single day, this is the classic resort location for anyone looking to have a magical time.

2. **Disney's Animal Kingdom** – If theme parks are your thing, there's nothing like Animal Kingdom. It's over 500 acres of rides, lush foliage, and exotic animals. Also, the Pandora—World of Avatar section is stunning and great fun to explore.

3. **Disney's Hollywood Studios** – With the addition of Star Wars: Galaxy's Edge and Toy Story Land, Hollywood Studios has become a prime destination at Walt Disney World. There are dozens of attractions from stunning shows starring the characters from *Beauty and the Beast* to thrilling rides like The Twilight Zone Tower of Terror and the Rock 'n' Rollercoaster. Nothing will blow your mind more than the immersive galaxy of *Star Wars* brought to life in this epic, real-life adventure!

4. **Epcot** – Though we've placed Epcot last, it shouldn't be forgotten. The 21+ crowd will love this theme park for its food and adult beverages, while kids will be entranced by its unique rides from the thrilling Test Track to the magical Frozen Ever After.

5. **The Water Parks** – We love Disney's creatively designed water parks. In contrast with the other theme parks, Disney's Typhoon Lagoon and Blizzard Beach can't compare. If you are deciding which of the two water parks to visit, we recommend Typhoon Lagoon since the attractions are generally in more variety. However, if you're staying at a hotel with a waterslide, you may have just as much fun relaxing there without the extra cost and travel time.

TIPS BEFORE YOU BOOK

PRE-BOOK YOUR HOTEL

The further out you book your vacation, the less expensive it tends to be. This is almost always true with flights, but the car rentals and hotels sometimes have better deals that fluctuate. If you are booking with the WDW Resort, they give you lots of wiggle room. You can change your bookings to add more dates or completely change your hotel just days before your travel dates. If the price changes or you cancel, you may have to pay a fee (usually around $50 for each package).

FLY INTO ORLANDO INTERNATIONAL AIRPORT

If you are planning to fly, we recommend Orlando International because it tends to be the least expensive and easiest to travel from. The airport is located right next to highways that will take you to WDW. We review more of that in the next chapter.

BUNDLE FOR BIGGER SAVINGS

Sometimes purchasing a flight/hotel/car package from WaltDisneyWorld.com or a third party travel website can save you a lot of money. If you collect points with airlines like Southwest or Alaska, you can get even better points with the bundle.

KNOW THE TICKET PRICE STRUCTURE

Park tickets vary in pricing for each day, sort of like a hotel or airline. If you book on a crowded day like a holiday weekend, the price will be more than if you book on a Tuesday or Wednesday outside of the busy season. Tickets are typically less expensive Monday through Thursday outside of summer and holiday.

GETTING THE BEST TICKET PRICE

Ticket prices decrease per day the more dates you visit. For example, a 2-day ticket could cost $101 per day, but a 5-day ticket could cost $78 per day. For this reason, sometimes it could save to book an extra day. It's best to play with ticket prices on WaltDisneyWorld.com before purchasing to score the best deal.

Tickets also have expiration dates depending on your number of days. This means that if your vacation lasts a week, but you only purchase a 4-Day ticket, you can space out your theme park visits over the course of a week.

FLEXIBLE DATE TICKETS

If you need more flexibility, the Flexible Dates add-on is about $20-$30 a day and allows tickets to be used any day before the end of the year (though they expire 14 days after the first use). Ticket terms may change, so always check the fine print.

TICKET EXPIRATION CHART

Number of Ticket Days	Number of Days Expired After Selected Start Date
1	Expires day of selection
2	4 days
3	5 days
4	7 days
5	8 days
6	9 days
7	10 days
8	12 days
9	13 days
10	14 days

PARK HOPPER TICKETS

If you want to visit two or more theme parks in a single day, a Park Hopper ticket is the ideal upgrade. Park Hoppers are an extra $50 - $60 for a single day (the pricing goes down with multi-day purchases). We highly recommend the Park Hopper option no matter your length

of stay. Since the Parks stay open later, you can take a break in the middle and head out at night to Epcot or the Magic Kingdom for more fun. Park Hoppers can also include the water parks for an additional cost that is usually a very good deal. For an extra $50 for a single day, you'll be able to go back and forth between both parks as much as you'd like.

DISCOUNTED TICKET OFFERS

Walt Disney World occasionally offers multi-day tickets at a discounted price. These deals occur seasonally when crowd levels and vacation package booking are at a low.

To get updated on these discounted offers, subscribe to our free e-mail newsletter: **www.magicguidebooks.com/signup**

· **Magic Tips** ·

Unless you plan on bouncing around parks, you may want to consider a **1 Park Per Day** ticket. For most guests who want to take in all of the magic of the theme parks during their visit, this ticket offer makes the most sense. It can also save a family of four *hundreds* of dollars compared to the Park Hopper option.

UK TICKET OFFERS

Disney has special offers for guests visiting from the United Kingdom. From a dedicated website, UK residents can book flight, hotel, and ticket bundles as well as access exclusive deals! The 14-Day Ultimate Ticket allows for park hopping at a heavily discounted price. Each year, Disney rolls out early free dining bundles for residents of the UK: **https://www.disneyholidays.co.uk/**

MEMORY MAKER

Disney PhotoPass is a fantastic way to save digital versions of your vacation photos taken by resort-wide photographers. Several key spots are located around the resort including in front of the Epcot Spaceship Earth ball, Cinderella Castle at Magic Kingdom, and character meets! Some rides like Tower of Terror and Seven Dwarfs Mine Train have special videos that automatically sync to your Memory Maker when you have a MagicBand! Saving photos and videos onto your device is easily done through the Walt Disney World app. You'll only need one Memory Maker for your party and buying ahead saves about $30 (typical price is $199).

DISCOUNT HOTELS

There are many ways to save on booking your stay. Some are better than others depending on the offer. Here are our most recommended choices based on how much they can save you:

BOOKIT.COM (877-742-9891)
highly recommended!
BookIt is a little-known travel website with some big discounts. It's ideal for discounted packages that include flights, hotels, and ticket options. While BookIt isn't *always* the best deal, we often unbeatable prices on here.

PROS
1. Payment plans available with no credit check.
2. Big discounts on flights when you book a vacation package.
3. We notice that Bookit.com has a different selection of available hotel rooms than other third party site.
4. WDW Resort Hotels available—and get all of the benefits including MagicBands and Extra Magic Hours, including bookings through third-party sites.
5. Lists WDW's "Good Neighbor Hotels" so you can see the closest hotels for what Disney recommends.

6. Bundle park tickets for discounts. Save on multiday park hopper tickets and tickets to other parks including Universal Studios Orlando and Islands of Adventure.
7. Discounted car rental options and inexpensive travel insurance available.

CONS

1. When you just book a hotel without airfare, this website can sometimes be more expensive than other third parties.
2. Some of the better deals cannot be cancelled.
3. Often cancellation comes with a fee. Many other companies offer free cancellation without this fee.

DISCOUNT CODES

Get limited-time deals on vacation packages: **www.bookit.com/ coupon-codes**

WALTDISNEYWORLD.COM (407-939-1936)

Disney's home website is the only place to get a "Magic Your Way" package where you can bundle a resort hotel, park tickets, and a Disney Dining Package. When WaltDisneyWorld.com has hotel sales, usually the third-party websites will as well—but not always. WaltDisneyWorld.com often has the most variety of room choices, but rarely discount tickets. At times, there may be a 1-park per-day discounted deal for multi-day tickets. These promotions aren't guaranteed and are often for off-season booking only.

Since discounted one-day theme park tickets are nearly impossible to find (sometimes you can save a few bucks a ticket through discounted sites), we recommend booking a hotel room with a third party website and your tickets through WaltDisneyWorld.com.

Summer Time (June – August) and Fall (September – October) typically have the lowest fares. WDW will offer discounts even for Spring and Winter getaways. Look for deals when booking on the website. Check the website for discounts on hotels and more. Here you can book any of the Resort hotels, purchase Theme Park tickets, and add features like Disney Memory Maker.

SPECIAL DISCOUNTS

Always check this link before booking to see if you're getting the best deal. This link provides discounts for Military, Group, and more: https://disneyworld.disney.go.com/special-offers

> **· Magic Tips ·**
> Sometimes the best deals come from using multiple sites. Try booking your hotel with Orbitz and your flight with an airline like Southwest or Alaska.

THE BEST WALTDISNEYWORLD.COM DEAL

The best promotion for WDW's website is the Free Dining Offer. The deal usually arrives in the spring (typically Mid-April) and is available for dates August through December. To qualify for this discount, you often must book a select, full-price WDW resort hotel and park hopper ticket package for each traveling member. In turn, you'll receive Disney Dining for free for each night of your stay per person. We've done the math and this deal can save you hundreds of dollars —if not thousands—during your stay! This deal is popular and reservations go quickly for the more popular resort hotels like Disney's Beach Club and Disney's Yacht Club.

PROS

1. For most packages, only $200.00 down is required to book. The balance is due around 30 days before your trip.
2. Larger selection of rooms that are not available on third-party sites (though the other way around can happen, too).
3. Bundle park tickets, dining packages, and features like Memory Maker.
4. You can add flights, transportation, character dining, and tickets to Theme Parks and Water Parks.
5. Often has flexible cancellation policies for full refunds.

CONS

1. The travel insurance is a lot pricier than most other sites.
2. Third party sites can generally save you more money.

ORBITZ.COM

highly recommended!
Get discounts on rooms for your vacation for hotels in and around WDW. We love Orbitz because you can often use their promo code to get a discount on many hotel rooms earn points that work like cash toward future bookings.

PROS

1. Option to pay in full upfront or at the checkin.

2. Big discounts on flights when you book a vacation package that includes a rental car.
3. Easy to use website with rewards program.
4. Promotional discount codes routinely available.

CONS
1. Some of the better deals cannot be cancelled.
2. Orbitz usually has limited availability of hotel rooms within Walt Disney World, so they often runout quickly.

Discount Codes: www.orbitz.com/deals

PRICELINE.COM
Great hotel selections and vacation packages on an easy to use site. It's hard to find promotional codes for Priceline, but they have great prices.
Sometimes third party websites will save you a bit on booking multi-day park hopper tickets, but not usually. There are some tricks to saving money and receiving extra perks like early park admission.

AAA, AMEX TRAVEL, ETC.:
There are almost countless other options. We've listed our favorites, but depending on your work discount or credit or club membership, you often can get discounted tickets. The best deals are typically a bundle of them together. Make sure that you check more than just one third-party site to ensure you are truly getting the best discount out there.

BOOKING MULTIPLE HOTELS
If you want to stay at multiple hotels during your stay, this is entirely possible. Disney can reconfigure your MagicBand per room reservation if you visit your hotel concierge before checkout. If both of your hotels are in the WDW Resort, tell bell services that you need your bags transferred to your new hotel. That way you can enjoy the parks and head to your new room afterward.

MAGICGUIDEBOOKS.COM
Our website announces the best deals on discounted tickets and vacation packages as they become available. Sign up for our free e-mail newsletter to get information on discounts directly to your inbox.

ANNUAL PASSPORTS

The Walt Disney World Resort offers several annual passes for its theme parks. Three of these passes are available to anyone, while the others are reserved for Florida Residents and Disney Vacation Club members. All passes are for ages 3 and up and include admission to all four theme parks, 20% off merchandise and dining, Disney PhotoPass (except water parks), plus complimentary parking and special passholder entrances into the theme parks.

While receiving the perks of an annual pass may seem tempting, the cost isn't always in your favor. Even if you visit WDW two consecutive weeks a year, Disney discounts multiway tickets and therefore, getting a Platinum pass won't make sense. A 10-day park hopper for an adult is about $500.00 versus an annual Platinum Pass starting around $850. If you visit two separate weeks a year, getting an annual pass could save you money.

DISNEY PLATINUM PLUS PASS
$1219 / $999 (Florida Residents & Disney Vacation Club)
Visit any park on any day, including the water parks. Also gives admission to Disney's Oak Trail Golf Course and the ESPN Wide World of Sports Complex. Visit any day of the year.

DISNEY PLATINUM PASS
$1,119 / $899 (Florida Residents & Disney Vacation Club)
Visit all 4 of the theme parks any day of the year, but *not* the water parks, golf course, or ESPN Sports Complex. Visit any day of the year.

WATER PARKS ANNUAL PASS
$139
Visit the water parks any day of the year (that they are open). Does not include any additional discounts or access to other theme parks.

DISNEY GOLD PASS
$699 (Florida Residents & Disney Vacation Club only)
Select blockout dates apply (around Holiday and Spring Break), but includes admission to the 4 theme parks.

FLORIDA RESIDENT PASSES

Disney offers several annual passes for Florida residents from weekday only to water park access after 2PM. There's also an Epcot After 4PM Pass for locals. Florida residents have monthly payment options without a credit check!

EVEN MORE BENEFITS

Free pins and collectable items are just some of the perks of having an Annual Pass. At times, Disney will also host special previews for new attractions, discounts on After Hours events, occasion "bring a friend" promotions, and lower costs on hotels.

For more AP information, details, and purchasing, visit:
https://disneyworld.disney.go.com/passes

· **Magic Tips** ·

If you visited the park and want to purchase an Annual Pass, you may use your park ticket toward the cost of your AP. Additionally, you may upgrade your Annual Pass to a higher tier at any time (this is at Disney's discretion).

SPECIAL EVENTS

AFTER HOURS EVENTS

If you want to visit Walt Disney World without the crowds, the After Hours Events are your best bet. Imagine being at the park with limited crowds, free snacks, and incredibly short wait times! This is exactly what you get with Disney's After Hours Events.

Magic Kingdom, Hollywood Studios, and Animal Kingdom throw these 3-hour events on select nights. Since space is limited, popular attractions like Toy Story Land and Pandora rides have very short wait times (usually 15 minutes or less). Tickets start at $139 (plus tax) per guest and come with complimentary ice cream, popcorn, and some beverages.

2020 MAGIC KINGDOM DATES
January 6, 13, 17, 20, 2020

2020 ANIMAL KINGDOM DATES
January 9, 16, 22, 30, 2020
February 6, 13, 19, 27, 2020
March 5, 12, 19, 26, 2020

Note: More dates will likely be added for Spring and Fall 2020.

EARLY MORNING MAGIC

Similar to the After Hours events, Magic Morning is an exclusive early event taking place before the parks open. These often are just 90-minutes, but come with breakfast. Prices start at $79 (plus tax) per guest.

Here are some tips for visiting during Early Morning Magic:

• Buy Ahead – This event is limited, so tickets could sell out.
• Get There Early – Guests who come early have been able to experience the attractions more frequently in the first 15 minutes.
• Wait to Eat – Everyone tends to eat at the start, but we recommend bringing a snack and eating after you've experienced the rides.

GO VIP

Walt Disney World offers several VIP tours to cut the lines, go behind the scenes, and see how some of the best dining experiences come to life. The 7-Hour Ultimate Day of Thrills VIP Tour starts at $349 per person and is offered on Monday, Tuesday, Fridays, and Saturdays starting at 8:30AM. You'll need a park hopper ticket for this amazing and unforgettable experience.

Want more exclusiveness and luxury? If you're visiting Walt Disney World—with $12,000 to spare—book the World of Dreams Ultimate VIP Tour. Essentially, Walt Disney World will grant you as many wishes as you want during this time. Cut the lines to the ride, enter Cinderella Castle's secret chambers, go behind the scenes in Star Wars: Galaxy's Edge and more! Disney VIP services are top-notch experiences with the best hosts in the world—so don't forget to tip!

DISNEY VACATION CLUB

For those wishing to visit Disney properties year after year, Disney Vacation Club (DVC) may be a right fit. We only briefly overview DVC because we feel that an entirely new book can be created based the ins and outs of this membership program. In short, Disney Vacation Club is a non-traditional timeshare. Members purchase points to use annually for stays at the Walt Disney World Resort, Disneyland Resort, Aulani in Hawaii, Disney Cruise Line and many other exciting Disney and non-Disney destinations around the world. Many people ask if DVC is worth purchasing.

THINGS TO CONSIDER BEFORE BUYING

1. It's not cheap. Disney is a premium company with premium prices, meaning that you will get the quality experience for the money that you pay. DVC points can cost over $200 each, and the lowest nightly hotel rates for 2020 are around 10 points.
2. How often do you plan to vacation at Walt Disney World? If you said every year or every other year, the DVC may be a great option that can save you money. It's more ideal if you can travel during the off-season (February or September) when hotels cost fewer points. The points also have a "use year" for when the month that they renew. You can bank your points up to one year and borrow from the next. For example, if your use year is in September, your new points will be available then. If you want your trip in July, you can borrow from the points that will be available in September and combine them with your current points. Disney may also allow you to "rent" some additional points for around $17 each if you don't have enough.
3. Points have home resorts, but they can be used at any DVC property. The benefit of a home resort is that you can book up to 11 months in advance there. For non-home resorts, you can book up to 7 months in advance.
4. The early bird gets the worm with DVC. Those who can plan 11 months ahead usually come out on top. They snag all of the best properties right away and leave everyone else with the scraps. Resorts like Old Key West and Saratoga Springs often have plenty of availability for last-minute decision makers—as long as those resorts fulfill their needs.

5. DVC has annual dues. The cost of these dues is per point and varies depending on which vacation property you purchase. These dues also go up every year.

6. Financing may be an affordable way to purchase, but it won't likely save you any money. Since DVC financing charges interest, it won't be a good deal in the end. The best way to purchase is upfront and in full.

7. The extra benefits aren't guaranteed. While Disney has amazing perks for members like discounted annual passes and free park nights like Moonlight Magic—where DVC members have exclusive access to a Disney theme park at no additional cost—these options don't always stick around. At one time, DVC offered discounted resort tickets—but not anymore. The only thing guaranteed is that your points won't lose value. Meaning, that if one hotel room price goes up a point, another one must go down a point.

8. Many times the DVC doesn't feel worth it until pricing goes up in a few years. This means that you may see a wash at first (or close to it), but when the prices for WDW resort hotels start to climb, and your DVC points buy the same, you'll be happy that you went there.

9. Buying resale may be cheaper, but you won't get the perks. Disney VISA cardholders and Disney annual passholders get many of the same perks including discounted dining and other deals.

10. Membership is limited. To keep the real estate at a specific value, only so many points can be sold per property. However, there may be a waitlist for a resort property of your choosing.

11. Disney has a first right of refusal for those selling their points. Since demand is so high, Disney may pay you for your points instead and resell them back to other members.

12. More resorts will be added in the future!

TIPS FOR PURCHASING DISNEY VACATION CLUB

1. If you want access to the membership perks of DVC, buy your first 100 points through Disney directly. As of now, this is the only way to get the extra benefits. Those who buy resale aren't privileged to a membership card that access the special events, discounts, and more. You can always purchase more points for cheaper through resale after your initial 100 and still keep your benefits.

2. If you're buying resale, we recommend that you haggle. Many sites like **www.dvcresalemarket.com** have listings with set

prices. However, saving $10 a point isn't a big enough deal to buy third party. Always try to negotiate.

3. Make sure you enjoy staying at your home resort. If you decide to purchase Saratoga Springs but always want to stay at the Beach Club Villas, you may be out of luck as Beach Club fills quickly. Disney's Beach Club is expensive and may not be worth buying. Not only are the points pricey, but so are the dues.

4. Disney will offer season deals such as bonus points or cash. These deals aren't always listed, so call for the benefits.

5. Again, any of the membership benefits may change at any time. So don't use them as a reason for purchasing. We anticipate the value of Disney Vacation Club to skyrocket in the coming years. As Disney increases the cost of points, new members are continuing to join.

· Magic Tips ·

Disney Vacation Club members receive several new benefits throughout the year from exclusive discounts to special access. DVC Members also get extra early access to events like Mickey's Not-So-Scary Halloween Party beginning at 2PM.

If you are interested in joining the Vacation Club, we highly recommend checking out one of their presentations at Old Key West during your visit.

Info: https://disneyvacationclub.disney.go.com

TRAVELING TO WALT DISNEY WORLD

INTRODUCTION

With the planning out of the way, it's time to bring your vacation to the Walt Disney World Resort. Getting there doesn't have to be tricky, but if you don't plan correctly, it might feel like a mess. Contrary to what many believe, WDW is not exactly the heart of Orlando, Florida. The Resort is located in Lake Buena Vista, Florida, which is about 20 miles southeast of the Orlando International Airport. It appears that most people who visit the Resort either drive or fly into Orlando International. If you have a family of three or more and live within a comfortable driving distance, then going by car might be your best bet. If you live on the other coast or the Midwest, driving might be a bit taxing. Thankfully, WDW has you covered no matter your form of transport. In fact, you can arrive at the Resort via bus, train, shuttle, or a taxi!

When we visit WDW, we typically fly into Orlando International (though we have driven there before). Flying is great because as soon as you arrive, there are plenty of options to get to your hotel. If you've booked a WDW Resort Hotel, Disney's Magical Express is a free bus service that takes you to your Hotel. We enjoy the Magical Express because it's located inside of the airport and the staff is extra friendly.

The Magical Express feels like any other bus, but it has its Disney touches with cartoons playing on small television screens. If you have kids, it's a great way to distract them as their excitement builds for the destination. The downside to the Magical Express is that you have to drop others off at their neighboring Resort hotels first. Sometimes this can be a little annoying, especially after a day of travel. For a free transport, it saves you a lot more than if you opted for a private shuttle or car. If you aren't staying at a WDW Resort Hotel, check with your hotel or vacation spot to see if they offer a shuttle. To better compete with Disney, they are often free. They tend to run less than the Magical Express, since those busses go all day and night.

Without Magical Express, we've use private car and rideshare apps (like Uber) to get to the WDW Resort. These are nice because the drivers tend to know the areas very well and they get you quickly to your hotel without stopping anywhere else. Typically, we've saved about 10-15 minutes in travel time. Expect to be charged anywhere from $30 or more each way. This is a standard price for these rideshare apps, and the private cars can cost up to $100. Whichever way you choose, we highly recommend planning ahead and having a back-up plan just in case. Taxis are always available in front of the airport to help get you to your destination. Just make sure to ask the driver if he or she has a flat fee. If you are driving yourself, the coastal routes are extremely scenic. We love driving up the middle and seeing Florida's flat, lush landscapes, many lakes, and wildlife along the route. By the time that you get to the Resort, you'll be ready to hit the pool for relaxing—or the bed for some much-needed sleep.

In this chapter, we review the several different methods of getting to the resort. How you get there is entirely up to you, but if you're feeling indecisive (or just need more information in order to choose), read thoroughly to get the best choices.

BY AIRLINE

If you aren't planning a road trip and live far away from the WDW Resort, flying will likely be your best option. While airlines can be expensive at times, there are several ways to save money:

- Compare airlines to see the best pricing.
- Check baggage fees and allowed carry-on items (we like Southwest because they give you 2 free checked bags). If you live on the east coast, Spirit Airlines is an à la carte option that can save you hundreds of dollars, especially on last-minute flights.
- Book early to get the best discounts.

OUR TOP CHOICE AIRLINES

SOUTHWEST

We love Southwest Airlines! If you grab their "Wanna Get Away" deals, you can score some great rates. Southwest works perfectly if you book ahead.If you are late to the game, they can get pretty pricey. Southwest's staff is friendly, the aircrafts are generally comfortable for long flights, they include snacks and soft drinks for free, and each passenger gets 2 free checked bags of luggage. This can be a *very* sweet deal if you plan on your Disney World vacation being longer than 5 days. This airline also does not charge for change fees, meaning, if you have to reschedule your flight for whatever reason, you can do so without charge during an allotted time period. Because Southwest offers first-come-first-served seating, we highly recommend paying the extra money to get the "Early Bird" option. This will allow everyone in your party to pick seats together for your flight. You can also ask any of their helpful flight attendants to assist with seating your family together, though it can't be guaranteed. Family boarding is called after the "A-list" section finds their seat (which is about one-third of the customers).

ALASKA

We also love Alaska. This is a great airline that is great with customer service. Book early enough and their rates are very affordable. Alaska gives you the free option to select your seat, but checked bags are often a moderately priced additional charge. They also offer free soft drinks and snacks for the flights. If you've never flown Alaska, we invite you to give them a try!

DELTA

Delta is a premium airline that excels in what it does. While it's not as innovative with its deals as Southwest, it does deliver fantastic flights and aircrafts. This is usually our third choice above other airlines like United or American because of its quality. Delta is often more expensive that Southwest or Alaska.

BUDGET AIRLINE OPTIONS

SPIRIT

This airline is *à-la-cart*, so the general price you see is just for a seat on the plane—everything else is an extra cost. The extra costs include: picking your own seat, checking a bag or putting a bag in the overhead compartment, drinks, and snacks. If you don't mind where you sit and only need to bring a personal item, Spirit can save you some big bucks. Once you pick a seat and opt to bring another bag (carry-on bags are also extra), the prices begin to stack. Also, Spirit Airlines doesn't have much of a customer service department in our opinion. We've had an issue with a delayed flight and no one was there to assist at the gate. We've had a good experience with them as well. Just understand that you usually get what you pay for and Spirit is no exception to that rule.

FRONTIER

Works similarly to Spirit and can get to be very pricey. We find that Spirit tends to have more comfortable seats than Frontier. If you're only on a two-hour flight or less, you may not mind.

FLYING INTO ORLANDO INTERNATIONAL

We recommend Orlando International because it tends to be the least expensive and easiest to travel from. The airport is located right next to the highways that will take you to the Walt Disney World Resort. This is also the airport where Disney's Magical Express is stationed.

DISNEY'S MAGICAL EXPRESS

If you've opted to fly into Orlando International and you're staying at Walt Disney World Resort, you can take the Magical Express coach from the airport to your hotel. The Magical Express is a bus with service on the baggage claim floor in the airport. To reserve your spot, you need to opt in when making your reservation, giving your flight times (you can also add this information later). During peak seasons, lines for the Magical Express can be long. Most of the time, you'll only wait about 15-30 minutes for your bus to arrive.

REASONS TO LOVE MAGICAL EXPRESS

1. It's complimentary with your WDW Resort booking.
2. The bus is efficient, air conditioned, entertaining (there are TVs with Disney programs!), and it doesn't cost the hefty fees of a taxi, Lyft/Uber, or rental car.
3. Before you arrive, Disney sends you free luggage tags with codes to your hotel (if you change hotels last minute, the tags still get to your hotel).
4. Conveniently located in the baggage claim area in the Orlando International Airport.
5. Comfortable charter bus seats.
6. Quick check-in using your MagicBand.
7. The bus has television screens that show fun things to do on your trip as well as Disney cartoons and quizzes.
8. Disney picks up your luggage for you at the airport and bell services deliver it straight to your hotel room.
9. The Magical Express drops your party off in front of your hotel lobby.
10. When you leave to return to the airport, the Magical Express will drop you off in the same location.

If you are flying with Alaska, American, Delta, JetBlue, Southwest, or United, most WDW hotels will allow you to drop off your luggage and print your tickets for you inside of the hotel. It's a fast and friendly service that takes a lot of the stress off of your departure. Keep in mind that the Magical Express picks up about 3 hours before your flight and that the Orlando International Airport lines can be long, including domestical.

> **· Magic Tips ·**
>
> Your bags will get to your room *after* you checkin (usually within an hour). Thus, we recommend bringing anything you might need with you to the hotel. This includes your MagicBand, which will be needed when you checkin at the Magical Express and hotel.

BY CAR

Whether you're on a road trip, staying in a neighboring city, or you live close enough to drive to the Resort, this can be a great method to take in the beautiful sights of Florida's wetlands before you head to the WDW Resort. If you're flying, then renting a car might be the best option. You won't have much of a need for a car if you are staying on the property. However, a trip to Universal Orlando or other attractions outside of Walt Disney World might be more cost effective if you have your own.

CAR RENTAL

We recommend Enterprise.com or Dollar.com for car rental as they typically have a great selection and the best pricing. Pre-booking before you arrive at the airport is advised.

- www.Enterprise.com – You can visit the company's website or see typically better deals on Priceline.com (or bundle with your airfare and hotel booking).
- www.Dollar.com – Click the "specials" tab for deals.
- www.Budget.com – Click the "deals" tab for offers.

PARKING

Theme Parks – Standard theme park parking costs $25 per day for a car or motorcycle and $30 per day for an oversized vehicle like an RV. Closer preferred parking can save up to 15 minutes in travel time into the parks and is $45-$50 per day (higher during summer, spring break, and holiday).

Water Parks – Typhoon Lagoon and Blizzard Beach offer complimentary parking.

Resort Hotels – Value resorts charge $15 per night, Moderate $20 per night, and Deluxe $25 per night.

Disability Parking – Closer parking spaces are available for those with disability parking permits all across the resort. Parking attendants will guide guests to disability parking spots.

· **Magic Tips** ·

If you are just planning on staying at the WDW Resort, we don't recommend a rental car. Parking can cost daily at certain Resort hotels (like the Walt Disney World Swan and Dolphin), and there are free transports around the Resort. If you plan on visiting Universal Studios or any other parts of Florida, it may be worth doing.

BY TRAIN

Taking the train can a be relaxing and beautiful way to travel to the Walt Disney World Resort. The trains let out at the Orlando Station (or Kissimmee) and you will need to have a second transport from the train station to the resort which is roughly 20 minutes away by car. We recommend renting a car for the best value. Taxis work great, too.

AMTRAK
www.Amtrak.com
Perfect for longer distances on a budget (and if you have the time to travel). Check the "Deals" tab for discounts on Amtrak's website.
There are a few great reasons to take the bus to the Walt Disney World Resort:

1. **Saves Money** – This is usually the top reason you might want to go with the bus. Airfare and the train can cost ten times the amount.
2. **It's Relaxing** – The bus can be a calming, easy way to travel from your home to WDW.
3. **A Discount** – Seniors and students can receive discounted rates on Greyhound.

BY BUS

We recommend Greyhound as our top pick for busses. They have a great reputation and are often the fastest way with the most options to get to Orlando. Keep in mind that the Orlando Bus Station is not near Orlando International or the Walt Disney World Resort. You'll need to take a private car into the Resort or to your hotel—and that might cost you a lot of money.

BY RIDESHARE APP

Ridesharing apps like Uber and Lyft make great choices for traveling during your vacation. Both of these services offer private drivers in clean cars (these are not cabs). Here are a few ways you can book:

UBER / LYFT MOBILE DEVICE APPS

To download one of these applications, open the App Store (Apple Devices) or Play Store (Android Devices) and search the application by its name. These applications will start you at approximately $35-$40 each way (depending on traffic). Lyft tends to be less expensive while Uber has a better selection of high-end cars and private options for a premium price.

DISCOUNT CODES

Uber: uber.com/promo
Lyft: www.lyft.com/promo-coupon-code-free-rides

The estimated ride-sharing costs are just that–estimations. The time of day and traffic does matter. In these apps, you can select an estimated fare by entering your destination. You don't have to tip on these apps and the drivers won't ask for one. However, you may leave an additional tip once the ride has completed.

BY TAXI

Hail a taxi in front of the airport and ask for a flat rate. The typical price is usually around $45 each way.

For a shuttle, we recommend Mears:
http://www.mearstransportation.com (they also have an app). They usually cost about $23 each way, per person. You can also pay up front for the round trip cost of $37 and they will pick you up from your hotel and return you to the airport at the end of your vacation.

Tip: It is customary to tip your cab driver 15–20%, depending on your experience with the drive.

Discount Code: WEB10 (to save 10%) with Mears

DISNEY TRANSPORT

If you are staying off of the Resort property and haven't elected to rent your own car, many hotels will offer a free or paid shuttle to the Walt Disney World Resort. Once inside of the Resort, Disney offers a free bus transport to the hotels, parks, and parking lots. These are clean, standard busses that run day and night. After 1AM, they will only run to the Disney World Hotels. Look for the Bus Stop signs outside of each Hotel, Theme Park, and Disney Springs. There are usually multiple locations outside of the gates from the Parks. The bus line you desire will have your location marked on the display in front of the bus. Sometimes you may have a stop or two before your destination.

We have a love/hate relationship with the WDW bus system. On one hand, it's free and has excellent air conditioning. On the other, it can feel crowded at times and slow to arrive. Sometimes you have to do a bit of walking to get to your stop. We much prefer using the boats and the monorail system when they are available because they are much more enjoyable to ride. WDW also offers free ferries between some of the parks and Disney Springs as well as a monorail system around the Magic Kingdom Park and Epcot, each with separate loops that connect near Disney's Polynesian Resort. The monorail takes you to Disney's Contemporary Resort, Disney's Grand Floridian, and Disney's Polynesian. The ferries travel to all of those locations with trips to many other resort hotels and to Disney Springs.

DISNEY SKYLINER GONDOLAS

This new gondola system connects several Resort hotels to Disney theme parks. These gondolas work very similarly to those at high-end ski resorts. A Disney feel with painted characters and music will play as you ride. This system will connect Disney's Art of Animation, Pop Century, Caribbean Beach Resort, and the new Riviera to Epcot and Hollywood Studios, emptying in front of the theme parks. The gondolas move at a moderate speed over land and water. While they aren't air conditioned, the cabins are designed with ventilation systems to keep them cool. Each gondola holds about ten guests and have benches for seating.

MINNIE VANS

Lyft and Disney have teamed up to create a unique on-demand transport within the Walt Disney World Resort! These polka dot vans look like Minnie Mouse's dress and use the Lyft application to order. The driver can also answer any questions you have about WDW during your ride. Rides range from about $25-$35 each way and the cars hold up to 6 passengers. Minnie Vans also drop off right in front of the theme parks, so if you're running late, this might be a great option instead of the bussing system. Minnie Vans will also take guests to Orlando International Airport.

CHAPTER FIVE

WHAT TO WEAR AND BRING

INTRODUCTION

Now that you've planned your vacation, it's time to figure out what to wear! Luckily, this part is easy (and to experienced theme park travelers, it's common knowledge). WDW is filled with people from all walks of life, style, and attitude. But everyone is there for the same reason: *to have fun*! The important thing is to be yourself! Here we explain how to maximize your fun through comfortable clothing and bringing the right items. Did you know that a bottle of water at the WDW Parks can cost $3 or more? Be aware that security will inspect your bags before you enter the parks. There also may be a metal detector. In this section, we review tips and tricks for a comfortable and cost-effective stay at the resort.

WHAT TO WEAR AND BRING

1. **Comfortable Clothing** – Shorts, t-shirts, sneakers (trainers), and tank tops are seen all around the Resort for a good reason: they are comfortable. You'll be standing in the hot (and often humid) Florida sun all day, so we recommend that you dress comfortably.

2. **Hats and Sunglasses** – Again, the Floridian sun! It's a wonderful thing, but you don't want to get burned. Be careful of hats and sunglasses on rides (most high-speed attractions will have a compartment on the ride to store your items).

3. **Sunscreen** – Even on a cloudy day the ultraviolet rays from the sun can give you an uncomfortable burn. Be careful and stay protected–you don't want to ruin your vacation by looking and feeling like a boiled lobster.

4. **Stroller** – Kids can get tired and WDW has zones to park these with attendants that watch them while you ride. You can bring your own or rent one at one of the parks. If you're worried that your child may be too tired to walk around all day, it's best to use caution and set aside extra cash for a stroller rental. For longer stays, the WDW Resort gives a bit of discount.

   Stroller Rental Cost:
   Single – $15 per day / $13 for multi-day
   Double Stroller – $31 per day / $27 for multi-day

   Disney Springs requires a $100 credit card deposit in addition to the daily cost. This is done for theft preventative reasons since anyone can walk in and out of Disney Springs and take the strollers they've rented.

5. **Jacket or Sweater** – Hot days the WDW Resort can become chilly nights. Therefore, we highly recommend bringing a jacket or sweater just in case.

6. **Water Bottles and Snacks** – You can save money (or help any picky eaters in your party) by bringing your own snacks. WDW will allow you to bring sealed bottles of water into the parks. Save yourself money and bring your own. If you don't mind fountain water, you can refill them at water fountains near any restroom for free.

7. **Hand Sanitizer** – Though we know that science tells us not to use hand sanitizer on a daily basis, it's virtually a must-have at the Parks. You'll likely touch handrails, seat cushions, and many other things that will require you to disinfect before eating.

8.   **Extra Phone Charger and Waterproof Cellphone Bag** – If you have a smartphone, we highly recommend an extra portable charger. We also recommend becoming familiar enough with your smartphone so that you can turn on the battery-saver mode in the settings. This will prevent you from running out of juice too early while you take pictures and use the Walt Disney World app. Also, if you plan on riding the water attractions like Splash Mountain or Kali River Rapids, you're likely to get soaked. The last thing you want is to accidentally drench your cellphone! We *highly* recommend the Frieq waterproof cellphone bags and we use them ourselves. They are often $9 or less and they come with a lanyard. The case is clear (so you can touch the screen and take photos). Since it's completely sealed, we've taken photos underwater and on the wettest rides without worrying about getting our phones drenched.

9.   **A Standard Backpack** – Carry your items in one of these. Make sure it's not too large to fit on the rides. Also keep in mind that your bag will be checked by security before entering the park area. If you don't feel like lugging it around all day, rent a locker and store it in there.

10.   **Money** – The WDW Resort accepts all major credit cards, cash, and Disney Gift Cards. If you are staying at a WDW Resort Hotel, you can link your MagicBand to your credit card for easy paying. The Walt Disney World Resort accepts the following credit cards: Visa, MasterCard, American Express, Discover, Diners Club, and the Japan Credit Bureau.

11.   **Identification** – For adults, make sure you plan on bringing your government-issued ID if you plan to drink alcoholic beverages. At times, you may be asked to present ID when purchasing at shops in Disney Springs.

12.   **Water Resistant Clothing** – Rainstorms in Orlando are highly unpredictable. In the summer, the rain will last under an hour, but you don't want to wear something that can't get wet. Leave the suede shoes and stick to cotton shirts. Just in case you don't want to deal with the rain, this is what we recommend bringing with you:

- Compact Umbrella – On rainy days, this is very handy. Don't bring a full sized umbrella, as it won't fit on rides and will be difficult to carry around.
- Poncho – It might be a bit of a fashion *faux pas* to some, but a poncho could keep you and your belongings dry. Many visitors love wearing these on the water rides.

· **Magic Tips** ·

If you forget any of these items, WDW sells them. Check the shops near the entrances to any of the parks for some of these items.

WHAT *NOT* TO WEAR AND BRING

1. **Ice** – Loose ice isn't permitted as a safety hazard, though ice packs are allowed. If you need ice, ask quick-service restaurants for a cupful.

2. **Selfie Sticks** – It seems like it would be so much fun to take photos with one of these, but WDW bans them for the safety of other guests.

3. **Adult Costumes and Masks** – Children under 14 are allowed to wear costumes; but as not to trick people into thinking a non-Cast Member is a character, WDW bans these for adults. During Mickey's Not-So-Scary Halloween Party, adults may dress in costume. For safety reasons, adults are not allowed to wear masks to the park.

4. **Skateboards, Rollerblades, Bikes, Roller Skates** – WDW bans these for safety reasons. Even those skates that slide out from kids' shoes are banned. If you need a vehicle, you may rent a scooter or wheelchair from Guest Services to the right of the WDW entrance gates.

5. **Remote Control Toys and Drones** – Sorry, but not allowed— even in Tomorrowland.

6. **Your Pet** – Animals are not permitted in any of the six parks, Disney Springs, most of the hotels, or any of the transportation at the WDW Resort. Though, some of the campsites at Fort Wilderness do allow dogs. If you need a place for your pet during your stay, the Resort offers pet boarding and kennels at the Best Friends Pet Care, located near Disney Springs and the Port Orleans Resort Hotels. The facility is huge, air conditioned, and a premium resort for your pet. They offer dozens of trained pet caregivers to accommodate your family's furry member when you enjoy the resort. Accommodations include play and grooming services for both dogs and cats. Your length of stay will determine the pricing. For more information, please visit:
    www.bestfriendspetcare.com (advanced reservations required along with proof of certain vaccines).

7. **Alcoholic Beverages** – These are not allowed in the parks (though adults 21 and over with a valid ID may purchase alcoholic drinks at all Theme Parks).

8. **Lawn Chairs** – You might be tempted to bring these to watch a parade, but WDW bans them. We assume it's to keep the Resort's aesthetics from looking like a 4th of July picnic.

9. **Glass Bottles** – Another safety precaution. However, small glass containers of baby food are allowed.

10. **Bags with Wheels and Hiking Backpacks** – It's okay to bring these into the hotels, but you'll need to leave them out of the parks.

11. **Wrapped Gifts** – For inspection reasons, you cannot bring wrapped gifts into the parks. If you plan on giving someone a present, use a gift bag.

12. **Cigarettes** – Walt Disney World has banned smoking inside its theme parks. Designated smoking areas are located outside of each theme park and water park entrance. Disney Springs and Walt Disney World Resort hotels have several smoking spots around their properties. Use the search tool on the Walt Disney World app to find a list of designated smoking areas around the resort.

BACKUP PLANS

Rent a Locker

There's no need to tire yourself out with a hefty backpack when a locker that fits your belongings starts at just $8/day plus a $5 key deposit. Larger lockers are $10/day with a $5 key deposit. You get the deposit back when you return the key. The water parks have a different cost at $10/day for regular-sized lockers and $15/day for large-sized lockers. The water park lockers work with a 4-digit pin that you create in order to keep your belongings safe and secure. Most theme parks have locker storage inside and outside of the entry gates.

Locker Locations

- Magic Kingdom – Just before Main Street, U.S.A. outside of the gates
- Epcot – Bus Stop outside of the park, International Gateway at the entrance, and near the Camera Center.
- Hollywood Studios – at the entrance and near the bus stop
- Animal Kingdom – Expedition Everest and Kali River Rapids
- Typhoon Lagoon – There are two: at the entrance and just after the entrance
- Blizzard Beach – There are two: at the entrance, and to the right after you enter.

Plan a Midday Return to Your Hotel – If you don't want to rent a locker, make a plan to return to your hotel midday. There you can eat, refill on drinks, and maybe take a power nap. When you're refreshed, head back to the parks for more fun!

Get Park Hoppers – Sometimes you don't get everything done in one day and if the extra cost works with your budget, the Park Hopper is the way to go. This pass allows you to visit any of the four main theme parks any time you want (though there is a water park option as well).

CHAPTER SIX

THE MAGIC KINGDOM

INTRODUCTION

The Magic Kingdom is Walt Disney World's epicenter and most beloved theme park. Designed after the original Disneyland concept, the Magic Kingdom offers a world-class experience into the heart of Disney. With 20 million annual visitors, the Magic Kingdom is the most-visited theme park in the world! It opened in 1971 and has over 100 square acres of classic rides, roller coasters, themed lands, delicious food, beautiful scenery, a massive lake, and, of course, the iconic Cinderella Castle.

The six sizable lands are all differently themed and have their own set of rides. Main Street, U.S.A. is the gateway into the stunning park. Though Main Street feels like a tempting beginning, the allure of the distant castle will have your feet moving toward Fantasyland with rides designed for families with young kids. Adventureland is like walking into a dense jungle, and Frontierland places you in the heart of the Wild West! Liberty Square rounds the classic experiences with its unique, American attractions, and Tomorrowland pulls guests into the future where anything is possible!

There are nearly countless things to do in the lands of the Magic Kingdom, but we've reviewed every single one of them to give you the best planning opportunity. In this section, we explore everything from the rides to the spectacular shows that bring the magic of Walt Disney's Kingdom!

MAGIC KINGDOM ROPE DROP STRATEGY

The Magic Kingdom Welcome Show—or rope drop—is a fantastic, mostly unlisted event. We highly recommend getting to the Magic Kingdom 30-minutes before opening to see a great show at the Cinderella Castle. This timing will allow you to get through security and head to the hub in front of the castle. This show is popular, dazzling, and makes for some great pictures of characters! There's a song, dancers, and a dozen characters, including Mickey and Minnie! It all ends with a *bang* before you start your unforgettable adventure in the park!

During the first hour, we recommend heading to Fantasyland to knock out several attractions in a row. You can also experience an attraction that you weren't able to book a FastPass+ reservation for like Space Mountain. Keep in mind that the Seven Dwarfs Mine Train tends to have long lines from morning until night, so put this first on your list if you don't have it in your FastPass+ selections.

"THE KISS GOODNIGHT"

Guests who stay until the closing of the Magic Kingdom are treated to a special, somewhat unofficial show. Cinderella Castle dazzles as an announcement plays over the speakers. Disney worked carefully on this special announcement, making certain that you'll feel the last bit of magic it has to offer before you leave. While the Kiss Goodnight isn't as spectacular as the Welcome Show, it still leaves you with some good feelings.

MAIN STREET, U.S.A.

The Magic Kingdom's iconic grand entrance is filled with shops, dining, and a magnificent view of the castle. The first thing you'll notice is the train station, beautiful flower arrangements, and smiling faces. Choose the left or the right side of the entrance to find yourself in a hub of horse-drawn street cars and Disney characters waiting to greet you.

Theme: Turn-of-the-century American town—specifically, Walt Disney's hometown of Marceline, Missouri in the early 20th century.

RIDES

WALT DISNEY WORLD RAILROAD
Best for: Young Kids, Adults 50+
Description: This iconic, relaxing steam train moves around the perimeter of the park. It's a 20-minute ride over a mile and a half of track. Other stops include Frontierland and Fantasyland.
Level: Everyone
Recommendation: Best if you are looking for a way to stay out of the sun and appreciate a leisurely experience. Tweens, Teens, and Thrill Riders may not enjoy this experience as much.
Line Length: Short / **FastPass+:** No
Refurbishment: This attraction may be closed into 2020 as construction begins on the *Tron* roller coaster (set to open in 2021).

MAIN STREET VEHICLES
Best for: Young Kids, Adults 50+
Description: Ride a horse-drawn streetcar, horseless carriage, or a double-decker bus that will take you down to Cinderella's Castle.

Level: Family
Recommendation: A fun ride for small children and guests who enjoy the classic appeal of Disney attractions. Thrill Riders might rather skip this and head straight to a ride like Space Mountain or Big Thunder Mountain Railroad.
FastPass+: No

SHOWS AND ATTRACTIONS

TOWN SQUARE THEATRE
Best for: Young Kids, Kids, Family
Description: Meet Mickey Mouse in this stunning theatre.
Level: Family
Recommendation: This is your best opportunity for a photo with Mickey Mouse. Other characters like Tinker Bell and Disney Princesses show up throughout the day. Check the Walt Disney World app for character times on the day of your visit.
FastPass+: No

MOVE IT! SHAKE IT! MOUSEKEDANCE IT! STREET PARTY
Best for: Young Kids, Kids, Family
Description: A dance party parade with Mickey, Minnie, Donald, Daisy, Goofy, and more!
Level: Family
Recommendation: This street party celebration is a lively midday event with heaps of classic character. See everyone from classic Disney characters to newer ones from Pixar. The route goes from Main Street and loops around the hub in front of Cinderella Castle. As with most parades, we recommend finding a spot about 20-30 minutes ahead of time for the best viewing. You can stop by this party any time for a great view and photos.

· Magic Tips ·
Main Street makes a great viewing spot for many of the parades and nighttime fireworks displays. Crowds line up along the streets typically 30-60 minutes before each show to get a great view. If you'd like to avoid the parades and shows, it's best to stay clear of Main Street around the show times.

HAPPILY EVER AFTER FIREWORKS

Best for: Everyone of all ages!

Description: An epic new fireworks and image projection show around Cinderella Castle!

Level: Everyone

Recommendation: Conclude your day with this stunning fireworks display that dazzles the sky. See your favorite Disney and Pixar characters from Aladdin to Zootopia as they overcome the impossible to live happily ever after. The best viewing is at the end of Main Street before the center "hub" with the statue of Walt Disney and Mickey Mouse. Here you can see the entire display. We recommend getting their early, either an hour on less-busy days and two hours early on busy days.

Outside Viewing: Grand Floridian Hotel guests can see the Magic Kingdom fireworks from the hotel's beach. Contemporary Resort Hotel guests also have fantastic views from select rooms. We recommend making a dining reservation at the California Grill for fantastic viewing around showtime. The restaurant also plays the fireworks theme music and dims the lights when the show starts!

MORE ATTRACTIONS

Harmony Barber Shop – Get a haircut in this charming barbershop. Look for the famous barbershop quartet, the Dapper Dans, singing in four-part harmony! Haircuts start at $19 for adults and $18 for kids. Harmony isn't a salon, so those with long, stylized hair may not prefer to visit this location. Reservations: (407) 939-7529

Browse Main Street – You can also discover the many shops, City Hall, and the Main Street Chamber of Commerce.

> **· Magic Tips ·**
> Guests can often shop on Main Street up to an hour after the park's closing time. Instead of shopping early and carrying bags around all day, shop as you leave!

FANTASYLAND

Classic Disney animated films come to life in this classic kid-friendly land located behind Cinderella Castle. The Magic Kingdom's Fantasyland is divided into three sections: the Castle Courtyard, the Enchanted Forest, and the Storybook Circus. In Fantasyland, you can ride classic attractions and meet your favorite Disney Princesses.

Theme: Land of Fairytales

RIDES

SEVEN DWARFS MINE TRAIN
Best for: Kids, Tweens, Teens, Adults, some Thrill Riders
Description: A family-friendly rollercoaster through the mines of the Seven Dwarfs. The carts move side to side, creating a unique experience like no other rollercoaster.
Level: Family (must be 38"/ 97cm or taller)
Recommendation: The Seven Dwarfs Mine Train is one of the park's most popular attractions. Thus, we recommend adding this to your FastPass+ selection list. If you aren't able to get a FP+ for this ride, come when the park at opening and ride this attraction first. Additionally, if you purchase the Memory Maker, you'll receive a video of your party on the ride—which makes this a great first-time roller coaster for a kid!
Line Length: Very Long / **FastPass+:** Yes

PETER PAN'S FLIGHT
Best for: Young Kids, Kids, Tweens, Adults 50+
Description: Fly along Peter Pan through London and Neverland on a pirate ship!
Level: Young Kids / Everyone
Recommendation: Perfect for all ages (kids love this ride) and a Disney classic that we also recommend Peter Pan's Flight for thrill-seekers looking to ride an all-ages ride.
Line Length: Very Long / **FastPass+:** Yes

> **· Magic Tips ·**
> If you don't get a FastPass+ selection for Peter Pan's Flight visit after dark for much shorter lines (when the younger kids have gone home).

THE MANY ADVENTURES OF WINNIE THE POOH
Best for: Young Kids and Kids
Description: A slow-paced ride through the brightly-colored world of Winnie the Pooh.
Level: Young Kids / Family
Recommendation: Great for Kids of all ages, but Tweens, Teens and Thrill Riders will likely want to skip it.
Line Length: Short/ **FastPass+:** Yes

DUMBO THE FLYING ELEPHANT
Best for: Young Kids and Kids
Description: Soar high while boarding Dumbo! You control how high or low Dumbo goes.
Level: Young Kids / Family
Recommendation: Perfect for families with Young Kids. We don't recommend FastPass+ for Dumbo since the ride is "queue-less". Instead of waiting in a traditional line, guests receive a pager and kids can play in the big-top tent playground while you wait.
Line Length: Short / **FastPass+:** Yes

MAD TEA PARTY
Best for: Everyone
Description: Disney's famous tea cups inspired by *Alice in Wonderland*! Spin with your friends (up to 3-4 adults per tea cup).
Level: Kids / Everyone
Recommendation: Perfect for all ages and a Disney classic that we also recommend to Thrill Riders (the tea cups can spin fast or slow, depending on how hard you turn them). If you get motion sickness easily, you might want to skip this spinning attraction.
Line Length: Short / **FastPass+:** Yes

PRINCE CHARMING REGAL CARROUSEL
Best for: Young Kids and Kids
Description: A classic carrousel with horses from Cinderella.
Level: Family

Recommendation: Perfect for families with Young Kids.
Line Length: Short / **FastPass+:** No

"it's a small world"
Best for: Young Kids, Kids, Families, Adults 50+
Description: A boat floats through several counties with children singing the "It's A Small World" theme song in different languages.
Level: Young Kids / Family
Recommendation: Perfect for families with young children. Adults may enjoy the ride as they beat the heat in the air-conditioned boat ride. Some may find this ride horribly annoying because of the endless singing children—we're not kidding!
Line Length: Short / **FastPass+:** Yes

THE BARNSTORMER
Best for: Kids and Tweens
Description: A kid-friendly outdoor rollercoaster starring Goofy as the Great Goofini.
Level: Family
Recommendation: Like the Seven Dwarfs Mine Train, this is a great introductory rollercoaster.
Line Length: Very Short / **FastPass+:** Yes

UNDER THE SEA ~ JOURNEY OF THE LITTLE MERMAID
Best for: Young Kids, Kids, and Tweens
Description: Board shell-shaped chairs as you travel "underwater" to see Ariel and her friends. There's music, special effects, fish, and the wicked Ursula!
Level: Family
Recommendation: Perfect for fans of The Little Mermaid.
Line Length: Medium / **FastPass+:** Yes

SHOWS AND ATTRACTIONS

CINDERELLA CASTLE WALKTHROUGH
Best for: Everyone
Description: Walk through the famous Castle! There's also a dining area called Cinderella's Royal Table.
Level: Everyone
Recommendation: Take a picture outside of the castle! If you don't have someone to snap your photo, there is often a Disney photographer outside of the castle. He or she will take your picture

for free (though you have to pay for the prints, unless you have PhotoPass/Memory Maker). Afterward, the Cast Member is happy to take a free photo of you with your camera or phone.
FastPass+: No

MICKEY'S PHILHARMAGIC
Best for: Young Kids, Kids, Tweens, Families
Description: A 4-D film show starring Mickey Mouse and his friends. Though, to be honest, it should be called Donald's PhilharMagic because most of the show stars him and Mickey just seems to make a cameo.
Level: Family
Recommendation: Great for show lovers of all ages. Awesome special effects and music. We recommend sitting in the center of the theater. Seats further up can seem blurring in the 3D glasses.
Line Length: Short / **FastPass+:** No

CASEY JR. SPLASH 'N' SOAK STATION
Best for: Young Kids and Kids
Description: A Dumbo-themed water playground for kids.
Level: Everyone
Recommendation: On the hottest days when your kids don't feel like waiting in lines, this can be a memorable attraction. It's best to plan to head back to the hotel afterward or bring a change of clothes. Though, many times, the hot Florida sun may be enough to dry them off.
FastPass+: No

FESTIVAL OF FANTASY PARADE
Best for: Young Kids, Kids, Tweens, Families
Description: An afternoon parade set to Disney music with impressive floats, singing, and dancing.
Level: Family
Recommendation: Great for parade lovers of all ages. Get there early for the best seating! We recommend being near the Cinderella Castle (on the Main Street side) at least 30 minutes before the parade begins. The park map will list showtimes as they can change from day to day.
FastPass+: No

BIBBIDI BOBBIDI BOUTIQUE
(inside the Cinderella Castle)
Best for: Young Kids and Kids
Description: Dress up in princess clothing and makeup.

Level: Kids and Young Kids

Recommendation: Perfect for children who are inspired Disney princesses (for pricing starting a $59.95, kids can get their makeup and hair done—and even a gown from their favorite Disney princess). There are more packages, including a "Knight Package" and a "Frozen Package".

FastPass+: No

CHARACTER MEETING SPOTS

ARIEL'S GROTTO
Best for: Young Kids, Kids, and Tweens
Description: Take photos with Ariel from Disney's The Little Mermaid.
Level: Family
Recommendation: Perfect for fans of The Little Mermaid.
FastPass+: No

PETE'S SILLY SIDESHOW
Best for: Young Kids, Kids, and Tweens
Description: Take photos with Daisy and Minnie or Donald and Goofy in this circus-themed meet-and-greet attraction. The characters are dressed in circus attire.
Level: Family
Recommendation: Perfect for those looking for any of these characters.
FastPass+: No

PRINCESS FAIRYTALE HALL
Best for: Young Kids, Kids, and Tweens
Description: Take photos with Cinderella and other Princesses in this royal hall.
Level: Family
Recommendation: Perfect for fans of Disney Princesses.
FastPass+: No

ENCHANTED TALES WITH BELLE
Best for: Young Kids, Kids, and Tweens
Description: Take photos with Belle from *Beauty and the Beast*.
Level: Family
Recommendation: Perfect for fans of Disney Princesses.

Line Length: Long
FastPass+: Yes

MEET MERIDA AT FAIRYTALE GARDEN
Best for: Young Kids, Kids, and Tweens
Description: Take photos with Merida at the Fairytale Garden
Level: Family
Recommendation: Perfect for fans of Brave.
FastPass+: No

THE TANGLED REST AREA

The *Tangled*-themed rest area is well-designed and to the west of Fantasyland, near Liberty Square and the Haunted Mansion. It may also be the best restroom area in all of WDW. Equipped with pristine toilets, sinks, and floors, you'll feel the spotless clean of these new restrooms. The stalls are also well-spread and have a great, private feeling for both women and men.

The tree stumps across from the restrooms are free cellphone charging stations. They use regular outlet plugs, so you'll need to bring your own cord. Take a break and rest your feet in a tranquil spot in the heart of the Magic Kingdom. There's also a nice waterfall and plenty of Tangled-themed landscapes to admire. You can also fill your water jugs here. The pipes are newer so they don't have some of the old Florida water taste that areas in Adventureland have in their fountains.

ADVENTURELAND

Discover adventure brought to life with some of Disney's best storylines and attractions set in a dense jungle. Brave a seas ruled by pirates and fly high on a magic carpet!

Theme: The jungles of South America, Asia, and Africa

RIDES

JUNGLE CRUISE
Best for: Young Kids, Kids, Families, Tweens, Adults 30+

Description: Venture down a massive river on a boat with your comedic tour guide. See animatronic Amazonian and African animals from monkeys and crocodiles to elephants and lions on this 7-minute long ride.
Level: Everyone
Recommendation: A classic, humorous Disney ride that most guests will enjoy. Teens, Young Adults, and Thrill Riders may want to skip it.
Line Length: Long / **FastPass+:** Yes
Holiday Overlay: Jingle Cruise (the holiday version of the Jungle Cruise) offers Christmas lights, a different script, and animals wearing Christmas hats. This attraction runs mid-November through the first week of January.

PIRATES OF THE CARIBBEAN
Best for: Everyone!
Description: Pirate-themed boat ride in the dark. Also a great air - conditioned ride to cool off on hot days.
Level: Everyone, though some young kids may be frightened by the drop, loud sounds, and darkness.
Recommendation: A must-see Disney Classic for all! Both thrill riders and families will love Pirates of the Caribbean for its stunning scenery, animatronics, and pirate humor. We also recommend a FastPass+ selection for this attraction. The boats load quickly, but this is one of the Magic Kingdom's most popular rides, so the line can be quite long.
Line Length: Long / **FastPass+:** Yes
Staying Dry: To avoid getting wet, sit near the center of the boat. If you are on the fourth or fifth row, and on the right side, a cannon blast can send a mighty splash of water your way. Avoid these seats if you want to stay dry.

THE MAGIC CARPETS OF ALADDIN
Best for: Young Kids, Kids, Families
Description: Looping flying carpets similar to the Dumbo the Flying Elephant ride.
Level: Families

Recommendation: Kids under ten enjoy this ride the most as they control the flying carpets to go high or low.
Line Length: Very Short / **FastPass+:** Yes

SWISS FAMILY TREEHOUSE
Best for: Young Kids, Kids, Tweens, Families
Description: A climbable treehouse themed after the 1960 *Swiss Family Robinson* film.
Level: Young Kids / Everyone
Recommendation: Kids ages 10 and under will enjoy this attraction that typically has a very short line (or no wait at all). There are also great photo opportunities from the top!
Line Length: Very short / **FastPass+:** No

SHOWS AND ATTRACTIONS

WALT DISNEY'S ENCHANTED TIKI ROOM
Best for: Kids, Adults 60+
Description: An animatronic show starring birds and Tikis in a tropical island setting.
Level: Family / Everyone
Recommendation: Have a Dole Whip while you watch the 15-minute long show. Tweens, Teens, Young Adults, and Thrill Riders will want to skip this one, as it's a classic attraction that can feel a bit dated.
Line Length: Short / **FastPass+:** No

PIRATE'S ADVENTURE~TREASURES OF THE SEVEN SEAS
Best for: Kids, Tweens
Description: Pirates of the Caribbean-themed walkthrough attraction. Help Captain Jack Sparrow discover treasures in this fun explorative mini-adventure!
Level: Kids and Tweens
Recommendation: Perfect for Kids and Tweens, but it may be too complex for Young Kids, and it's not aimed for Adults.
Line Length: Short / **FastPass+:** No

> **· Magic Tips ·**
> Complete the adventure and Captain Jack Sparrow will give you a FastPass to Pirates of the Caribbean!

PIRATE'S LEAGUE
Best for: Young Kids, Kids
Description: Transform into a swashbuckling pirate with makeup beard and all. Kids can also look undead and learn the swagger of a pirate!
Level: Kids and Tweens
Recommendation: Perfect for pirate fans with an extra cost starting at $39.95.

FRONTIERLAND

Immerse yourself in the wild west near the Rivers of America. Ride the high-speed Big Thunder Mountain Railroad or catch a lighthearted show at the Diamond Horseshoe.

Theme: North America's wild west

RIDES

SPLASH MOUNTAIN
Best for: Tweens, Teens, Adults, Thrill Riders
Description: Water-based log ride starring the singing critters from Song of the South. Prepare to hear the classic Disney song, "Zip-A-Dee-Doo-Dah"!
Level: Thrill Ride (must be 40"/102cm or taller)
Recommendation: If you love drops and getting wet, this is the ride for you! There are several drops in this ride, including a 50 foot drop at 45 degrees at the end. This ride typically has the longest lines in Frontierland, especially during the hotter days and can be well over an hour wait. This is why we highly recommend making it a FastPass+ selection.
Line Length: Long / **FastPass+:** Yes
Staying Dry: Sit near the back to avoid getting as wet (though you will still likely get wet). Tell a Cast Member at the end of the queue that you'd like to sit in the back and they will help accommodate you. If it's a cold day or you just don't feel like getting your clothes wet, either buy or bring a poncho or skip this attraction altogether.

BIG THUNDER MOUNTAIN RAILROAD
Best for: Kids, Tweens, Teens, Adults, Thrill Riders
Description: A fast rollercoaster with a few dips called "The Wildest Ride in the Wilderness!"
Level: Thrill Ride (must be 40"/102cm or taller)
Recommendation: Many families and thrill riders will love this fast rollercoaster with short dips and great special effects. If you're unsure whether to take your child on this rollercoaster, have them ride the family-friendly Seven Dwarfs Mine Train first in Fantasyland.
Line Length: Long / **FastPass+:** Yes

TOM SAWYER ISLAND
Best for: Kids, Tweens
Description: Explore a remote island in the center of the Magic Kingdom's famous river. You must get there by raft!
Level: Family
Recommendation: We recommend this island playground for kids. There are hideaways and trinkets for them to play with, though teens, adults and Thrill Riders will likely want to skip this one. Tom Sawyer's Island closes before sunset, so make sure that you get this attraction done earlier in the day if it's on your list.
Line Length: Short / **FastPass+:** No

SHOWS AND ATTRACTIONS

COUNTRY BEAR JAMBOREE
Best for: Young Kids, Kids, Adults 50+
Description: A country music-filled jamboree featuring the classic animatronic Country Bears. There are over twelve songs in this nearly 16-minute long show.
Level: Everyone
Recommendation: Perfect for nostalgic Disney World-goers, but the theme may feel lost on others. The Country Bear Jamboree might be a classic, but the crowds have thinned over the years and the show doesn't have the same excitement from its previous fans.
Line Length: Short / **FastPass+:** No

MORE ATTRACTIONS

- **Walt Disney World Railroad** – A station for the park's iconic train.
- **Frontierland Shootin' Arcade** – A paid experience where you can shoot targets with laser-guided toy rifles.

LIBERTY SQUARE

A colonial America-themed land filed with shops, treats, and one of the park's most popular rides, the Haunted Mansion. Catch sight of Liberty Bell and Liberty Tree replicas, dine, or catch a parade near the Rivers of America.

Theme: 18th-Century New England

RIDES

HAUNTED MANSION
Best for: *Kids, Tweens, Teens, Adults*

Description: A slow-paced ride through a haunted house. Filled with illusions, animatronics, and creepy sounds, this attraction is uniquely Disney.
Level: Everyone – though young children may become frightened
Recommendation: It's a Disney classic that many thrill-riders may want to skip for it's slow movement and effects that are only scary enough to terrify young kids. You can fit 2-3 people per "Doom Buggy" chair. We've sat 3 adults together, but it's not very comfortable.
Line Length: Average / **FastPass+:** Yes

SHOWS AND ATTRACTIONS

HALL OF PRESIDENTS
Best for: Young Kids, Adults 50+
Description: Animatronics show hosted by US Presidents.
Level: Everyone
Recommendation: Another Disney classic that may bore some guests uninterested in US History.
Line Length: Short / **FastPass+:** No

LIBERTY BELLE RIVERBOAT
Best for: Young Kids, Adults 50+
Description: Explore a beautiful American-style riverboat over the Rivers of America.
Level: Everyone
Recommendation: For those looking to cool off and ride on a large river boat.
Line Length: Short/ **FastPass+:** No

TOMORROWLAND

A futuristic land filled with rides for thrill seekers and sci-fi fans. Tomorrowland is also home to Space Mountain and Buzz Lightyear!

Theme: The land of the future

RIDES

SPACE MOUNTAIN
Best for: Thrill Riders
Description: A rollercoaster in the dark.
Level: Thrill Riders (must be 40"/ 102cm or taller)
Recommendation: A must for Thrill Riders! Space Mountain at the Magic Kingdom feels a little bit dated with its worn carpet in the queue and 70's-style exterior. However, the ride hasn't lost its unique charm as you blast through outer space! We highly recommend this unique experience for Thrill Riders, so select this as a FastPass+ (and consider you may want to ride this twice).
Line Length: Very Long / **FastPass+:** Yes

TOMORROWLAND SPEEDWAY
Best for: Kids and Tweens
Description: Where kids can drive cars around a track.
Level: Kids / Family (must be 32"/81cm or taller to ride; must be 54"/ 137cm to drive alone).
Recommendation: Designed for kids and tweens to drive motorized go-kart style vehicles.
Line Length: Long / **FastPass+:** Yes

TOMORROWLAND TRANSIT AUTHORITY PEOPLEMOVER
Best for: Young Kids, Kids, Adults 50+
Description: A futuristic, slow-moving vehicle through Tomorrowland.
Level: Kids / Family
Recommendation: Perfect for those looking for a break. The PeopleMover is a 10-minute long ride and a great way to beat the heat as the ride travels through air-conditioned spaces.
Line Length: Very short / **FastPass+:** No

BUZZ LIGHTYEAR'S SPACE RANGER SPIN
Best for: Everyone
Description: Compete against others in this fun *Toy Story*-themed ride. It's fun for everyone to blast the laser guns and try to rack up the points.
Level: Everyone (including most thrill riders)
Recommendation: A crowd favorite for everyone to enjoy.
Line Length: Medium / **FastPass+:** Yes

Scoring Big: There are special targets on the robot and alien enemies that give different points. It's not clear how much these are worth unless you know these tips.

1. You can hit the targets as many times as you'd like, including the ones worth the most.
2. Orange Robot (first room) – Shoot the inside of its glowing hands for 100,000 points.
3. Volcano (second room) – Aim for the volcano with green lava in the back of the room and get 25,000.
4. Alien Ant – There's an ant with a target on its rear worth 50,000.
5. Zurg's Ship – There's a difficult target at the bottom of the crab-like ship that's worth 100,000.
6. Hyperspace Warp – There's a huge spaceship at the end with a target worth 100,000.

ASTRO ORBITER
Best for: Young Kids and Kids
Description: Orbit a solar system model on rocket ships (similar to Dumbo).
Level: Kids / Family
Recommendation: Fun for Young Kids
Line Length: Medium / **FastPass+:** No

STITCH'S ALIEN ENCOUNTER
May operate seasonally
Best for: Kids and Tweens
Description: Character Meeting
Level: Everyone (must be 40"/ 102cm or taller)
Recommendation: Meet the lovable alien from Lilo and Stitch.
Line Length: Short / **FastPass+:** No
Possible Ride Closure: This character greeting takes place at the former Stitch's Great Escape! During peak season, Stitch's Great Escape may run instead. The ride is fairly unpopular, so Disney will soon replace it with a permanent attraction.

SHOWS AND ATTRACTIONS

MONSTERS, INC. LAUGH FLOOR
Best for: Young Kids and Kids
Description: A comedy club-style show with digital puppetry that allows characters on a screen from Monsters, Inc. to interact with the audience.

Level: Kids / Family
Recommendation: Fun for Families with Kids
Line Length: Short / **FastPass+:** Yes

WALT DISNEY'S CAROUSEL OF PROGRESS
Best for: Young Kids and Adults Ages 50+
Description: Watch as animatronic characters bring you the future of gadgets in a turning carousel-like building.
Level: Everyone
Recommendation: Another great way to cool down, but there is a lot of standing. The ride is more for those looking for nostalgia, though Young Kids can appreciate the characters more than Tweens, Teens, and Young Adults.
Line Length: Short / **FastPass+:** No

CHAPTER SEVEN

EPCOT

INTRODUCTION

Since its opening in 1982, Epcot has been a staple of the Walt Disney World experience. Its name is an acronym for Experimental Prototype Community of Tomorrow. It's a place where "joy, hope, and friendship" are launched into a space of creativity, exploration, and innovation.

We are asked a lot: "Is Epcot worth visiting?" For us, the answer is a clear *yes*. Epcot is like the Magic Kingdom's Tomorrowland, fully expanded over 300 acres. It's a world of tomorrow and today where guests can ride futuristic attractions, try delicious food from all over the world, and also party into the night. However, those looking just for thrills may feel disappointed by Epcot's lack of ride attractions. Disney is fixing this by adding at least two new rides by 2021, a roller coaster based on the *Guardians of the Galaxy* and a family-friendly dark ride based on Pixar's *Ratatouille*. In the mean time, we recommend booking dining reservations and checking the rides that Epcot has to offer—you never know what will feel exciting!

Epcot is divided into two sections: Future World, with the most rides, and the World Showcase which consists of representations of eleven countries. Whether you are a thrill rider looking for unique experiences, a foodie craving something different, or a kid yearning to make some Disney memories,

Epcot is the place. With attractions like Soarin' and Frozen Ever After, as well as delicious wine and gourmet delights, there's something for everyone in Epcot!

EPCOT ROPE DROP STRATEGY

Epcot has the least exciting rope drop. Perhaps it's because the space is so large and so few guests show up for it. Or it could because they often have Extra Magic Hours before the actual Park opens. Epcot has two official rope drops, one for each entrance. The first is in Future World, where you are led near the center. Cast Members will allow you to move to one of the Future World attractions after that. We recommend experiencing Soarin' or Test Track first.

The second rope drop is in the World Showcase entrance between the United Kingdom and France. It's the least climactic one as it opens much later in the morning than the other Parks, so only a tiny amount of people appear. You might want to head to Frozen Ever After from there, but since it's on the complete opposite side, we recommend accessing it from Future World.

> **· Magic Tips ·**
> Epcot is often open late, allowing for locals to wine and dine around it's beautiful, massive lake in the center of the World Showcase. Because of this, it's sometimes best to avoid the weekend crowds—unless you're open to them!

BACK ENTRANCE

Epcot has two entrances: one at the Main Entrance near Spaceship Earth, the second between the United Kingdom and France sections in the World Showcase on the other side of the park. The second entrance is known as "The International Gateway."

Typically, the two sections have different opening times. The Future World opens earlier (usually about two hours) than the World Showcase. This is because Future World has more rides and World Showcase is mostly shops and restaurants. The World Showcase often is open two hours after Future World closes.

FUTURE WORLD

The first half of Epcot is home to its iconic, golf ball-like centerpiece. This structure is actually considered a "spaceship" and contains the captivating ride, Spaceship Earth. Epcot's many flowers bloom here, especially in the spring during the Flower and Garden Festival. Future World has a new attraction, Soarin', which now takes guests to choice locations around the world. It's an experience not to be missed by any Disney fan!

Theme: Future World of Tomorrow

RIDES AND ATTRACTIONS

MISSION: SPACE
Best for: Tweens, Teens, Adults, and Thrill Riders
Description: A dizzying astronaut training excursion into outer space with a new mission!
Level: Everyone
Recommendation: Thrill Riders should choose the more intense experience, while those who experience motion sickness should choose a stationary option—or skip this ride altogether.
Line Length: Medium / **FastPass+:** Yes

IMAGINATION!
Best for: Young Kids, Kids, and Tweens
Description: This pavilion explores imagination for its fun and importance to the human experience. Its main attraction is Journey Into the Imagination with Figment, a classic dark ride with a scientific twist that explores our senses!
Level: Everyone
Recommendation: Great for families with Kids.
Line Length: Very Short / **FastPass+:** Yes

TEST TRACK
Best for: Tweens, Teens, Adults, Thrill Riders
Description: Zoom along a simulated test track in a futuristic car. The vehicle races at over 60-miles per hour with turns and movement inside and outside of a building.

Level: Thrill Ride
Recommendation: Perfect for Thrill Riders. If the line is long and you missed a FastPass+ reservation, use the Single Rider line.
Line Length: Very Long / **FastPass+:** Yes

SPACESHIP EARTH

Best for: Everyone
Description: A slow-moving dark ride set inside of the Epcot sphere. The ride has animatronics and more as it discusses humans' ability to communicate on Earth throughout time.
Level: Everyone
Recommendation: A ride that is more fun that it seems. Thrill Riders might want to head directly to Test Track instead.
Line Length: Short / **FastPass+:** Yes

Note: Disney has plans to reimagine Spaceship Earth, so we expect it to be close for most of 2020.

LIVING WITH THE LAND

Located in the Land pavilion
Best for: Everyone
Description: A slow-paced, informative ride that beautifully describes how we harvest the land for food.
Level: Everyone
Recommendation: Perfectly informative and fun. Thrill Riders may want to skip this slow-paced ride and head straight for Soarin'.
Line Length: Very Short (Living with the Land) / High (Soarin')
FastPass+: No

SOARIN'

Located in the Land pavilion
Best for: Kids, Tweens, Teens, Adults, and Thrill Riders
Description: An all-new update to the park's popular Soarin' ride. Fly over some of the world's most famous landmarks in this unique hang glider simulation.
Level: Kids to Adult
Recommendation: Small children and those with a fear of heights may want to skip this one, though the ride feels very relaxing.
Line Length: Long / **FastPass+:** Yes

THE SEAS WITH NEMO & FRIENDS

Best for: Everyone

Description: Learn about the oceans in this Finding Nemo-themed attraction. The ride loads quickly with seats similar to the "doom buggies" in the Haunted Mansion. There are also massive aquariums with live fish, manatees, and more!
Level: Everyone
Recommendation: A spectacular ride with plenty to see and experience. Thrill Riders may want to skip out unless they are interested in seeing the aquariums.
Line Length: Short / **FastPass+:** Yes

TURTLE TALK WITH CRUSH
Inside The Seas pavilion
Best for: Young Kids and Kids
Description: Interact with Crush the turtle from Finding Nemo in this unique and hilarious theatre-like event designed for Young Kids.
Level: Everyone
Recommendation: Young Kids
Line Length: Short / **FastPass+:** Yes

DISNEY & PIXAR SHORT FILM FESTIVAL
Best for: Young Kids, Adults 50+
Description: The creative geniuses behind the Academy Award winning Pixar films bring an 18-minute show. Experience Pixar shorts like never before with 4-D effects!
Level: Everyone
Recommendation: A must for Pixar lovers, but those looking for thrills might want to skip this one.
Line Length: Very Short / **FastPass+:** No

MORE ATTRACTIONS

INNOVENTIONS – Hands-on experiences that help guests explore science in a fun way!

AWESOME PLANET (Inside The Land Pavilion) – An emotional film showcasing the most magnificent places on Earth.

WORLD SHOWCASE

While Future World dives us into "what could be" in the universe, the World Showcase at Epcot is designed to enlighten you about the dining, entertainment, and splendor of the world around us. Made up of 11 countries — Canada, China, France, Germany, Italy, Japan, Mexico, Morocco, Norway, United Kingdom, and the United States — you can try the food and beverages of these lands, plus ride along to discover their culture. While the World Showcase doesn't initially feel as Disney-themed as the other parks, there are sprinkles of its magic like the Norway pavilion which houses the Frozen Ever After ride. At night, see fireworks over a massive lake, dazzling gardens, and architecture from Japanese pagodas to Mayan temples!

Year round, there's always something new and exciting happening at Epcot. The annual Food and Wine Festival that takes place in the fall is a fan favorite for its delicious world-class bites and adult beverages. These meals and beverages come at an additional cost, and there's something fun for all to try. We also love the waiters at Epcot, because they are authentically from their respective country (many of the times), and they are some of the happiest employees in all of WDW.

We invite you to step into Epcot with an open mind and heart as you have the opportunity to fall in love with the splendor of the World Showcase. If you're an adult, you might just walk away thinking that this was your favorite land of all.

Theme: A Showcase of Worldly Traditions

RIDES AND ATTRACTIONS

FROZEN EVER AFTER
Location: Norway
Best for: Everyone
Description: Explore the culture of Norway and the magic of Disney's Frozen in this unique boat ride.
Level: Everyone / Family
Recommendation: The World Showcase's most "daring" ride, though it's fun for the whole family. There are some small dips and senses of danger, but the Frozen characters keep young kids happy.

Line Length: Long / **FastPass+:** Yes

REMY'S RATATOUILLE ADVENTURE

Opening Summer 2020!
Location: France
Best for: Everyone
Description: A trackless dark ride fit for the entire family! Journey along Remy the rat from Pixar's Ratatouille as you dash through a kitchen.

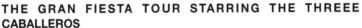

Level: Everyone / Family
Recommendation: This exciting dark ride uses physical sets and 3D elements. We recommend it for kids and adults!
Line Length: Very Long / **FastPass+:** Yes

THE GRAN FIESTA TOUR STARRING THE THREEE CABALLEROS

Location: Mexico
Best for: Everyone
Description: Explore the culture of Mexico in a boat ride with music.
Level: Everyone
Recommendation: We recommend experiencing the ride for its fun with Donald Duck and his pals.
Line Length: Very Short / **FastPass+:** No

DISNEY PHINEAS AND FERB: AGENT P'S WORLD SHOWCASE ADVENTURE

Best for: Kids and Tweens
Description: A scavenger hunt around the showcases.
Level: Family
Recommendation: Unless you have Kids or Tweens who are fans of Phineas and Ferb on the Disney Channel, it's best to skip the Agent P adventure.
Line Length: None / **FastPass+:** No

MORE PAVILIONS

There is a lot to do in the World Showcase and you may not have time to do it all. Most of the attractions are family-oriented, though all ages can enjoy them. See the recommendations in each section to see which ones you should explore in case you don't have the time to experience them all.

FRANCE

Best for: Everyone

Description: Watch Impressions de France, an 18-minute cinematic film showcasing the wonders of the country. Beginning January 2020, the "Beauty and the Beast Sing-Along" rotates with this show.

Level: Everyone

Recommendation: It's a small pavilion and great to walk through. If you enjoy French cuisine, we highly recommend eating at Les Chefs de France. Many of the employees come from Disneyland Paris to give an authentic French vibe. Just don't forget to make a reservation!

CHINA

Best for: Everyone

Description: Wondrous China is a circle-vision 360 movie exploring the beauty of the country.

Level: Everyone

Recommendation: The China pavilion is well-done, but not as memorable as Mexico or Norway.

Line Length: Very Short / **FastPass+:** No

CANADA

Best for: Everyone

Description: See a humorous, circle-vision 360 movie exploring the country. This new film debuts January 2020.

Level: Everyone

Recommendation: Everyone may enjoy this circle-vision 360° movie. Adults will enjoy the lager and handcrafted merchandise.

Line Length: Very Short / **FastPass+:** No

JAPAN

Best for: Everyone

Description: Impressive pagodas and traditional structures make this land a temptation for the eyes. Many of this pavilion's employees are from Disneyland Tokyo and they are happy to guide you through their culture.

Level: Everyone

Recommendation: Check out the shops and take photos by the amazing architecture.

THE AMERICAN ADVENTURE
Best for: Everyone
Description: Epcot's showcase of Americana with an animatronic cast on a stage who review the history of the country.
Level: Everyone
Recommendation: It feels like a bit of a repeat from what is shown in Liberty Square at the Magic Kingdom, so it's not as popular as Norway, Germany, Japan, or France.
Line Length: Very Short / **FastPass+:** No

MOROCCO
Best for: Kids, Adults 30+
Description: Explore a Moroccan city with mosaics and artwork created by Moroccan artists. There are several shops, dining experiences, and musical acts throughout the pavilion. Aladdin and Jasmine also make daily appearances.
Level: Everyone
Recommendation: Adults will love the food and the scenery while Kids will look forward to taking photos with Aladdin and Princess Jasmine.

UNITED KINGDOM
Best for: Everyone
Description: Stroll down the streets of London or the old countryside of England while listening to British rock cover bands.
Level: Everyone
Recommendation: Perfect for shop-lovers.

ITALY
Best for: Kids, Adults 30+
Description: See the sweeping scenes of Italy as recreations of its famous landmarks and artwork are put on display in this pavilion. The Via Napoli restaurant has some of the best pizza in Orlando! Pinocchio also shows up for photo opportunities.
Level: Everyone
Recommendation: Adults will love the food and the scenery while Kids will look forward to taking photos with Pinocchio.

GERMANY
Best for: Adults 21+

Description: Quaint German towns, food, and Biergarten beverages make up this unique pavilion.

Level: Everyone

Recommendation: Germany feels more like a land for Adults who enjoy beer and classic German food. Kids may want to skip it for attractions like Frozen or to see the shops in Japan.

SHOWS

EPCOT FIREWORKS
Epcot Forever & Harmonious

Best for: Everyone

Description: "Epcot Forever" is a limited-time show celebrating the worldly history of the theme park. Special effects spark from around the lake near World Showcase. For those looking to experience some Disney theme park nostalgia, head to Epcot for this celebration with fireworks, music, and dazzling kites! We expect Epcot Forever to be replaced with a new nighttime show, "Harmonious," likely in the fall of 2020.

Level: Everyone

Recommendation: Conclude your day with this fireworks display.

FastPass+: Yes—If you reserve a FastPass for this, you will stand near the entrance to the World Showcase. For many, this is the best spot.

Best Seating: If you didn't select a FastPass+ reservation for the fireworks at Epcot, make sure you reserve a spot 30-60 minutes before the show. Sit as close to the lagoon by Mexico or the Mitsukoshi Store in Japan. On busier days, you'll want to claim your spot about 90 minutes ahead of time. If you don't get there early, find standing room where you can. You can also request a patio or window seat at any of these restaurants for firework viewing: Rose and Crown Pub (United Kingdom), Bistro de Paris (France), Cantina de San Angel (Mexico), La Hacienda de San Angel (Mexico), Tokyo Dining (Japan) all have great viewing.

Exiting: The crowds pour from Epcot after the show. Most of the time, the International Gateway, between Great Britain and France, is the best exit. There are a few ways out of the park after the fireworks: bus, monorail, boat, or your own car. The first three are much easier as Disney has this system down for getting guests back to their hotels. If you don't have a hotel and drove, it's sort of a mad rush to the parking lot. To avoid this, we recommend being one of the first to leave through the International Gateway.

· **Magic Tips** ·

Disney's Boardwalk Inn guests can see the fireworks from the hotel's outdoor walkway. It's not the best viewing, but it beats the crowds, and you can see plenty of the fireworks in the sky. Another (more expensive) option is dining at Spanish steakhouse, Capa, in the Four Seasons Orlando. You'll have a 17th-floor view of Epcot's fireworks! Make a dining reservation of the Walt Disney World app before you go.

CHAPTER EIGHT

DISNEY'S HOLLYWOOD STUDIOS

INTRODUCTION

Previously known as MGM Studios—until it was revamped in 2008—Disney's Hollywood Studios is a park dedicated to Hollywood's Golden Age in the 1930's. Disney felt inspired to bring a movie-themed park to its Resort as Universal Studios eyed Orlando for its next project. With thrilling rides like The Twilight Zone Tower of Terror and stunning shows like *Fantasmic!*, Hollywood Studios brings famous films and characters to life in a spectacular way!

Hollywood Studios is also home to immersive themed areas like Toy Story Land—where guests shrink down to the size of a toy—and Star Wars: Galaxy's Edge—where guests begin their own *Star Wars* adventure! This theme park heavily focuses on Pixar, Star Wars, and Disney Junior attractions designed with the entire family in mind.

Disney's Hollywood Studios has many shows. So if you are just looking for rides, you might want to consider doing Hollywood Studios and Epcot on the same day. They are 15-minute walk (or 10-minute boat ride) from one another. We recommend starting at Hollywood Studios and then heading to Epcot in the late afternoon.

> **Note:** We cover the Star Wars: Galaxy's Edge attractions in the next chapter.

HOLLYWOOD STUDIOS ROPE DROP STRATEGY

Hollywood Studios has one of the more expansive pre-opening areas. Guests are allowed to stroll down Hollywood Blvd as well as parts of Echo Lake. We recommend getting there 30 minutes early for the security before being allowed into the park. There is a welcome announcement with Cast Members.

We recommend heading to the back of the park for Star Wars: Galaxy's Edge and riding Rise of the Resistance first (unless you've scored a FastPass+ selection for it). Afterward, we recommend exploring Galaxy's Edge, riding the Millennium Falcon: Smugglers Run, or heading to Toy Story Land for Slinky Dog Dash.

HOLLYWOOD BOULEVARD

The grand, golden age-themed entrance of the Park. You'll feel like you're walking down a glamorized version of the real Hollywood Boulevard in the same way that Walt Disney experienced it when he first moved to Los Angeles. There are shops, a coffee joint, and loads of Hollywood golden-age glamour!

Theme: Golden Age Hollywood entrance

RIDES

MICKEY AND MINNIE'S RUNAWAY RAILWAY

Best for: Everyone
Description: A family-friendly dark ride with "2 1/2-D" and projection mapping special effects! Join Mickey and Minnie in this unique and funny attraction located in the Chinese Theater.
Level: Everyone
Recommendation: Due to the newness of this attraction and the rising popularity of Hollywood Studios, lines are long for Mickey and Minnie's Runaway Railway. We advise riding this attraction at park open or closer to night.
Line Length: Very Long
FastPass+: TBA

SHOWS AND ATTRACTIONS

WONDERFUL WORLD OF ANIMATION

Description: A 12-minute stunning nighttime projection show displays on the iconic Chinese Theatre. See the magic of Disney movies come to life with special effects and projections!

Recommendation: If you love nighttime shows, this is a unique one that celebrates the legacy of Disney animation. We recommend waiting about 30 minutes before the scheduled show time in front of the palm trees and stage. If you're too far back other trees might block your view. Ten minutes after is a showing of the stunning Star Wars: A Galactic Spectacular in the same location!

STAR WARS: A GALACTIC SPECTACULAR FIREWORKS

Best for: Everyone

Description: The music and images from the Star Wars films come to life on the Chinese Theatre with an epic fireworks display.

Level: Everyone

Recommendation: For every fireworks and Star Wars fan. To get the best views, wait 20-30 minutes before Wonderful World of Animation shows in the same spot. Then wait another ten minutes or so for this show to begin.

ECHO LAKE

This land is a bit of a hodgepodge of themes from George Lucas films like Star Wars and Indiana Jones, with the addition of theaters that recreate the palm-tree crowded Southern California feel from just outside of Hollywood.

Theme: Mock studios around a central lake.

RIDES

STAR TOURS – THE ADVENTURES CONTINUE
Best for: Kids, Tweens, Teens, Young Adults, Thrill Riders
Description: A Star Wars themed 3D motion simulator hosted by C-3PO. During the ride, you visit two of nine planets from the films, but they mix them up. Ride multiple times and get a different experience each time!
Level: Thrill Riders (must be 40"/ 102cm or taller)
Recommendation: A perfect ride for *Star Wars* fans. If you get motion sickness, you may want to skip this ride.
Line Length: Medium / **FastPass+:** Yes

SHOWS AND ATTRACTIONS

FOR THE FIRST TIME IN FOREVER: A FROZEN SING-ALONG CELEBRATION
Best for: Young Kids, Kids, Tweens, Adults 50+
Description: A 30-minute theatre show at the Hyperion Theatre starring Elsa, Anna, and their Frozen friends with music and more from the massively popular film.
Level: Family
Recommendation: Bring every *Frozen* fan that you know.
Line Length: Short / **FastPass+:** Yes

INDIANA JONES EPIC STUNT SPECTACULAR!
Best for: Everyone
Description: A 25-minute live stunt show starring Indiana Jones. See the action of *Raiders of the Lost Ark* in this epic attraction.

Level: Everyone
Recommendation: Great for everyone, though Young Kids who have a hard time sitting still for long or don't enjoy loud noises may want to skip this attraction.
Line Length: Short / **FastPass+:** Yes

GRAND AVENUE

Grand Avenue is home to LA-style shops, dining, and fun attractions starring the Muppets!

Theme: Present-Day Downtown Los Angeles

SHOWS AND ATTRACTIONS

MUPPET*VISION 3D
Best for: Young Kids, Kids, Tweens, Adults 50+
Description: A hilarious 15-minute 4D show with special effects and silly surprises starring Kermit the Frog and nearly every other character from *The Muppet Show*.
Level: Family
Recommendation: Perfect for families with Kids and fans of *The Muppet Show*.
Line Length: Very Short / **FastPass+:** Yes

· **Magic Tips** ·

Muppet*Vision was one of director and creator Jim Henson's final films. Unfortunately, he passed away before its debut in 1991, but it's exciting to know that his legendary work is still entertaining audiences every day.

ANIMATION COURTYARD

Venture into a studio lot dedicated to the art of Walt Disney Animation Studios. See live shows as well as meet characters in this unique land.

Theme: Walt Disney Animation Studios

SHOWS AND ATTRACTIONS

DISNEY JUNIOR DANCE PARTY!
Best for: Young Kids
Description: A live action dance show starring Disney Junior characters designed for preschool-aged children.
Level: Young Kids
Recommendation: Families with young children.
Line Length: Short / **FastPass+:** Yes

VOYAGE OF THE LITTLE MERMAID
Best for: Young Kids, Kids, Tweens
Description: A family-friendly live show that brings to life the characters, adventure, and music of Disney's *The Little Mermaid*. The entire show is 17 minutes in length.
Level: Family
Recommendation: Great for families with Young Kids and fans of Disney's *The Little Mermaid*. Others might want to check out the Indiana Jones show or Beauty and the Beast.
Line Length: Short / **FastPass+:** Yes

WALT DISNEY PRESENTS
Best for: Teens and Adults
Description: See sneak peeks of upcoming attractions as well as exhibits detailing how Disney brings its theme parks to life.
Level: Everyone

Recommendation: We recommend this attraction for theme park enthusiasts or those who like to explore the history of Walt Disney World.
Line Length: Short / **FastPass+:** None

SUNSET BOULEVARD

A fictionalized version of the famous Sunset Boulevard and see the harrowing Hollywood Hotel in the distance. There are also iconic shows and fantastic shops in this area.

Theme: Hollywood Street

RIDES

THE TWILIGHT ZONE TOWER OF TERROR
Best for: Tweens, Teens, Adults, Thrill Riders
Description: Plummet down thirteen treacherous stories in this *Twilight Zone*-themed thrill ride.
Level: Thrill Riders (must be 40"/ 102cm or taller)
Recommendation: Only those looking to be scared! If you decide to skip the FastPass, we recommend riding Tower of Terror in the evening. The line for this ride tends to get shorter later in the day once everyone has already ridden it. For optimal thrills, sitting front row can make a difference. If you want to sit in front, ask a Cast Member at the end of the queue.
Line Length: Long
FastPass+: Yes

· **Magic Tips** ·
The library room (with the black and white TV) shuffles guests around. If you want to be the first group to ride, move to the back of the room where you'll see a closed door. That's the quickest way to the final line once the preshow finishes.

ROCK 'N' ROLLER COASTER STARRING AEROSMITH
Best for: Teens, Adults, Thrill Riders
Description: Similar to Space Mountain, this coaster is indoors and fairly dark. You are launched into loops, corkscrews, and inversions to get your blood flowing! Aerosmith sets the tone and music to this epic attraction.
Level: Thrill Riders (must be 48"/ 122cm or taller)

Recommendation: We notice that the lines can be quite long for this ride as there aren't many options for Thrill Riders in Hollywood Studios. If you are looking forward to riding this attraction, make sure that you book a FastPass+ reservation. To avoid much of the line, move to the far left near the doors when you enter the recording studio room with Aerosmith. You'll bypass the crowd when entering the final line.
Line Length: Very Long
FastPass+: Yes

SHOWS AND ATTRACTIONS

LIGHTNING MCQUEEN'S RACING ACADEMY
Best for: Young Kids, Kids, Tweens
Description: An animated theater racing show with characters from Pixar's *Cars*.
Level: Family
Recommendation: Great for kids! Stay afterward to meet Cruz Ramirez.
Line Length: Short
FastPass+: Yes

BEAUTY AND THE BEAST – LIVE ON STAGE
Best for: Young Kids, Kids, Tweens, Adults 50+
Description: A 25-minute live Broadway-style musical starring the cast of Disney's animated film, Beauty and the Beast.
Level: Everyone
Recommendation: Perfect for fans of Broadway-style musicals
Line Length: Short
FastPass+: Yes

FANTASMIC!

Best for: Everyone

Description: The stunning Hollywood Hills Amphitheater brings to life the 26-minute Disney spectacular, Fantasmic! See Mickey and more in this epic show of light, music, and special effects all on the water. But be careful because the Disney Villains are on the loose!

Level: Everyone

Recommendation: Everyone should see this show at least once. After Fantasmic! you'll either want to leave or head to the Star Wars Fireworks show. Either way, head near the entrance to watch the fireworks.

Line Length: Medium

FastPass+: Yes – If you opt for the FastPass+, you will be placed in a special section in the front and near the center. If you miss the FastPass+ option, get to the Amphitheater at least 30 minutes beforehand and sit as close to the center of the seating for the best views.

Reserved Seating with Dining: Reserve a Dining Package and receive a voucher for seating in the center. We recommend the Hollywood & Vine or Brown Derby dinner packages.

STAR WARS LAUNCH BAY – Meet Chewbacca, Darth Vader, and Jawas while seeing replicas of props used in the original *Star Wars* films.

· Magic Tips ·

Why are *Star Wars*-themed attractions outside of Star Wars: Galaxy's Edge? Star Tours and Star Wars Launch Bay mostly focus on themed elements from the first two movie trilogies while Star Wars: Galaxy's Edge is based around the newer trilogy starring Rey. We expect most *Star Wars* attractions outside of Galaxy's Edge to eventually get reimagined.

TOY STORY LAND

A land based around Pixar's *Toy Story* film series. Shrink down as you enter Andy's backyard to experience like the size of a toy!

Theme: Pixar's *Toy Story*

RIDES

SLINKY DOG DASH
Best for: Everyone
Description: A family-friendly launch rollercoaster through Andy's backyard. Andy has placed his slinky dog on the RC racer track!
Level: Kids, Tweens, Teens, Adults, Thrill Riders (must be 38"/ 97cm or taller)
Recommendation: Great for rollercoaster lovers of all ages.
Line Length: Very Long
FastPass+: Yes
Holiday Overlay: The same attraction changes with sleigh bells and season decorations beginning in November.

ALIEN SWIRLING SAUCERS
Best for: Everyone
Description: Get flicked and whirled around on flying saucers while escaping the ominous claw!
Level: Family (must be 32"/ 82cm or taller)
Recommendation: Perfect for families with kids looking for a fun and thrilling ride. Thrill riders might also enjoy this unpredictable attraction!
Line Length: Long
FastPass: Yes
Holiday Overlay: The same attraction changes with holiday music beginning in November.

TOY STORY MANIA!
Best for: Everyone
Description: A 4D game where riders attempt to score the most points by shooting at animated targets with a plunger canon.
Level: Everyone

Recommendation: All ages will enjoy this ride from Young Kids to Thrill Riders. Not recommended if you have trouble seeing with 3D glasses.

Line Length: Very Long

FastPass+: Yes

Scoring Big: Many "pro" riders hold the plunger between two fingers with their palm facing them—be careful not to pull too hard of course! While most riders aim for the middle of the screen, the higher points are often at the bottom. Also look for bonuses in these scenes:

- Scene #1 (Hamm and Eggs) – Hitting the pigs on the fence will make a cat show that can be hit multiple times for big points.
- Scene #2 (Rex and Trixie) – Pop the lava balloons on the volcano to make it erupt with 500-point balloons.
- Scene #3 (Green Army Men) – Look for the yellow-tinted plates that are worth 2,000 points.
- Scene #4 (Alien Ring Game) – On the far sides are rocket ships and aliens worth big points.
- Scene #5 (Woody's Western Theme) – Aim for the doors of the saloon to reveal higher point targets. At the end of this scene there are mine carts that roll toward you. Look for the bats above the mine carts that are worth some major points.

CHAPTER NINE

STAR WARS: GALAXY'S EDGE GUIDE

For decades Disney theme parks have gone virtually unmatched by competitors. Not only are they the most popular theme parks in the world, but the Disney brand is practically synonymous with themed entertainment. All of that changed when The Wizarding World of Harry Potter opened in Universal's Islands of Adventure in Orlando. Suddenly, there was a theme park expansion so stunningly immersive that tourists were planning trips to become part of the Harry Potter storyline.

It became abundantly clear to Disney that these immersive worlds were the next generation of theme park entertainment. But what would Disney build? They dropped the ball some years back when the theme park's rights to Harry Potter fell through (that's right, Disney originally had the rights to the Wizarding World). Thus, two years later Disney purchased Lucasfilm which brought Star Wars into the lineup of their properties.

Star Wars is the perfect answer to Harry Potter. In its 40-year history, the franchise has earned an estimated $65 billion in merchandise, box office, home video, and more. Its fandom is also wide-reaching and multigenerational, making the storylines familiar to millions of potential park guests.

So, what was Disney going to do with Star Wars? Transport visitors to a galaxy far, far away, have them become Jedis, fly the Millennium Falcon, and meet Chewbacca? Well, yes! With Star Wars: Galaxy's Edge, Disney has created its most massive, most immersive expansion to date. There are Stormtroopers marching down ancient streets, a secret hideaway where guests can learn the ways of the Jedi, and even a shopping district where visitors can haggle with aliens!

The party gets started when guests enter Oga's Cantina, which is much like the one found in the first *Star Wars* film—though no one hopefully gets their arm chopped off! Disney also went as far as omitting signage in Galaxy's Edge and used alien writing instead to make the land feel as authentic as possible. Some of this writing is a bit easy to read while others require your mobile phone to decode (more on that later).

Galaxy's Edge stretches across 14 acres, which is roughly the same size as 2-3 lands in a typical Disney theme park. The magic is in the details, which took Imagineers about two years just to complete the rock work and paint needed to bring Galaxy's Edge to life. One half of the land is crowded with shops, dining, and the Millennium Falcon! This is where guests can explore and also fly the famous ship on the flight simulator, Millennium Falcon: Smugglers

The other half is the hiding spot of the Resistance. This area isn't as populated, but there are some iconic ships and characters to take photos with. The Resistance side is supposed to look unassuming as it holds a hidden path to the land's signature attraction, Star Wars: Rise of the Resistance. This jaw-dropping dark ride has guests join the Resistance to battle the First Order in an epic intergalactic confrontation!

In this chapter, we review the story, attractions, and tips for exploring Star Wars: Galaxy's Edge. It's like visiting a theme park within another theme park and feels like nothing ever created before!

THE STORY

Star Wars: Galaxy's Edge is an entirely immersive land with a vibrant backstory. Set on the fictional planet of Batuu at the edge of the Star Wars galaxy, this ancient destination is home to a variety of creatures. Black Spire Outpost is the main area guests explore in Batuu. It's an old trading area once used as a ship  refueling station before hyperspace was invented. Black Spire gets its name from an enormous dark, petrified tree at its center. At night, all of the petrified spires around the outpost glow with vibrant hues!

Today, Black Spire Outpost is the home of rogues looking to escape the clutch of the First Order. In this timeline—set shortly after the events of *Star Wars: The Last Jedi (Episode VIII)*—the wicked First Order has indeed arrived. Kylo Ren and his fleet of Stormtroopers scour Black Spire Outpost for "rebel scum." Meanwhile, Resistance members like Rey and Chewbacca hide on the outskirts of Black Spire.

Now, if Batuu doesn't sound familiar, it's because Disney invented the planet for its theme parks. They wanted a new, yet familiar land for Galaxy's Edge. Nearly every major element from

across *Star Wars* films and animated TV series can be found on Batuu. The round-top buildings of Black Spire Outpost are reminiscent of Naboo while the lush surroundings look like Alderaan. Oga's Cantina feels a lot like the one found on Tatooine. As you browse the Merchant Row, you'll see creatures and items from the entire Star Wars Universe. This includes species found around Jabba the Hutt's palace like the amphibious Worrt (located in Oga's Cantina) and a Kowakian monkey-lizard (purchasable in the Creature Stall shop). There's even a "live" baby Sarlacc (the sand monster that ate Boba Fett in *Return of the Jedi*) in Dok-Ondar's Den of Antiquities.

Disney made it so that every crevice of Batuu is sprinkled with Star Wars charm. For anyone doubting that a land like this belongs in a Disney theme park, guess again. There's nothing but magic, fantasy, and dazzling storytelling throughout Galaxy's Edge. Even if you've never seen a *Star Wars* film, the spectacular production is mind-blowing. The world appears real, and the fun is abundant. No matter what your expectations are, you're certainly in for a wild ride.

ENTERING GALAXY'S EDGE

The easiest time to visit Galaxy's Edge is at the start of the day. Once the land hits capacity, Disney may issue mobile "boarding passes" with group numbers. This pass can be accessed on your mobile device via the Walt Disney World app. If you miss the cut off point, simply apply for a free boarding pass on your phone and wait until you receive a pop up notification with your return time. Boarding passes are only distributed on *very* busy days, so this system is may not be in effect during your visit.

MAP OF GALAXY'S EDGE

Toy Story Land Entrance

Grand Avenue Entrance

a. Star Wars: Rise of the Resistance (ride)
b. Market (shopping)
c. Docking Bay 7 Food & Cargo (dining)
d. Droid Depot (droid build)
e. Savi's Workshop (lightsaber build)
f. Millennium Falcon: Smuggler's Run (ride)
g. Oga's Cantina (bar)
h. Milk Stand (drinks)

RIDES

There are two featured rides in Star Wars: Galaxy's Edge. The first is Millennium Falcon: Smugglers Run, a flight simulation ride where guests collaborate to fly Han Solo's famous ship. It's incredible to see that Disney built the Falcon from the ground up. We don't mean a *part* of it or a *model* of it. Disney built the entire ship *to scale*—and you get to fly it!

Seeing the Falcon for the first time brings many visitors to tears. It's like meeting a long lost friend in an unexpected place. Disney effectively unveils the ship by making visitors peak around a corner or step down stairs as it comes into view. After the initial shock, you might want to touch the thing, but there's a rusty-looking barrier surrounding the Falcon that keeps us humans at bay. Luckily, Disney photographers happily snap photos in front of her. Best of all, these shots don't get other guests in the background!

Finally, you get to fly the Millennium Falcon! But not so fast —there will likely be a wait. Luckily, the queue is riddled with Star Wars surprises. There are engine parts, defunct droids, and an unfinished game of Sabacc. Best of all, there are dozens and dozens of easter eggs to look for when you're in the queue—what can you spot? (Hint: look for Porgs!)

> · **Magic Tips** ·
> Disney PhotoPass works widely around Galaxy's Edge, including a spot in front of the Millennium Falcon. Photos taken by Disney photographers will show up on your Walt Disney World mobile app usually within a couple of hours after being taken. Remember that Disney photographers will gladly take a photo with your phone camera— just ask.

Just before entering the Falcon, you'll meet Hondo Ohnaka, Disney's second-most advanced animatronic (the first being the singing Na'vi shaman in Pandora—The World of Avatar). The way that Hondo moves around the space makes him appear more like an actor than a robot. Hondo's believable performance is essential to the ride as he gives details about the mission. Finally, you'll walk into the famous halls of the Millennium Falcon and will receive a placeholder with one of three roles (we'll get into those next). This placeholder will come with a color group, and you'll explore the Falcon before your group is called into the cockpit.

The best part about the attraction is exploring the Falcon. Take a photo with the Dejarik board—a holographic game played on the ship (it doesn't work here though)—or one of Chewy's bed. There's tons to see and very little time before your color group is called—so use it wisely.

Now, of course, you're not actually inside the ship we described earlier. Instead, Disney built several mock cockpits for the simulation. Once inside the cockpit, you'll take the seat according to your placeholder. There are three jobs: pilot, gunner, or flight engineer. Each requires pushing buttons, flipping switches, and/or cranking the ship into hyperspace! Engineers sit in the back, followed by gunners in the center, and pilots in front. Engineers and gunners press buttons which light up when it's time to fire or activate something. Gunners fire at objects (you can manually target or select the recommended automatic setting) and flight engineers help repair damage from attacks and poor flying. Pilots have most of the physical work. The left pilot flies side movements, and the right is in charge of up, down, and launching into hyperspace.

· **Magic Tips** ·

Flying the pilot position has the best views of the screens, but it also requires the most work. Sadly, you can't choose which job you play. If you're wanting to pilot, we recommend asking the Cast Member and waiting your turn until they can issue you a pilot position. You can also ask others in your group to switch positions.

Flying the Falcon means crashing into things, causing explosions, and stealing cargo from another ship. There are some Star Wars enemy crafts and a select few other elements, but the entire thing feels like a giant, detailed video game. Since it is like a game, this ride might not be for everyone. We also think that if you're well-versed in playing video games, you'll have an easier time with the controls. If you win, you're rewarded with some virtual credits—if you lose, you'll notice a very banged up ship as you exit the hallway.

Also, when riding the Falcon, you can earn credits for how well your mission goes. Disney keeps track of these in the Play Disney app. When you first open the app, it'll ask to leave the Bluetooth feature on—this piece is essential for recording your credits on your flight.

· **Magic Tips** ·

Keep in mind, if you get motion sickness on rides like Star Tours, this attraction is another flight simulator that may cause the same sensation.

The Millennium Falcon ride experience also changes day and night. For example, fly during the day, and you'll see the sun out. At night, it's much darker around Black Spire Outpost!

MILLENNIUM FALCON: SMUGGLERS RUN

Best for: Kids, Tweens, Teens, Adults, Thrill Riders
Restrictions: 38" / 97cm
FastPass+: Yes

STAR WARS: RISE OF THE RESISTANCE

Best for: Kids, Tweens, Teens, Adults, Thrill Riders
Restrictions: 40" / 102cm
FastPass+: Yes

SHOWS

The shows of Galaxy's Edge don't have the same style as the traditional theatrical productions at Disney theme parks. Instead of running on a schedule, they appear to occur at random before unsuspecting guests. The two main stages are located on opposite sides of Black Spire Outpost. The first being Kylo Ren's ship where the First Order dramatically welcomes their leader to Batuu. The second stage is near the back of the Market, where rebels like Vi Moradi take on the First Order. This show is even more explosive than the one with Kylo!

> · **Magic Tips** ·
> Shows in Galaxy's Edge mostly occur during the day, as do most character meetings (though Rey and Chewbacca have been spotted in the evenings). Just keep this in mind if you are planning on visiting at night.

If you don't know who Vi Moradi is, you're not alone. She's a fairly new character, only having debuted in a *Star Wars* novel back in 2017. Vi Moradi, a rebel spy, is easy to pick out of a crowd. She has black and blue hair and usually wears a bright orange rebel vest. Vi was sent to Batuu by General Leia Organa to spy on Kylo and his troops.

We love the shows in Galaxy's Edge because guests become part of the storyline. Talk to Vi Moradi, and she might tell you about her mission. Kylo Ren also walks through the crowd as he looks for rebels. These are ideal times to snap a photo with your favorite Star Wars characters.

DINING

Disney has created out-of-this-world dining experiences for Star Wars: Galaxy's Edge! There's a lively cantina serving alcoholic (and non-alcoholic) beverages, a rustic dining hall, and a stand with the famous blue milk!

The food in Galaxy's Edge is somewhat eclectic. Disney purposely made the flavors hard to place so that each bite seems foreign. For foodies, this is great. There are a wide variety of new treats in store for them across the entire land. For many children and picky eaters, getting something to tickle their tastebuds might be a bit challenging. If this pertains to your traveling party, we highly recommend reviewing the menu options on the Walt Disney World mobile app before visiting.

OGA'S CANTINA

This high-energy cantina feels incredibly authentic to the Star Wars Universe. The ancient-looking building houses a hodgepodge of equipment, creatures, and a droid DJ! The owner, Oga Garra, is a Blutopian who also runs the cantina. She doesn't take any sass and expects all guests to follow her rules. We never really see Oga, but her staff talks wildly about her as if she's a well-known threat.

For those who recall the captain of the first Star Tours attraction, you're in for a treat. DJ R-3X (voiced by Paul Reubens, a.k.a. "Pee-wee Herman") spins day and night as bartenders deliver fizzing, bubbling, and steaming drinks to their patrons. Each of the cocktails is named after a Star Wars theme or creature—and comes with a high price tag starting at $14 for an alcoholic beverage. There are drinks for kids, too, like the Blue Bantha with a cookie on top!

Oga's Cantina also serves separate breakfast and lunch/

dinner options. Morning beverages include coffees, juices, and drinks like the Bloody Rancor (Bloody Mary). For lunch/dinner, guests can sample the regular menu with dozens of drinks including cocktails, beers on tap, and hard cider on tap. The cantina serves most styles of alcohol from vodka and rum to beer and wine. If you're visiting in the morning and don't like the selection, ask your waiter or bartender for the standard menu.

Note: We highly recommend grabbing a reservation at Oga's Cantina as this is one of the most difficult bookings to make in Walt Disney World. Book through the app or at WaltDisneyWorld.com.

OGA'S CANTINA RECOMMENDATIONS

Spiran Caf / Type: Breakfast Alcohol
A hot coffee with rum, orange marmalade, and vanilla whipped cream

Dagobah Slug Slinger / Type: Lunch/Dinner Alcohol
A semi-sweet drink made with tequila, blue curacao, ginger, herbs, citrus juice, and bitters

T-16 Skyhopper / Type: Lunch/Dinner Alcohol
A bold drink made with vodka, melon liqueur, half and half, and served with a kiwi candy garnish

Oga's Obsession / Type: Non-Alcoholic Provision
A gelatinous mix of lemonade and cotton candy flavors served with dried fruit eaten with a spoon

Carbon Freeze / Type: Non-Alcoholic Drink
Lemon-lime and wild strawberry juices with blueberry and green apple "popping pearls"

Secret Menu Item: Charcuterie Board
A large plate of dried meats, cheeses, pickled veggies, and dipping sauces. This cheese and meat board has some wild flavors that we only recommend for adventurous eaters.

· **Magic Tips** ·
The Cantina may also limit your experience to two drinks per person and a 45-minute max time slot.

DOCKING BAY 7 FOOD AND CARGO

This rustic quick-service diner serves a variety of alien eats for guests to enjoy. We think that the food here closely resembles Asian-fusion cuisine with some surprising twists. For example, the sweet and spicy Smoked Kaadu Ribs comes with a blueberry corn muffin. Additionally, there aren't forks and knives in Galaxy's Edge (for now). Instead, guests must use a spork-like utensil to cut, scoop, and eat. Yes, this can be a little tricky at first, but it doesn't take long to get the hang of the spork. It's these unexpected touches that give Black Spire Outpost its alien feel.

DOCKING BAY 7 DINING RECOMMENDATIONS

Smoked Kaadu Ribs / Type: lunch and dinner entree
Pork ribs slathered in a sweet and lightly spicy sauce and served with a melt-in-your-mouth blueberry corn muffin and cabbage slaw

Braised Shaak Roast / Type: dinner entree
Savory beef pot roast served over pasta with cooked kale and mushroom

Moof Juice / Type: all-day non-alcoholic beverage
A very sweet concoction of fruit juices and chipotle-pineapple

Oi-oi Puff / Type: lunch and dinner dessert
A delectable creamy raspberry puff with passion fruit mousse

Other eats are located at the Milk Stand near Oga's Cantina and Kat Saka's Kettle (popcorn) in the Market. The Milk Stand line gets long but moves fairly quickly. Here you can try blue and/or green milk from the *Star Wars* films. These "milks" are plant-based (dairy-free) and served cold like a slushy. Each milk has a unique flavor with blue tasting somewhat like blueberry candy and the green having more a light melon flavor. We recommend the blue milk, and most surveyed guests seemed to enjoy this flavor as well.

Kat Saka's Kettle popcorn is covered in a sweet and spicy glaze. It's a delicious flavor of kettle corn not found anywhere else! The mix is designed to be eaten by the handful, mixing all of the flavors together with each bite.

If you're still hungry, try Ronto Roasters. Look for the droid spinning meat under a podracer engine and enjoy some of the fresh delicacies. We recommend the Ronto Wrap made with pork sausage, peppercorn sauce, and tangy slaw wrapped in pita bread. Drinks also look a bit different on Batuu. Coke bottles, for example, are in the round shape of a thermal detonator. These items add to the fun and storytelling behind Galaxy's Edge.

· Magic Tips ·

The Milk Stand and Docking Bay 7 both take mobile orders via the Walt Disney World mobile app. If the lines are long, use this method to order.

SHOPPING

There are seemingly infinite items to purchase in Galaxy's Edge including cute Porg plushies and Jedi robes! You can also purchase a Kowakian monkey-lizard puppet (the small creature found with Jabba the Hutt) that sits on your shoulder and moves with your commands. If this sounds familiar, it's because the monkey-lizards work similarly to the banshees in Pandora—The World of Avatar in Disney's Animal Kingdom.

If you're searching for a gift, try the Toydarian Toymaker, a small shop with plenty of handmade toys for kids. Or head over to the Jewels of Bith for t-shirts, bags, or a misting fan. Disney also sells a metal gift card in Galaxy's Edge called the Batuuan Spira (a coin of Batuu). These gift cards are available with a minimum load of $100, and you can keep the coin as a gift after using.

Sadly, some of the better experiences in Galaxy's Edge come at an extra cost. Savi's Workshop and the Droid Depot are amazingly fun, but you might spend hundreds of dollars entertaining your family. Here we review these experiences to help decide what's best for your visit.

SAVI'S WORKSHOP
CUSTOM LIGHTSABERS REVIEW

Savi's Workshop is a secret backdoor area—sort of like a speakeasy —where those seeking the Force can become a Jedi! In other words, you find a secret entrance in a scrap metal yard to build a custom lightsaber for around $200. Because of the hefty price tag, we only recommend this experience for those who are serious Star Wars fans.

These lightsabers are as good as real. They have metal hilts, and the blades make sounds as they draw in and out. You can choose one of four handles: Peace and Justice (Republic-era Jedi), Power and Control (dark side/Sith), Elemental Nature (wild Jedi), or Protection and Defense (ancient Jedi). There are also four different kyber crystals that change the color of the blade: blue, red, green, or violet.

The lightsaber building experience includes a moving pre-show where guests are taught the ways of the Jedi until they are finally sworn in by a mystical guest (give you a hint of who it is, we will...) For true Star Wars fans, Savi's Workshop will be one of the best moments of their trip. Having a "working" lightsaber that both looks and feels real is one thing, but becoming part of the Jedi order is absolutely mind-blowing. John Williams, the original composer of the Star Wars films, scored new music to fit this stunning experience. While we wished for some extra animatronics, Savi's Workshop delivers with great storytelling through script, lighting, and sound. We believe that adults and kids 5 and older will greatly appreciate this experience. Savi's Workshop only allows one guest to accompany each builder, so plan accordingly.

If you're not a big Star Wars fan, you might want to skip this one if $200 sounds out of your price range. Sure, it's a fantastic show, but some of the magic might be missed if you don't appreciate the folklore from this franchise. The lightsabers are also huge—about 45 inches (114 cm)—so small children will have a difficult time wielding these. Also keep in mind that your lightsaber doesn't easily break down, so something this size won't fit in a rental locker. For this reason, you may want to schedule Savi's Workshop around the end of the day or when you can take time to place it somewhere. Otherwise, you'll be riding rollercoasters like Space Mountain with it between your legs!

· **Magic Tips** ·
Savi's Workshop takes around 80-90 guests an hour. Thus, time slots can become full very quickly with demand. If you're planning on building a lightsaber, reserve your experience at **WaltDisneyWorld.com**.

If you want a different saber hilt, visit Dok-Ondar's Den of Antiquities and see if you can barter or trade for one. Individual lightsaber parts and pieces are sold outside of Savi's, and are limited to two parts per purchased lightsaber.

DOK-ONDAR'S DEN OF ANTIQUITIES

Our favorite shopping spot in Galaxy's Edge is Dok-Ondar's Den of Antiquities. Inside, you'll see an extensive collection of rarities from exclusive kyber crystals to exotic creatures. Most impressive is the animatronic Dok-Ondar, a finicky Ithorian who might trade with you for one of his prized lightsaber helms—or you can uncover your own treasure within his collection. Dok-Ondar sells white and yellow kyber crystals that change the color of lightsaber blades. Additional blue, red, green, and violet crystals found in Savi's Workshop are sold, too!

· **Magic Tips** ·
Those who buy a red kyber crystal may discover a secret black one with a special note! We've been told that these black crystals are fairly rare!

There are seemingly countless collected goods in Dok-Ondar's Den of Antiquities. Look at the second level of the the shop to spot some classic *Star Wars* and other Lucasfilm items. There's also the Arc of the Covenant prop from *Indiana Jones*!

DROID DEPOT

See a working factory where guests can make their very own remote-controlled droid! You pick the parts to customize a BB-8 or R2-D2 unit. The droids start around $100 each and are fun to build for kids and adults (we recommend ages 6 and older, though Disney lists 3 and older). The Droid Depot doesn't have the show elements found in Savi's Workshop, but it likely makes a better take-home toy. Kids might play with lightsabers a bit, but a remote-control toy is fun for just about everyone.

Droid Depot is also home to some luxury finds. Guests can buy and design a fully animatronic R2-D2 for $25,000! If you're dropping the dough on this one, R2 can be customized with personality and a battle-worn appearance. If $25,000 is just a *little* bit out of your price range, R2 also hangs out at the depot for pics and chats with guests!

> · **Magic Tips** ·
> The best droid parts may run out toward the end of the day. If you're looking for a variety, head to the Droid Depot early on during your visit.

THE MARKET

Black Spire's prime marketplace is home to a gallery of small shops. Set up like a co-op, guests can browse the shelves and hidden elements within these stores. Most of the items appear handmade, so as to add to the authenticity of visiting an alien planet with realistic merchandise.

Black Spire Outfitters – Pick up a Jedi robe and other costumes inspired by characters like Rey and the dark-sided Sith. Clothing pieces come in multiple sizes for kids and adults. Unfortunately, Disney prevents those aged 14 and older from wearing these costumes throughout the park. This ban may be removed in the near future as demand increases for guests to live out their Star Wars story in full garb.

Creature Stall – Set up like a small pet store, this shop is filled with *Stars Wars*-inspired toys from porg puppets to plush tauntauns. There are also several small animatronics here including a sleeping loth-cat found in a crate near the entrance. Loth-cats are furry alien critters made famous from the animated series *Star Wars Rebels*. Outside of the Creature Stall is a small register with Kowakian monkey-lizards, sinister-looking critters that work as puppets that sit on guests' shoulders. These monkey-lizards—like the one found in Jabba the Hutt's palace in *Return of the Jedi*—run about $70 each.

Jewels of Bith – The Bith were an alien race from the planet of Clak'dor VII. They were known for their highly evolved mental and motor skills for playing music and creating fine wares. If you're looking for more day-to-day clothes, this store sells everything from t-shirts and jackets to hats and trinkets. Pick up misting fans, keychains, pins, and several other gifts in this shop. To keep with authenticity, nothing in this store will say "Star Wars: Galaxy's Edge" but instead read "Black Spire Outpost" or "Batuu."

Toydarian Toymaker – Discover wooden and hand-sewn toys perfect for collectors of all ages. There are also instruments and games for sale here. The store gets its name from the flying alien species, Toydarians, like Watto who appeared as a junk dealer in *The Phantom Menace*. You can see the Toydarian shop owner, Zabaka, flying around her shop through a foggy window.

OTHER STORES

The Resistance Supply – Kiosks found near the Rise of the Resistance attraction selling various gifts, clothes, and toys.

First Order Cargo — A store near Kylo Ren's ship that sells goods fitted for the light or the dark side. Buy everything from clothing to trinkets made famous by Star Wars characters. Look above First Order Cargo and spot Stormtroopers on the roofs!

MORE TO EXPLORE

The Play Disney mobile application has a special data pad designed just for Galaxy's Edge. Open the app, click on the icon in Galaxy's Edge, and follow the instructions to hack, decode, and interact with the world around you. You'll earn points as you crack simple codes, and assist your chosen side—the Resistance or the First Order!

SECRETS OF GALAXY'S EDGE

Super-Zoom Droid

There's a super-zoom camera located near First Order Cargo. Ask a citizen of Batuu (Cast Member) to have your photo taken by this droid. You'll need Disney PhotoPass to download it on your device.

The Language

Learn the language of Batuu from the locals! They say many words and phrases that aren't used on Earth. Some are a bit self-explanatory while others can be somewhat confusing to hear for the first time. For example, there are several ways to say "hello" or "goodbye" when visiting Batuu. To keep you up to speed, here are several of the phrases we've gathered:

BATUUAN SPEAK	ENGLISH MEANING
Datapad	mobile device/phone/credit card machine
Credits	dollars (money)
Credentials	Disney Annual Pass or Disney Vacation Club Card
Credit Reducer	Disney Annual Pass or Disney Vacation Club Card
Hydrator	water fountain
Scans	photos
Image Data Card	Disney PhotoPass Card
Image Scanner	camera / phone camera
Cargo	personal items such as backpacks and cameras
Cargo Manifest	receipt
Holograms	Magic Shots (added effects to Disney PhotoPass images
"Good Run!"	"Good Luck!"

"Bright Suns!"	"Good Day!" or "Hello!" said in the daytime
"Rising Moons!"	"Good Evening!" or "Hello!" said at night
"Under the Shadow of the Spire!"	"Cheers!"
"May the Spires Keep You!"	"Goodbye!"
"Till the Spire!"	"Goodbye!" or "Until We Meet Again!"
"Good Journey!"	"Goodbye!"
"For the Order!"	a First Order salute
"May the Force Be With You"	a Resistance salute
"Only the ancients know…"	"I don't know…"
Travelers/Off-Worlder	park guests
Inhabitants	Cast Members working in Star Wars: Galaxy's Edge
Youngling/Padwan	child
Youngling Transporter	stroller

ADVENTURE AWAITS...

Virtually every corner of Galaxy's Edge has some hidden surprises awaiting you. For example, drink from the water fountain near the Market and spot a dianoga—the trash monster found in the original *Star Wars* film! With so much to see and do, you'll want to set aside plenty of time (and maybe a chunk of cash) before visiting Galaxy's Edge. You might not be able to do it all in a single day, which will only increase your desire to return to this beautiful and unique land.

CHAPTER TEN

DISNEY'S ANIMAL KINGDOM

INTRODUCTION

Completed in 1998, Disney's Animal Kingdom is a unique theme park dedicated to both the classic Walt Disney World attractions as well as animal conservation. With lions, tigers, and elephants living in the Park, it would seem that Animal Kingdom is Disney's version of a zoo. That couldn't be further from the truth. The Park is breathtaking in its seamless foliage between specialized lands and perfect environments for its animals. As you travel through the jungle, you'll meet Disney favorites like meerkats and warthogs as well as critically endangered species. Disney takes this park seriously and works its hardest to be the best for its animal inhabitants.

Set on more than 500 acres of land, Animal Kingdom is not only the largest park in WDW, it's the largest theme park in the world! The centerpiece is the famous Tree of Life, a 14-story replica of the same tree from Disney's *The Lion King*. Animal Kingdom perfectly ties together fun and information in 6 distinct lands: Oasis (the lush main entrance), Discovery Island (a central hub including The Tree of Life), Africa (an African village with safaris), Rafiki's Planet Watch (a family-friendly outpost), Asia (excursions of the East and home of the towering Expedition Everest ride), DinoLand U.S.A (where dinosaurs roam the Earth once again), and Pandora—The World of Avatar (an alien planet inspired by the James Cameron film, *Avatar*).

While some informative attractions in Epcot and Hollywood Studios can seem a bit boring and dated, Animal Kingdom feels new and exciting in all of its exhibits. Perhaps it's that you are seeing the actual animals roam as you ride on an African-style safari while you learn about the many habits of the spectacular creatures before you. Or maybe it's that Animal Kingdom feels perfectly nestled in the Floridian weather, bringing you a sense that you are climbing the steps of Asian countryside or deep in the heart of the jungle. Then again, it could be the blend of family-friendly attractions, beautiful animals, and expansive thrill rides that gives something to everyone at this unique Park. Whatever the reason, Animal Kingdom is flawless and perhaps the best park in all of Walt Disney World. In this chapter, we review each of the lands as well as give you an index of animal locations throughout the park.

ANIMAL KINGDOM ROPE DROP STRATEGY

We recommend getting to the Animal Kingdom park 30-minutes before opening. This will allow you to get through security, then head through the Oasis and onto Discovery Island where guests crowd in front of the Tree of Life. There's also a special surprise for those who get to the Park early. About 10 minutes from opening time, you'll hear an announcement. A pleasant voice will welcome you to the Animal Kingdom, and a small showing of beautiful parrots will glide overhead. It's a stunning display and not to be missed!

If you didn't score a FastPass+ selection for AVATAR: Flight of Passage, ride this attraction first. You'll notice that most guests head this way (since the line for this ride can easily exceed two hours later in the day). After Flight of Passage, we recommend the Navi River Journey, Kilimanjaro Safaris, and then DINOSAUR. You'll bounce around the park a bit doing this method, but you can easily go back to spots like Pandora—The World of Avatar later on for more exploration.

THE OASIS

The lush entrance to Disney's Animal Kingdom. Here you will find several walkways through bush and along rivers filled with exotic plants and animals that find their home here. The Rainforest Café is also located here. There are no rides in the Oasis, so this land feels a lot like a well-designed animal sanctuary.

Theme: Tropical Oasis

ANIMALS
Mammals: Barbirusa, Giant Anteater, Swamp Wallaby
Reptiles: Florida Cooter, Rhinoceros Iguanas
Birds: African Spoonbill, Bufflehead, Chiloe Wigeon, Exotic Duck, Hooded Merganser, Indian Spotbill, Macaw, Medium Sulpher-crested Cockatoo, Reeves' Muntjac, Teal

DISCOVERY ISLAND

The centerpiece or "hub" of Animal Kingdom. It's home to several animals, shops, and the Park's signature Tree of Life. Discovery Island is surrounded by the Discover River and connects to nearly every land in the Park.

Theme: An Animal-Inhabited Island

SHOWS AND ATTRACTIONS

TREE OF LIFE AWAKENING
Best for: Everyone
Description: See the Tree of Life come to life with four different animations that magically project on the tree at night.
Level: Family

Recommendation: This nighttime show can best be seen as you walk toward it from the Oasis. Views and details are better seen closer to the tree. Since this show occurs throughout the night, crowds usually stop forming after the first hour or so.
Line Length: None / **FastPass:** No

IT'S TOUGH TO BE A BUG!
Best for: Everyone
Description: A 9-minute family-friendly 4D show starring characters from Pixar's *A Bug's Life*. With special lighting effects and a large 3D screen, you'll feel as small as a bug as you laugh along to this hilarious attraction.

Level: Everyone
Recommendation: Though Disney originally planned this attraction to please families with Kids, everyone appears to get a kick out of this attraction. The theatre is large, so if there ever is a wait, it's usually just until the next show loads. For the best viewing, we recommend sitting in the center of the 4th-7th rows.
Line Length: Short / **FastPass+:** Yes

WILDERNESS EXPLORERS
Best for: Young Kids, Kids
Description: Inspired by Pixar's Up, kids can earn up to 30 Wilderness Explorer badges by completing challenges.
Level: Kids
Recommendation: A playground for kids of all ages.
Line Length: Very Short / **FastPass:** No

DISCOVERY ISLAND TRAILS
Best for: Everyone
Description: Follow pathways around the Tree of Life to see waterfalls, unique animals, and meet Timon.
Level: Everyone
Recommendation: Great for animal lovers. Check out the many carvings in the Tree of Life and watch them magically come to life at night!
Line Length: None / **FastPass+:** No

HAKUNNA MATATA DANCE PARTY – Celebrate *The Lion King's* 25th anniversary with this new dance party! A live street band plays Disney classics while you dance like Timon and Rafiki!

ANIMALS

Mammals: African Crested Porcupine, Otters, Axis Deer, Cotton-top Tamarin, Lemur, Kangaroo

Birds: Black Neck Swan, Cockatoo, Exotic Duck, Teals, West African Crowned Crane, White Stork

Reptiles: Galapagos Tortoise, Lappet Face Vulture, Flamingo, Macaw, Saddle-Billed Stork

---

· Magic Tips ·
Visit Otter Grove to see the adorable animals swimming and sliding around this renovated attraction!

AFRICA

A popular land for safari excursions, African animals, and eateries, Africa in centered around Harambe, a fictional Kenyan village. This area has he most animals spread throughout its unique attractions. The best way to see the most animals is on the family-friendly Kilimanjaro Safari ride. Many of these animals can also be seen from the Pangani Forest Exploration Trail.

Theme: African Village and Safari

RIDES

KILIMANJARO SAFARIS

Best for: Everyone

Description: Hop aboard a guided caravan tour of Africa. From the jungles to the savanna, you'll see everything from wildebeest to giraffes to rhinos and lions. The animals are in "cage-less" enclosures (except for the carnivores, of course), so watch them roaming free before your eyes.

Level: Everyone

Recommendation: The Kilimanjaro Safaris is one of the best attractions in Animal Kingdom. This ride does get a bit bumpy, so beware in case you have issues with that. Disney also just opened the ride for nighttime safaris. Sadly, most of the animals are almost impossible to see at night, and portions of the ride are closed as well.

Line Length: Medium / **FastPass+:** Yes

ANIMALS

Mammals: Addax, African Elephant, African Wild Dog, Antelope, Ankole-Watusi, Bong, Bontebok, Cheetah, Duiker, Eland, Giraffe, Greater Kudu, Hippopotamus, Hyena, Impala, Lion, Okapi, Oryx, Ostrich, Mandrill, Nyala, Rhinoceros, Waterbuck, Warthog, Wildebeest, Zebra

Birds: African Ducks, African Geese, African Pelican, African Pintail, African Stork, Blue Crane, Flamingo, Helmeted Guineafowl, Teal, White-breasted Cormorant

Reptiles: Nile Crocodile

SHOWS AND ATTRACTIONS

FESTIVAL OF THE LION KING

Best for: Young Kids, Kids, Tweens, Adults 30+

Description: An interactive 30-minute stage show set to the characters and music of Disney's The Lion King.

Level: Family

Recommendation: Easily one of WDW's best live shows, the Festival of the Lion King entertains guests with dancing, puppetry, and fantastic costumes. We highly recommend seeing this one! The theatre is divided into four sections, so depending where you sit, you'll have a slightly different experience. Each section is represented by an animal and the show's four hosts interact with their respective section.

Line Length: Very Short / **FastPass+:** Yes

PANGANI FOREST EXPLORATION TRAIL
Best for: Everyone
Description: Walk along the Kilimanjaro Safaris to see animals you can't explore from the caravan. There are more primates, reptiles, and even insects on this trail. There's also a large aviary filled with African birds.
Level: Everyone
Recommendation: We recommend this to anyone craving to see more African animals. The walk is short at little over a 1/3 of a mile, so kids will love this one.
Line Length: Very Short / **FastPass+:** No

ANIMALS
Mammals: Colobus Monkey, Duiker, Gerenuk, Gorilla, Hippopotamus, Lion, Meerkat, Naked Mole Rat, Okapi, Oryx, Zebra
Birds: African Duck, African Geese, African Parrot, African Pigeon, African Pelican, African Pintail, African Starling, African Stork, Blake Crake, Brimstone Canary, Blue Cran, Collared Kingfisher, Hamerkop, Hoopoe, Kori Bustard, Shrikes, Taveta Weaver, Teal, White-bellied Go-Away-Bird
Reptiles: Boa Constrictor, Shield-tailed Agama, Spiny-tailed Lizard
Arachnids and Fish: Lake Victoria Cichlid, Tarantula

WILD AFRICA TREK – VIP EXPERIENCE
Best for: Teens, Adults
Description: If you're looking for an expanded safari experience, we highly recommend this attraction. Get closer to the animals, move across rope bridges through the jungle, and ride on a specialized caravan safari during the second half. This is a 3-hour tour with a separate cost.
Pricing: $189-$249
Level: Adults
Recommendation: Because this VIP excursion is so long, we don't recommend it for kids or those who have trouble walking. Guests must be 18 or older or 8 years old with an adult. You must be able to wear harness gear and weigh under 300 lbs.
Line Length: None – Reservation
FastPass+: No
Booking: (407) 939-8687

RAFIKI'S PLANET WATCH

A section connected to Africa that highlights how to practice conservation to save the Earth's animals from harm and extinction. This area is hosted by Rafiki from *The Lion King*. It's fun to travel by the Wildlife Express Train, although it's a bit of a bore for many. Young Kids will enjoy the petting corral known as the Affection Section.

Theme: Africa / Global Conservation

RIDES

WILDLIFE EXPRESS TRAIN
Best for: Young Kids, Adults 50+
Description: A slow-paced steam railroad to Rafiki's Planet Watch. The 7-minute ride (5-minute return) takes guests behind the scenes of the habitats before emptying onto the Planet Watch.
Level: Family
Recommendation: If you have curiosity about Rafiki's Planet Watch and want to see some behind the scenes areas where the animals live, we recommend this ride.
Line Length: Short / **FastPass+:** None

SHOWS AND ATTRACTIONS

Note: We recommend all of the attractions here for kids ages 3-8. Older kids may like the Wildlife Express Train and the Animation Experience.

CONSERVATION STATION — A special care facility designed to help animals in the park. You can interact with some of them as well as watch a 3D movie about the rainforest, see backstage cameras, see cases with crawling insects, and watch the veterinarians care for animals (no FastPass selection).

HABITAT HABIT! — Walk along trails to discover cotton-top tamarin monkeys playing (no FastPass+ selection).

AFFECTION SECTION — Pet and feed cows, donkeys, goats, pigs, and sheep in this petting corral (no FastPass+ selection).

THE ANIMATION EXPERIENCE — Draw Disney cartoon animals in this family-friendly experience (FastPass+ available).

ASIA

Discover the fictional Asian land of Anandapur (Sanskrit for "Place of Many Delights") as you journey along a river village and deep into the Himalayan mountains. Asia is home to unique animals from beautiful tigers to stunning birds, as well as rides that can thrill the entire family.

Theme: Asian villages and the Himalayas

RIDES

EXPEDITION EVEREST
Best for: Tweens, Teens, Adults
Description: Costing Disney $100 million to make, Expedition Everest is one of the world's most expensive roller coasters! Lift high into the peaks of a mythical mountain deep in the Himalayas. You'll cruise at high speeds and end up rolling backward when attacked by the mountain's terrifying resident—a yeti!
Level: Thrill Riders
Recommendation: Perfect for those who enjoy high-speed rollercoasters. Expedition Everest also offers a Single Rider Line. Put this to use on busy days! To access the Single Rider line, look for the sign next to the regular line queue entrance.
Line Length: Long / **FastPass+:** Yes

> **· Magic Tips ·**
> Thrill riders craving a front-row experience have two options. Since the coaster goes backward at certain points, riding in the back is another great experience! Everest has two special lines at the end of the queue for those wishing to ride in the front or the back. Just ask a Cast Member for the seat of your choice.

KALI RIVER RAPIDS
Best for: Kids, Tweens, Teens, Adults
Description: A family-friendly raft ride through the Asian jungle. You will likely get soaked on this 12-person water ride!
Level: Families, Thrill Riders
Recommendation: This wet ride is great for hot days! There are dips and spills, so if you're not looking to get wet, you might want to avoid this one.
Line Length: Medium / **FastPass+:** Yes

> **· Magic Tips ·**
> Kali River Rapids has shorter lines in the morning when it's cooler and very long lines in the hot afternoons. The shortest wait times are at night just before Animal Kingdom closes.

SHOWS AND ATTRACTIONS

MAHARAJAH JUNGLE TREK
Best for: Everyone
Description: A walking trail slightly over 1/3 of a mile, showcasing some of the most exotic animals in all of Asia. From tigers to komodo dragons, the Maharajah Jungle Trek is both informative and delightful for all.
Level: Everyone
Recommendation: Not to be missed for those looking to see spectacular and rare animals.
Line Length: Very Short / **FastPass+:** No

RIVERS OF LIGHT: WE ARE ONE

Best for: Everyone

Description: A vibrant nighttime show set along the Discovery River. See light-up floats, hear the music from Disney films, and watch the amazing special effects in this one-of-a-kind, nature-themed show.

Level: Everyone

Recommendation: While the colorful water floats of the Rivers of Light are stunning, the show might feel a bit boring to younger viewers. However, the show is only 15 minutes and doesn't drag. If you can't get a space in the theatre to watch the show, stand around the perimeter for some great views! The later showings usually have a lot less viewers.

Line Length: Medium / **FastPass+:** Yes

UP! A GREAT BIRD ADVENTURE

Best for: Young Kids

Description: A stage show with live birds and characters from Pixar's *Up!*

Level: Family

Recommendation: Best for kids 8 and under!

Line Length: Short / **FastPass+:** No

Holiday Script: This show spreads holiday cheer beginning in November.

ANIMALS

Mammals: Banteng, Bengal Tiger, Gibbon, Malayan Flying Fox, Sumatran Tiger, Water Buffalo

Reptiles: Komodo Dragon

Birds: More than 50 Species of Asian birds like Starling, Duck, Parrot, Peafowl, Pheasant, Barbet, and Kingfisher.

DINOLAND U.S.A.

This land takes guests on a journey to the past when the magnificent —and sometimes terrifying—dinosaurs roamed the Earth! There are dino-themed rides, fossil replicas, and a carnival-themed area.

Theme: Dinosaur Lab and Roadside Attraction

RIDES

DINOSAUR
Best for: Kids, Tweens, Teens, Adults, Thrill Riders
Description: Get sent back to the age of the dinosaurs in a special SUV time machine. Themed after Disney's Dinosaur film, there's rocky terrain in this unique dark ride similar to Disneyland's Indiana Jones Adventure.
Level: Thrill Riders (must be 40"/ 102cm or taller)
Recommendation: Perfect for Thrill Riders though some Kids may become frightened of the scarier dinosaurs.
Line Length: Long / **FastPass+:** Yes

PRIMEVAL WHIRL
May operate seasonally
Best for: Kids, Tweens, Teens, Thrill Riders
Description: Twist and turn over a zany rollercoaster track.
Level: Family
Recommendation: Designed for the Kids and Tweens, this ride is also enjoyed by many Thrill Riders.
Line Length: Medium / **FastPass+:** Yes

TRICERATOP SPIN
Best for: Young Kids, Kids
Description: Similar to Dumbo's Flight at the Magic Kingdom, riders control brightly colored triceratops as they soar in the air.
Level: Kids
Recommendation: A perfect ride for Young Kids.
Line Length: Medium / **FastPass+:** No

SHOWS AND ATTRACTIONS

DINO-SUE
Best for: Young Kids, Kids, Tweens, Adults 50+
Description: A replica of one of the largest Tyrannosaurus Rex fossils ever found.
Level: Everyone
Recommendation: A great walkthrough attraction for lovers of fossils. It's impressive to stand next to Sue, the massive T-Rex!
Line Length: Low / **FastPass+:** No

FINDING NEMO–THE MUSICAL
Best for: Young Kids, Kids, Tweens, Adults 50+
Description: A 40-minute live Broadway-style musical starring the cast of Pixar's Finding Nemo—and yes, Dory is there, too! Puppetry, lighting, and special effects bring this stunning show to life!
Level: Family
Recommendation: Perfect for fans of Broadway musicals and the animated film *Finding Nemo*. Get there about 30 minutes ahead for the best seating. On less crowded days, this may not be necessary.
Line Length: Medium / **FastPass+:** Yes

FOSSIL FUN GAMES
Best for: Young Kids, Kids, Tweens
Description: Additional cost carnival games with stuffed animal prizes.
Level: Family
Recommendation: Fun for Kids who love carnival games.

THE BONEYARD
Best for: Young Kids, Kids
Description: A playground where Kids can dig up dinosaur fossils.
Level: Kids
Recommendation: A great time for parents to take a break while the kids play.

MORE ATTRACTIONS

DONALD'S DINO BASH!

Meet Donald Duck and his family (including rare characters like Scrooge McDuck) as they celebrate their ancestral connection to dinosaurs! Other characters greet guests here, too, like Chip and Dale in their dino suits!

PANDORA–THE WORLD OF AVATAR

Enter a breathtaking alien world with mysterious flora and fauna that welcome you to their planet! See the famous floating mountains and experience some of the newest, state-of-the-art adventure rides anywhere in the world! Based around James Cameron's Avatar film series, Pandora is a not-to-be-missed land at Animal Kingdom.

Theme: Alien planet based on the Avatar film series

PANDORA AT NIGHT

When the sun goes down, the world of Avatar changes. Watch the bioluminescent world come to life under the stars as the magnificent creatures and plants light up in stunning ways. We don't want to give away too much, but we highly recommend that you make your way to this unique land for some unforgettable magic!

> **· Magic Tips ·**
> Need water? Check out the wattle bottle refill stations at the drinking fountains in Pandora. It's a free and easy way to keep hydrated.

RIDES

AVATAR FLIGHT OF PASSAGE
Best for: Thrill Riders, Tweens, Teens, Adults
Description: Fly high on a winged alien banshee as you soar over Pandora's nature in this unique flight simulator.
Level: Thrill Riders (must be 44" or taller)
Recommendation: If you like rides like Star Tours and Soarin', Flight of Passage takes this simulation experience to the next level!
Line Length: Very Long / **FastPass+:** Yes

NA'VI RIVER JOUREY
Best for: Young Kids, Kids, Adults 50+
Description: Explore the bioluminescent world of Pandora in this gentle boat dark ride.
Level: Everyone
Recommendation: This is a fun and gentle boat ride with some very cool Disney magic! The animatronics are awesome and the lighting is breathtaking!
Line Length: Very Long / **FastPass+:** Yes

PANDORA FASTPASS+ TIPS

The attractions in Pandora are notoriously difficult to book with FastPass+. If you reserve your FP+ sixty days before your trip, you still may not see time slots for either ride. This is because anyone with a WDW Resort vacation that begins before yours has access to those selections first. Another challenge is that only one of Pandora's two attractions can be reserved in advance (you choose which one). Still, there are ways to grab the Pandora FastPass+ selection that you desire.

The AVATAR Flight of Passage ride is the most sought-after FastPass+ selection in Animal Kingdom, so we recommend snagging this one first. Later in the day—on the date of your visit—the Na'vi River Journey often becomes available (though sparsely). If you don't manage to pre-book one of these attractions on your first attempt, keep checking back. We've seen several time slots become released as our vacation came closer. On the day of, even when FastPass+ selections were gone, we were able to book the Flight of Passage ride several times as guests cancel and more times became available. Check back on the Walt Disney World app until you see a time slot become available.

CHAPTER ELEVEN

DISNEY WATER PARKS

INTRODUCTION

Walt Disney World opened its original water park, Disney's River Country, in 1976. This Park has since been closed (as of 2001), as the massive popularity of its newer parks, Typhoon Lagoon (1989) and Blizzard Beach (1995) conquered the scene. Combined, the Disney Water Parks bring in nearly 5 million visitors annually—with Typhoon Lagoon being slightly more popular. Each Water Park is set in a different location within the Walt Disney World Resort. Typhoon Lagoon is near Disney Springs, and Blizzard Beach is on the other end near Animal Kingdom and between the All-Star Sports Resort and Disney's Coronado Springs Resort hotels.

Typhoon Lagoon is themed after a paradise bay—shortly after a storm has hit! There are pirate ships, streams, waterfalls, palm trees, and dozens of attractions. Blizzard Beach pulls its theme from ski lodges where the snow melts in the summer heat. It's an interesting hodgepodge of ideas with log cabins and snowy slopes—only without the cold! Each park has a similar layout with a mountain peak in the center, a wave pool below, and a lazy river around the perimeter.

Many adults who visit without children may want to skip the water park and just lounge at the pools in their Resort hotel. Remember, most of the hotels have their own waterslides. In fact, if you are staying less than five nights, it may be difficult to fit a full day in at the water parks and still see all of the theme parks. It's tricky to choose, so we give you concise information on which slides and attractions will benefit your vacation.

KEEP IN MIND

1. The water parks sometimes have Extra Magic Hours for Disney Resort hotel guests. Check the calendar during your stay to see when these are.

2. The water parks may close due to severe weather. Lightning doesn't mix well with water!

3. The Water Parks have extended hours during the summer (sometimes as late as 8pm), and cut back hours in the fall. During the winter, they can often be under refurbishment.

4. These may be the only parks that don't need a set of outlined plans. The line lengths can change frequently (but expect up to 30-minute wait times during the summer peak season for the most popular slides). Since everyone can go at their own pace, the water parks are a perfect time to find relaxation during your stay.

5. If you are feeling adventurous, you can do both water parks in one day. We recommend spacing these out by going at opening to one and heading over to the next in the afternoon when the crowds have lessened. Just remember that you might not get your choice of lounging area at the second park you choose.

6. There are no FastPass+ selections for Typhoon Lagoon, as the average wait time is usually only 10-15 minutes (with some of the popular attractions having 30-minute waits).

7. Get to the water parks at opening to reserve the best lounge chairs for your family. Prime spots are near the wave pool or just outside of it near the lazy rivers.

8. Keep your belongings safe. There's a general safe feeling all around the park, so you can leave some items like sunscreen and visors unattended (or under your towel). We recommend storing away your cellphone and car keys in a rental locker.

> **· Magic Tips ·**
> Cold weather and other harsh weather conditions can unexpectedly shutdown the water parks. Have a backup plan just in case this occurs.

WHAT TO BRING

The water parks have nearly everything you'll need for poolside fun—but with a cost. That's why we recommend bringing these items with you into the parks:

1. Sunscreen – You'll be out in the sun all day, after all.
2. Beach towels – Rentals are available. You can bring the towels from your hotel if you want, though WDW doesn't recommend this (and we're not saying that you should). However, people do it from time to time.
3. Change of clothing – It's not vital, but we recommend it if you plan to go somewhere afterward. If you forget anything, the shops at the water parks sell quality sunscreen, sunglasses, and visors—for a premium price.

RENTALS

LOCKERS

We highly recommend keeping your things here. There are two locker rental stations in each park near the entrance. Pricing is $10/day for a regular (12.5 inches by 17 inches) and $15/day for a large (15.5 inches by 17 inches). Lockers take credit cards and cash and your items are kept safe with a 4-digit code that you set. Lockers can sell out, so make sure you get to the park early to reserve one.

CABANAS

The Beachcomber Shacks at Typhoon Lagoon and Polar Patios at Blizzard Beach are reserved areas that come with lounge chairs, a personal locker, and a cooler for up to 6 guests (though you can pay more for 7-10 guests). Prices vary (usually $200-$350), and spaces are limited, so reserve yours as early as possible before your visit by calling: (407) 939-7529.

UMBRELLA AND LOUNGE CHAIRS

If you don't want to fork out the money for a cabana, you can always reserve an umbrella. These come with two loungers, two chairs, and towels for up to 4 guests. If you have two adults, we recommend splitting up at the start of the day to reserve a locker and lounge chairs. Sometimes the "rope drop" at the start of the day can get crowded. Have one person reserve the chairs in your desired section and the other rent a locker. You don't want to miss out on either! If we had to pick one over the other, we'd pick a lounging space and take our chances that the lockers will still be available. Pricing varies from $40-$50 per reservation. Like the cabanas, these are limited, so call ahead to reserve: (407) 939-7529.

TYPHOON LAGOON

Escape to the wild tropics in this water park built around a Caribbean beach, complete with a sunken ship perched high on a mountain!

Theme: Post-Typhoon Caribbean Beach

RIDES AND ATTRACTIONS

TYPHOON LAGOON SURF POOL

Best for: Tweens, Teens, and Adults
Description: A wave pool with waves that reach up to 6 feet.
Level: Everyone
Recommendation: This massive pool is wildly popular. Kids, Tweens, Teens, and Adults will love to splash in the blue waves. The waves aren't constant, as they come every couple of minutes. Young Kids should be kept near the beach part where the waves are just a couple of inches in height.

CASTAWAY CREEK

Best for: Family, Adults
Description: An expansive, 2000-foot long lazy river that slowly

travels around the perimeter of Typhoon Saloon. The entire journey takes about 20 minutes. Hop aboard one of the many floating rafts as you cruise down this gentle river.

Level: Everyone

Recommendation: Best for adults looking to relax, though Young Kids and Kids enjoy splashing around this area as well. You can stay in Castaway Creek for as long as you'd like. There are several entry points for all to enjoy.

KETCHAKIDDEE CREEK
Best for: Young Kids, Kids

Description: A water play area perfect for Young Kids under 48 inches.

Level: Young Kids and Kids

Recommendation: A great space to take your kids who want to ride water slides and splash in an area designed for them.

KEELHAUL
Best for: Kids, Tweens, Teens, Adults, Thrill Riders

Description: A beautiful waterslide with an inner tube.

Level: Family

Recommendation: Perfect for Kids to Adults, but Young Kids may want to sit this one out.

MAYDAY FALLS
Best for: Kids, Tweens, Teens, Adults, Thrill Riders

Description: A rapids-themed waterslide on a tube. Go over bumps and small drops as you adventure quickly down a river.

Level: Family

Recommendation: Great for Kids to Adults, but Young Kids may want to sit this one out. This one can be a bit rough!

GANGPLANK FALLS
Best for: Kids, Tweens, Teens, Adults, Thrill Riders

Description: A giant inner tube that seats four takes you down a wide waterslide.

Level: Family

Recommendation: Perfect for kids to adults, but Young Kids may want to sit this one out.

HUMUNGA KOWABUNGA
Best for: Tweens, Teens, Adults

Description: One of the Park's steepest slides—and it's in the dark. Travel alone through a treacherous path that leads to a plunge.

Level: Thrill Riders (must be 48" or taller)
Recommendation: Best for those looking for a thrill.

STORM SLIDES
Best for: Tweens, Teens, Adults, Thrill Riders
Description: A set of three waterslides that plummet from the ship-wrecked mountain top. Each of them dunk into a pool.
Level: Family
Recommendation: Best for those looking for a family-fun thrill.

CRUSH 'N' GUSHER
Best for: Tweens, Tween, Adults, Thrill Riders
Description: A high-speed "water coaster" on a raft that holds 2-3 people.
Level: Thrill Riders
Recommendation: A fun bobsled waterslide experience!

BAY SLIDES
Best for: Young Kids, Kids
Description: A water play area perfect for Young Kids under 60 inches.
Level: Young Kids and Kids
Recommendation: A great space to take your kids who want to ride water slides and splash in an area designed for them.

Mountain Trail
Best for: Young Kids and Adults 30+
Description: Green, tree-filled walkways beneath Typhoon Lagoon's famous mountain. There are palm trees, beautiful Caribbean structures, and rope bridges.
Level: Everyone
Recommendation: Perfect for those looking for a stroll, though we recommend this part mostly for Adults, as Kids and Teens may find it boring.

MISS ADVENTURE FALLS
Best for: Kids, Tweens, Tween, Adults, Thrill Riders
Description: The newest slide at Disney's Typhoon Lagoon! Discover the legend of Captain Mary Oceaneer as you discover her fabled lost fortune in this unique attraction. Disney designed Miss Adventure Falls with the entire family in mind. Hop aboard a family-sized raft and climb to the top before descending into a raging river.
Level: Family / Thrill Riders
Recommendation: Great for those wanting to board with their entire family.

MORE ATTRACTIONS

SURF LESSONS
Learn to surf in Typhoon Lagoon's signature wave pool! Hop aboard a surfboard in a 3-hour event for swimmers of all surf levels. Disney stops the guest list at 25 people so that everyone has ample time to catch waves. The instructors are fantastic and make the experience enjoyable for all! Lessons are $190 per person for guests ages 8 and older. Booking: (407) 939-7529

H2GLOW NIGHTS
During the summer months, Disney's Typhoon Lagoon throws a rave-style nighttime party. The entire resort glows with neon lights and most of the attractions are open. See special characters, usually from Pixar, in festive rave-style gear while music bumps in the background. With advanced tickets ranging from about $60-$70 a night, this event is a lot of fun for the entire family. The warm Orlando weather during these nights also makes jumping in a wave pool and heading down a waterslide even more enjoyable—and you don't have to worry about a sunburn! Hours run from 8PM-11PM on select nights usually from May through August. Early entry begins at 6PM.

BLIZZARD BEACH

Enter a ski resort on the brink of summer as the snow melts into a stunning water park! Disney's Blizzard Beach is as fun as it sounds– but without the cold! And what's ice and Disney without a little *Frozen*? Yes, there are also areas designed after one of the world's most beloved animated films. The park is built around a snowy summit with three color-coded sections: the Green Slopes, the Purple Slopes, and the Red Slopes.

Theme: Snowy Ski Resort Water Park

RIDES AND ATTRACTIONS

MELT-AWAY BAY
Best for: Kids, Tweens, Teens, and Adults
Description: A wave pool filled with rafts and small waves along rocks.
Level: Family
Recommendation: This large pool is wildly popular for families. The waves are constant, but are small and easy to ride.

CROSS COUNTRY CREEK
Best for: Family, Adults
Description: A calm, winding river journey that expands for 3,000 feet around the perimeter of Blizzard Beach. Hop aboard one of the many floating rafts as you cruise down this gentle river near waterfalls, lush foliage, and some of the thrill rides.

Level: Everyone
Recommendation: Best for adults looking to relax, though Young Kids and Kids enjoy splashing around this area as well. You can stay in Cross Country Creek for as long as you'd like. There are 7 points around the creek to enter.

SKI PATROL TRAINING CAMP
Best for: Kids, Tweens
Description: A water play area, short slides, and an obstacle course that's perfect for Kids and Tweens under 60 inches.
Level: Kids
Recommendation: A great space to take your kids who want to ride water slides and splash in an area designed for them.

TIKE'S PEAK
Best for: Young Kids, Kids
Description: A water play area perfect for Young Kids under 48 inches. There are mini water slides with and without rafters, shallow pools, and soft ground incase small kids slip!
Level: Young Kids and Kids
Recommendation: A great space to take your kids who want to ride water slides and splash in an area designed for them.

GREEN SLOPE

SUMMIT PLUMMET
Best for: Thrill Riders
Description: A single body slide that takes thrill riders through a high-speed plunge from the Park's centerpiece, Mt. Gushmore.
Level: Thrill Riders (must be 48 inches or taller)
Recommendation: Thrill Riders only.

SLUSH GUSHER
Best for: Thrill Riders
Description: A body slide that takes thrill riders through a high-speed plunge from this 90-foot tall slide.
Level: Thrill Riders (must be 48 inches or taller)
Recommendation: Thrill Riders only.

TEAMBOAT SPRINGS
Best for: Kids, Tweens, Teens, Adults, Thrill Riders
Description: A massive inner tube that seats 6 as it takes you down a long, wide waterslide.
Level: Family
Recommendation: Perfect for the family, but you might want to leave the Young Kids out of it as it does get a bit scary.

CHAIRLIFT
Best for: Kids, Tweens, Teens, Adults, Thrill Riders
Description: What's a ski resort without a ski lift? Take the Chairlift to the top of Mt. Gushmore to ride the Green Slope Rides.
Level: Family (must be 32" or taller)
Recommendation: A fun way to the top, but we don't recommend heading up there if you have a fear of heights.

PURPLE SLOPE

TOBOGGAN RACERS
Best for: Kids, Tweens, Teens, Adults, Thrill Riders
Description: Fly down wavy slopes on slick mats—a family favorite!
Level: Family and Thrill Riders
Recommendation: Perfect for Kids and older. The hills are steep, so if someone has an issue with heights, this might not be the ride for them.

SNOW STORMERS

Best for: Kids, Tweens, Teens, Adults

Description: Built to look like sledding slopes in the snow, Snow Stormers is another fun mat slide.

Level: Everyone

Recommendation: Great for those who want to try a mat slide without the scary heights. We don't recommend this ride for Young Kids.

DOWNHILL DOUBLE DIPPER

Best for: Tweens, Teens, Adults, Thrill Riders

Description: Race against friends and family in these side-by-side, snow-covered tubes in the wilderness.

Level: Thrill Riders (must be 48 inches or taller)

Recommendation: These are short slides with drops, and are very fun to race. The height requirement won't allow many Kids to ride, though they may want to.

RED SLOPE

RUNOFF RAPIDS

Best for: Kids, Tweens, Tween, Adults, Thrill Riders

Description: Three different slides change up the thrills as you travel on inner-tubes over and through the lush wilderness of Disney's Blizzard Beach. Each slide carries you in fun swirls down Mt. Gushmore.

Level: Family

Recommendation: Each slide is different, but all empty into a large pool. This ride allows you to travel alone or with a companion in a double tube. The center slide is completely enclosed (and dark) and made to look like there are stars coming through from the outside light. The outer slides open with different paths down the mountain.

CHAPTER TWELVE

HOTEL GUIDE

INTRODUCTION

Booking the right place to stay on your vacation is important. You likely have a list of "must-haves," and whether or not you've been to the Walt Disney World Resort before, you may not know which is the best Hotel for you. In fact, we believe that booking the hotel is the hardest part! After all, there are so many choices. Some of the WDW Resort Hotels are within walking distance of a Park or two while others might be a bit far away. Generally, the closer you are to a Park, the more expensive your room might be. In this chapter, we outline the pros and cons of every hotel in the WDW Resort. We give you our recommendations and the hotel details to help you make your decision with ease.

DISNEY WORLD RESORT HOTELS

There are several hotel properties on the resort, each with their own unique sense of themed magic from a wilderness lodge to a New England beachside hotel. There's something for everyone here, but sometimes it's hard to decide since each has its own perks, whether it's the amenities, the views, or the overcall cost.

ON-SITE HOTEL BENEFITS

1. MagicBand for hotel room access, park tickets, easy payment, Disney Dining, and more.

2. Disney's Magical Express*
3. "Extra Magic Hours" get hotel guests into the park earlier (or later) than anyone else on select dates.
4. A wide variety of Disney-themed guest rooms
5. Closer proximity to the parks
6. Free merchandise delivery to your hotel from any of the Disney shops in the parks. The following day you can pick them up from the bell services in your hotel.
7. Gorgeous pools with waterslides
8. Free Wi-Fi
9. Disney Dining Plan*

Walt Disney World Dolphin and Swan not included.

> **· Magic Tips ·**
>
> Guests can now purchase MagicBands with Disney designs at a discounted price. Select from Marvel, Pixar, and classic Disney characters printed right on your band for around $10 each. Solid-color MagicBands are still complimentary.

RESORT TYPES

VALUE

The least expensive per night. These Resort hotels are typically further away from the parks, only include bus transport, and have fewer amenities. Value resorts make up for fewer features with heavy Disney themes. Many of these properties will suit families on a budget. Those looking for larger beds and more spacious rooms may want to look elsewhere. Most of the value resorts only have double beds (full size) and some of the smallest rooms in WDW.

MODERATE

More amenities, closer theme park locations, and better landscaped resort properties than that of the Value resorts. Moderate properties often cater to convention crowds, so the rooms aren't as detailed with Disney extras, but many of them have upgrade options. Moderate hotels often have fantastic pool areas and many amenities of the deluxe resorts without the high price.

· Magic Tips ·

Guests staying multiple days at a value or moderate resort can opt out of Mousekeeping (room cleaning services). Many hotel rooms will have a card near the television with an invitation to skip Mousekeeping in exchange for a Disney gift card! These cards are usually worth $10 a day (not including your checkout day). If you don't see the card, call the front desk or concierge and ask if this option is available for your stay.

DELUXE

The Walt Disney World Resort's best properties. These are located in prime locations with several travel choices to the parks from the monorail system, boats, or via walking paths. Deluxe resorts usually have full amenities from gyms to spas and other options for leisure. All of these can come with a premium price tag.

· Magic Tips ·

The experience between value, moderate, and deluxe resorts is noticeable. Disney certainly puts its A-list hotel staff in the more expensive hotels, thus giving guests a more pleasant stay. That isn't to say you won't enjoy the staff at the value and moderate hotels (though we find it hit or miss), but expect impeccable service at the deluxe resorts.

ROOM TYPES

When booking your accommodations, you may notice a room description and price difference. Rooms with the best views and locations are usually more expensive.

STANDARD

These rooms don't promise special views. Many times, standard rooms have windows that face the parking lot or the hotel roof. In value and moderate resorts, this may not make a difference as the windows are small and even if you have a better view, you may not see much anyway. Deluxe resorts like the Animal Kingdom Lodge may feel overpriced without a view of the savanna, which is not guaranteed with a standard view. If you're okay with a non-exciting view, book one of these rooms. If a standard room is the only available option (or only within your price range), you can always request a room with a partial view of the garden or pool which may be available. It's very rare that Disney will upgrade a hotel room for free at checkin, though you can always ask if something becomes available during your stay.

GARDEN, POOL, LAKE, AND THEME PARK VIEWS
For those looking for scenery outside of your room window, getting a view of the garden, pool, or body of water may be your top choice. Often, the garden view rooms aren't much more than the cost of a standard view. Keep in mind that garden views aren't always spectacular. You may only see hedges and some grass—but to many, that's better than a view of a parking lot! Still, we've discovered that the pool and lake views are usually very stunning (though they do come with a higher jump in price). If you can grab a room with a theme park view, you'll pay a premium, but will have views of the fireworks at night. Near the Magic Kingdom, there's something special about seeing the Cinderella Castle in the distance.

STUDIOS AND SUITES
Studios are usually small and often have just one bed while suits house larger spaces with extra furniture like couches and small dining tables with chairs. Though, the Old Key West Resort has studios with two queen beds and extra space. Family Suites are perfect for large families and have a kitchenette and pull-out sofa for up to six guests. These rooms are located in the Art of Animation hotel.

PREFERRED ROOM
Since many of the WDW Resorts are spread out like Pop Century and Coronado Springs, having a room closer to the amenities and bus stops may make your vacation easier. These preferred rooms have closer access to busses, restaurants, and the amenities.

> **· Magic Tips ·**
> If you can't book a preferred room, you can always call Disney before 5-7 days before checkin with your location choice. While it's not guaranteed, sometimes the other rooms will have options for closer proximity.

VILLAS

These rooms were defined for Disney Vacation Club members, but can also be booked by non-members. Villas are often more spacious , come with a kitchen or kitchenette, and can sometimes have a washer/dryer in unit. Unfortunately for those with families, many of the villas will have two beds in the form of a king and an often uncomfortable pull-out couch.

> **· Magic Tips ·**
> Studio villas have kitchenettes with a microwave, sink, mini fridge, plates, and sometimes a dishwasher. Full kitchens are available for 1-bedrooms and larger (these include stoves, full-sized refrigerator with freezers, and extra pantry space).
>
> Grocery delivery is available for a $6 fee per order. However, you can pick up groceries yourself for free in the lobby. We recommend ordering through Garden Grocer which has everything from food to sundries to pet supplies. Link: https://www.gardengrocer.com

CLUB LEVEL

Some of the resorts will offer club rooms with extra amenities such as lounge access for light bites and a cocktail hour. Club levels will come at a premium cost, but are not always worth the extra expense. Often, for just a bit more in price, you can purchase a Quick-Service dining plan instead.

TREEHOUSE, BUNGALOW, CABIN, ETC

These special types of rooms are larger and contain more beds than a standard room. Often, they come with a high, premium price for their adventurous feel and spaciousness. The Polynesian Village

Bungalows are popular for their on-the-water island vibes and unmatched views of the Magic Kingdom!

> **· Magic Tips ·**
> Disney's housekeeping staff is call "Mousekeeping!" If you are getting excellent service and would like to tip, we recommend $5 cash per day.

THINGS TO KNOW

PARKING FEES
Walt Disney World Resort parking fees vary by hotel:
- Value Resorts: $15/night
- Moderate Resorts: $20/night
- Deluxe and Villa Resorts: $25/night or $33 for valet

HOTEL AAA RATINGS
The AAA Automobile Club ranks hotels based on their amenities, features, and value. AAA takes these rankings very seriously and so does Disney. Most of their Resort Hotels have a status in these categories of either 4-Diamond or 3-Diamond. These luxury levels suggest that the hotels will have a prominent elegance and several amenities for guests to enjoy. The 4-Diamond award is given to more stylish hotels with a bump in service and refineries not found in 3-Diamond. AAA is a bit vague on how they determine these rankings, but the differences in a 3-Diamond and 4-Diamond are noticeable, as each are very nice, yet the 4-Diamond excels.

REFURBISHMENT
Like the attractions in the Parks, the hotels also undergo refurbishment from time to time. This process may seem unsavory, but these can often work in your favor! In fact, some of the nicer hotels will go on sale during refurbished periods—and you may never notice that they are under construction! If you see that refurbishment is occurring during your travel period at a hotel, contact WDW to ask specifics about these refurbishments.

ROOM REQUESTS
Disney rarely will upgrade your room for free, but you can always ask for room placement. Whether you're looking for a high-up floor or

something with less walking distance to the lobby, be sure to include this within the notes once you've checked into your resort. If you don't see the room request, contact Disney by phone: (407) 939-1936.

> **· Magic Tips ·**
>
> Rooms near the pool and theme park views may be much noisier than rooms with garden views. If your party has noise sensitivities (or would just like some quiet), book accordingly or request a room furthest away from the crowds.

SPLIT STAYS

If you're staying a week or longer, you may want to consider booking a split stay at multiple hotels. We highly recommend split stays because they are a fun and adventurous way to enjoy more of Walt Disney World. Best of all, Disney will transport your belongings from one resort hotel to the next—we just recommend tipping bell services $1-$2 a bag.

BOOKING HOTEL DISCOUNTS

1. Always check third party travel websites for better deals (i.e.: Orbitz.com, Bookit.com, Expedia.com) and compare to WaltDisneyWorld.com.
2. Sometimes you can save quite a bit per night with third-party websites. Click on their "deals" or "promotions" tab to find discount coupons on the sites.
3. Though many websites offer packaged deals, sometimes these are not the lowest cost. We recommend checking the pricing of hotels and flights separately before you commit to a vacation package.
4. Seasonally, WaltDisneyWorld.com will offer discounted hotel pricing (usually 20-30% off). We recommended booking early when you see these deals! When you book online on the website or over the phone, you can often just put $200 down on a reservation (this includes any bundled park tickets and added items such as Memory Maker) and pay the remaining balance closer to your arrival date.

DISNEY'S ANIMAL KINGDOM LODGE

Best for: Everyone (especially animal lovers)
Theme: African Savanna Lodge
AAA Rating: 4-Diamond
Cost: Deluxe / Disney Vacation Club (select rooms)
Location: Furthest west, close to Disney's Animal Kingdom Park.
Pool: Yes, with Waterslide
Transport to Parks: Bus only
Amenities: Savanna views, Magical Express, Wi-Fi, Paid Laundry and Dry Cleaning, Multiple Pools, Waterslides, Jogging Trails, Movie Nights at the Pool, Playground, Club Access for Certain Rooms, Spa and Fitness Center, crafts for kids at Simba's Activity Center, and Arcade

OUR REVIEW

The Animal Kingdom Lodge is gorgeous! You'll feel transported to Africa where over 30 species of wildlife roam outside of your hotel room window. The savanna view rooms are breathtaking and an unforgettable experience. The animals range from zebras and giraffes to warthogs and exotic birds. The animals are in a "fenceless" savanna that comes right up to your room (a hidden fencing system keeps the animals from getting too close). While it's the closest hotel to the Animal Kingdom Park, it's still about a mile (1.5 km) away by bus.

　　The Lodge feels like a wilderness hotel with a breathtaking entrance, well-decorated rooms, authentic African art, views of the savanna, and a massive pool with waterslide and real flamingoes. The rooms aren't as big as some of the other Deluxe Resorts and the bathrooms could use brighter lighting.

　　Animal Kingdom Lodge is split into two sections: Jambo House and Kidani Village. Most of the activity and restaurants are in Jambo House, the main area of the resort. Kidani Village has the

perks of Disney Vacation Club rentals with condo-like villas equipped with kitchens. If your family needs a little more room, you may want to book at Kidani Village, though the rooms are further away from many of the resort's amenities (though Kidani does have its own pool). Jambo House also has villas with a bit more space.

The hotel has a smaller pool with its own waterslide, but a bigger space for the savanna. The hotel is beautiful, but if you don't have a savanna-facing room, we don't think it's worth the cost. We wish that the Lodge and Villas were within walking distance to Animal Kingdom, but we've found that this resort has the most efficient bussing system in all of WDW. Some of the non-savanna facing rooms still have partial views of the animals. Request one of these rooms if you can, through its not guaranteed. Otherwise, each floor has a balcony that faces the savanna.

· Magic Tips ·

Save a little on a 1-Bedroom price by booking a "value" villa at Disney's Animal Kingdom Lodge. These are converted standard rooms made into villas with full kitchens. You'll get a less square footage than a standard 1 Bedroom Villa, but will save about 10% on the total cost. Some of the value villas also have views of the savanna!

Some standard rooms also have partial views of the savanna! If you're willing to risk it, save money and book a standard room. Then, 5-7 days before your trip, call Disney and request a room with a partial view of the savanna. Of course, this is not guaranteed.

BOTTOM LINE
Gorgeous, African-inspired resort with a collection of on-property animals. Only the rooms facing the savanna are worth the high price from the resort far away from the theme parks.

PROS
- Stunning Savanna views with over 200 African animal
- Multiple pools, one with waterslide
- Delicious variety of food
- Gorgeous lobby and rooms
- The Villas sleep larger families

CONS
- Far away from the Parks
- Only transport option are the busses
- Poor room lighting (though this was done on purpose for the animals)
- Not worth the price without a savanna view

DISNEY'S BEACH CLUB RESORT

Best for: Teens, Adults, Epcot Fans
Theme: Beach Resort
AAA Rating: 4-Diamond
Cost: Deluxe
Location: Central to Epcot and Hollywood Studios
Pool: Yes, with waterslide, sand-bottom, and lazy river
Transport to Parks: Boat, Walk, Busses
Amenities: Magical Express, Wi-Fi, Paid Laundry and Dry Cleaning, Multiple Pools, Waterslides, Jogging Paths, Movie Nights, Playground, Volleyball and Tennis Courts, Bike Rentals, Boat Rentals, Fishing, Club Access for Certain Rooms, Spa and Fitness Center, Child Care, Mini Golf, and Arcade

OUR REVIEW

Our top choice resort! Beach club is a highly sought after property for its walking distance proximity to Epcot and Disney's Hollywood Studios. The resort has a quaint feel along a massive lake with water taxis taking guests to the theme parks and Disney's Boardwalk. There is timeless beach appeal to the building that will be appreciated by adults and teens alike. Most of the standard rooms have Juliet balconies while larger rooms with have full-sized balconies with seats.

Kids will love the Stormalong Bay pool with a shipwreck waterslide and sandy-bottom. Adults will enjoy the spacious beach chairs, comfortable rooms, and fine dining in this large pool area. The boardwalk is right across the way for nightlife and Epcot is just a 5-minute walk straight into the back entrance by the World Showcase for drinking and dining (especially popular during

Epcot's Food & Wine Festival). You'll find some of the finer service here and a leisurely boat ride to Hollywood Studios isn't to be missed.

BOTTOM LINE
Gorgeous property with stunning pool and service. Walking distance to Epcot and several great restaurants. Book Beach Club if you can!

Pros
- 3 acres of pool area at Stormalong Bay with a sandy bottom, waterslide, beach loungers, bars, and lazy river with inner tubes.
- Fine dining.
- Gorgeous lobby and rooms.
- Shared amenities with Disney's Yacht Club
- 5-minute walk or boat ride to Epcot and 15-minute walk or boat ride to Hollywood Studios.
- The Villas sleep larger families.
- See the Epcot fireworks from the beach.

CONS
- Longer bus wait times for the Magic Kingdom, Disney's Animal Kingdom, and Disney Springs
- Often difficult to book in advance.

> **· Magic Tips ·**
> Guests at the Beach Club and Yacht Club share pool areas. For a less-crowded pool, head to Disney's Yacht Club next door!

DISNEY'S YACHT CLUB

Best for: Teens, Adults (especially beach lovers)
Theme: New England Beach Resort
AAA Rating: 4-Diamond
Cost: Deluxe
Location: Central, walking distance to Epcot and Hollywood Studios
Pool: Yes, with Waterslide, sand bottom and lazy river
Transport to Parks: Boat, Walk, Busses

Amenities: Magical Express, Wi-Fi, Paid Laundry and Dry Cleaning, Multiple Pools, Valet, Waterslides, Jogging Paths, Movie Nights, Playground, Volleyball and Tennis Courts, Bike Rentals, Boat Rentals, Fishing, Club Access for Certain Rooms, Spa and Fitness Center, Child Care, Mini Golf, and Arcade

OUR REVIEW

If you can't get a room at Disney's Beach Club, stay at the Yacht Club. They were built in the same year and have many of the same features, layout, and amenities. In fact, these properties share the stunning Stormalong Bay pool, but the Yacht Club also has its own quiet pool near the back. This property is a bit spread out and walking to the rooms from the lobby, pool, or busses can be a bit of a journey. Still, the rooms are beautifully decorated with several Hidden Mickeys in the décor. You'll find spacious rooms and quiet at the Yacht Club all while being centrally located to Epcot and Disney's Hollywood Studios. Since the Resort is spread out and the vibe is more adult, Young Kids and Kids may not enjoy this property other than its pool.

BOTTOM LINE

Ideal for an adult experience at WDW while keeping the fun of the Beach Club.

· Magic Tips ·

There's not much of a difference between the different room views. The pool views are far more expensive and are often just of the Admiral Pool on the far end of the property. We suggest saving money and select a Garden or Woods view.

PROS

- 3 acres of pool area at Stormalong Bay with a sandy bottom, waterslide, beach loungers, bars, and lazy river with inner tubes
- Fine dining and character dining
- Gorgeous lobby and rooms
- 5-minute walk or boat ride to Epcot
- 15-minute walk or boat ride to Hollywood Studios
- See the Epcot fireworks from the beach
- Rooms have balconies

CONS

- Longer bus wait times
- No quick-service restaurants (only at Beach Club, Disney's Boardwalk, and Boardwalk Inn)
- Often very difficult to book in advance

DISNEY'S BOARDWALK INN

Best for: Kids, Teens, Adults
Theme: Boardwalk Hotel
AAA Rating: 4-Diamond
Cost: Deluxe
Location: Central, walking distance to Epcot and Hollywood Studios.
Pool: Yes, with Waterslide.
Transport to Parks: Boat, Walk, Busses
Amenities: Magical Express, Wi-Fi, Paid Laundry and Dry Cleaning, Multiple Pools, Waterslides, Jogging Paths, Movie Nights, Playground, Tennis Courts, Bike Rentals, Boat Rentals, Fishing, Club Access for Certain Rooms, Spa and Fitness Center, Valet, Child Care, Mini Golf, and Arcade

OUR REVIEW

The Boardwalk Inn and Villas are directly across the water from the Beach Club and Yacht Club. This makes the Boardwalk Inn a prime spot for transport to the Parks. Like the Yacht and Beach Clubs, there is a timeless feel at the Boardwalk Inn, but the pool is a little weird. Cartoon statue elephants spray water and the waterslide looks like a roller coaster with a massive clown face at the end (we think it's a bit creepy looking). Kids will enjoy this pool, but adults might want to stick to some of the side pools without the carnival feel. Being able to walk or boat to Epcot or Hollywood Studios is a huge benefit, and the boardwalk-facing rooms are stunning if you don't mind a little noise.

BOTTOM LINE

Fun, central property that appeals to Families with Kids more than the Yacht Club or Beach Resort.

PROS

- Rooms have balconies
- Carnival-themed pool with waterslide

- Fun Boardwalk arcades, dining, and dancing
- Gorgeous lobby and rooms
- 5-minute walk or boat ride to Epcot
- 10-minute walk or boat ride to Hollywood Studios
- The Villas sleep larger families
- See the Epcot fireworks from the beach

CONS

- Longer bus wait times
- Very spread out with longer walks from the lobby to some of the rooms and villas
- The pool is large, but has a strange carnival theme with a massive clown face slide that might turn off many guests.

DISNEY'S CONTEMPORARY & BAY LAKE

Best for: Teens, Adults
Theme: Contemporary Hotel
AAA Rating: 4-Diamond
Cost: Deluxe
Location: Next to the Magic Kingdom Park
Pool: Yes, with Waterslide
Transport to Parks: Monorail to Magic Kingdom and Epcot, Boat, Busses, Walk to Magic Kingdom
Amenities: Magical Express, Wi-Fi, Paid Laundry and Dry Cleaning, Multiple Pools, Waterslides, Jogging Trails, Movie Nights, Playground, Volleyball and Tennis Courts, Cabana Rentals, Fishing, Club Access for Certain Rooms, Spa and Fitness Center, Salon, Child Care, and Arcade

---

Note: The Bay Lake Tower is a Disney Vacation Club property, thus the rooms have a kitchenette or full-sized kitchen.

OUR REVIEW

The Contemporary Resort opened the same year as the Magic Kingdom Park in 1971 and is based on the design concepts in Tomorrowland. The hotel has kept its charm over the years, even when something contemporary could feel dated, it doesn't. The resort décor is clean and bright and everything feels streamlined and somewhat futuristic—the monorail even goes through it! The Bay Lake Tower opened in 2009, so it's our priority choice to stay though the rooms aren't as large. But, Chef Mickey's can be a bit noisy around this Hotel Resort, it's a fun atmosphere to dine and meet characters. Something about this Resort feels like a high-end condo building or Las Vegas Hotel (without the casino or cigarette smoke) that's walking distance to the Magic Kingdom Park. In fact, if you stay here, skip the morning monorail rush and head straight into the Magic Kingdom by foot. Contemporary has a more adult feel though Kids will enjoy the pool area and little-known butterfly garden on property. Though there are options for Park views, we don't recommend them as they are pricey and much of it is just a view of the parking lot area. You still get a great view of the fireworks at night. If this doesn't interest you, book a bay view.

BOTTOM LINE
Beautifully designed modern Resort with a monorail system to Epcot and the Magic Kingdom.

PROS
- Pool with Waterslide
- See the Electric Water Pageant from the bay
- Fine dining and character dining
- Gorgeous lobby and rooms
- 5-10 minute walk to the Magic Kingdom Park
- Monorail to Epcot
- Boat to Polynesian, Fort Wilderness, or Grand Floridian
- See the Magic Kingdom fireworks from this Resort

CONS
- Doesn't feel as Disney themed as some of the other hotels
- Not as close to the other Parks (other than Magic Kingdom)
- Can be a bit noisy at times
- May not be ideal for larger groups and families

DISNEY'S GRAND FLORIDIAN RESORT

Best for: Tweens, Teens, Adults
Theme: Sophisticated Southern Resort
AAA Rating: 4-Diamond
Cost: Deluxe
Location: Next to the Magic Kingdom Park
Pool: Yes, with Waterslide

Transport to Parks: Monorail to Magic Kingdom and Epcot, Boat, and Busses

Amenities: Magical Express, Wi-Fi, Turn Down Service, Paid Laundry and Dry Cleaning, Multiple Pools, Waterslides, Jogging Trails, Movie Nights, Playground, Volleyball and Tennis Courts, Private Cabana Rentals, Boat Rentals, Club Access for Certain Rooms, Spa and Fitness Center, and Arcade

OUR REVIEW

Easily the WDW Resort's most regal hotel. With a magnificent southern theme, you'll feel swept away by the magic and pristine styles of the Grand Floridian. Typically, this Hotel is the most expensive, so we only recommend it if you are looking for a more romantic feel to your stay. Some of the best dining in WDW is located in this Hotel. The Grand Floridian comes with a certain prestige from Disney World fans, and sometimes that adds to its appeal. The Resort isn't close to any of the Parks other than the Magic Kingdom, and can feel a bit isolated. Kids tend to like Animal Kingdom Lodge, for the animals, or the Beach Club, because of the pool, more than they'd like the Grand Floridian.

BOTTOM LINE

If you're looking for the finest Resort Hotel that WDW has to offer without the heavy Disney theming, this is your place. Otherwise, look elsewhere.

PROS

- Exquisite décor
- Pools with a waterslide at the Beach Pool
- Walkway to the Magic Kingdom
- Views of the Electric Water Pageant
- Fine dining and character dining
- Gorgeous lobby and rooms
- Monorail to Magic Kingdom and Epcot
- Boat to Magic Kingdom
- See the Magic Kingdom fireworks from this Resort
- Villas ideal for larger groups and families

CONS

- Not as Kid-friendly as other hotels
- Not as close to the other Parks (other than Magic Kingdom)

DISNEY'S POLYNESIAN VILLAGE

Best For: Everyone (especially fans of the Hawaiian Islands)
Theme: Island-themed Resort
AAA Rating: 4-Diamond
Cost: Deluxe
Location: Close to the Magic Kingdom Park
Pool: Yes, with Waterslide
Transport to Parks: Monorail to Magic Kingdom and Epcot, Boat, and Busses
Amenities: Magical Express, Wi-Fi, Multiple Pools, Waterslide, Jogging Trail, Movie Nights, Playground, Volleyball Court, Boat Rentals, Fishing, Club Access for Certain Rooms, Spa and Fitness Center, and Child Care

OUR REVIEW

The Polynesian Village is stunning. The tropical plants and island smells in the lobby instantly transport you to the Pacific islands. In fact, with Florida's humidity, you might actually feel like you're in Hawaii. The Polynesian Village Resort is well laid out, though it is a bit spread. The rooms are spacious and there are several options from bungalows on the water to villas. The price tag is high on this Resort Hotel because of its many amenities. From Disney-themed spaces to large pools and a view of the lake with the Magic Kingdom Park in the distance, the Polynesian Village Resort is nearly impossible to beat in style and fun. If your group needs more space, the Bora Bora Bungalows sleep up to 8 guests, have 2 bedrooms, 2 full baths, and a washer and dryer. The bungalows also have stunning views of the Magic Kingdom Park from the water and a unique, island feel. However, these are a bit difficult to book since their priority goes to the Disney Vacation Club members.

BOTTOM LINE

If you love the idea of staying in Hawaii with the appeal of Disney, this is the place for you.

PROS

- Island Resort feel
- Pool with Waterslide at the Lava Pool
- See the Electric Water Pageant from the Bay
- Fine dining and character dining

- Gorgeous lobby and rooms
- Monorail to Magic Kingdom and Epcot
- Boat to Magic Kingdom
- See the Magic Kingdom fireworks from this Resort
- Villas ideal for larger groups and families. They have kitchenettes and balconies
- Trader Sam's Grog Grotto bar is 21 and up after 8pm

CONS
- Not as close to the other Parks (other than Magic Kingdom)
- No easy walk to Parks
- May have to walk far from the pool and lobby to your room
- No on-site fitness center

DISNEY'S WILDERNESS LODGE
INCLUDING BOULDER RIDGE & COPPER CREEK

Best for: Everyone (especially Wilderness lovers)
Theme: Forest Lodge
AAA Rating: 4-Diamond
Cost: Deluxe (more affordable than others in this category)
Location: Close to the Magic Kingdom Park
Pool: Yes, with Waterslides
Transport to Parks: Boat and Busses
Amenities: Magical Express, Wi-Fi, 2 Large Pools, Paid Laundry and Dry Cleaning, Valet, Waterslides, Jogging Trail, Movie Nights, Water Playground, Volleyball Court, Bike and Boat Rentals, Fishing, Club Access for Certain Rooms, Spa and Fitness Center

OUR REVIEW
The Wilderness Lodge is a beautifully set Resort near the Magic Kingdom Park. It's on a massive piece of land with campgrounds and forests in its background and a bay lake in the foreground. Sadly, the monorail doesn't travel to the Wilderness Lodge, but its other amenities bring it up to the Deluxe Resort status. However, it doesn't

have the same appeal as the Grand Floridian and Polynesian or the central placement of the Beach and Yacht Clubs. Because of this, the Wilderness Lodge can be hundreds of dollars a night less than the other Resort Hotels.

A popular time for the Wilderness Lodge is during the holiday season where the many fir trees come to life with Christmas lights and spirit. It's also a lot of fun to take a boat ride to the Magic Kingdom Park. The busses can move a little sluggish when visiting other Parks. Families with Kids may like the Wilderness Lodge better because of the affordable cost and Kiddie pool area.

The Boulder Ridge and Copper Creek Villas add extra style and spaciousness for large families. These homey, yet chic villas are filled with fine details on the furniture and living spaces. These villas don't run cheap, but during the holidays they are our most recommended villas for some Christmas cabin vibes at the Wilderness Lodge!

BOTTOM LINE
A forested resort with several differently themed areas and room sizes to choose from. The Wilderness Lodge is also one of the least expensive deluxe resort properties.

Fire Rock Geyser
Between the main pool and the lake is a Fire Rock Geyser. This erupting beauty evokes the splendor of natural attractions such as Old Faithful in Yellowstone National Park. Fire Rock Geyser erupts every hour like clockwork.

PROS
- See the Electric Water Pageant from the Bay
- Pools with Waterslide at the Silver Creek Pools
- Fine and character dining
- Gorgeous lobby and rooms
- Boat to Magic Kingdom
- Stunning at Christmas time
- Most rooms aren't far from lobby or amenities

CONS
- Not as close to the other Parks (other than Magic Kingdom)
- No walking to Parks
- No larger rooms for big groups
- Longer bus wait times

> **· Magic Tips ·**
> Larger parties should to consider a cabin at Copper Creek. These beautiful and stunning cabins sleep up to 8 adults and boast views of Bay Lake. They are also very close to the main pool area and boats to the Magic Kingdom.

DISNEY'S FORT WILDERNESS
CABINS AND CAMPGROUNDS

Best for: Large Groups and Families (especially Wilderness lovers)
Theme: Camping in the Woods
AAA Rating: 3-Diamond
Cost: Varies
Location: Close to the Magic Kingdom Park
Pool: Yes, with Waterslide
Transport to Parks: Boats to Magic Kingdom and Busses to others
Amenities: Magical Express, Wi-Fi, Pool with Waterslide, Paid Laundry and Dry Cleaning, Animals at Tri-Circle-D Ranch, Jogging Trail, Holiday Sleigh Rides (seasonal), Archery, Wagon Rides, Movies in an Outdoor Theater, Campfire sing-a-longs, Fishing, Volleyball and Basketball Courts, Playgrounds, and Arcade

OUR REVIEW
Cabins: If you've ever heard of "glamping" (glamorous camping), this is the Disney version. Stay in a 750-acre forest with your family in a specially designed cabin. You'll have access to several beds (each cabin sleeps up to 6) and outdoor seating. There is also a country music show called Hoop-Dee-Doo, a pool with a waterslide, and a kitchen. Bring your own groceries or order your own on DisneyWorld.com and have them waiting in the fridge for your arrival. Keep in mind, this is still a camping feeling so insects and other critters could be sneaking around.

Campgrounds: If you're not looking to "glamp" and would rather pitch your own tent or bring an RV, you might want to check out the Fort Wilderness campgrounds. With all of the same perks of the Cabins, just without the housing, you'll be able to pitch a tent, plug in your RV, or stay inside a pop-up tent deep in the woods of Walt Disney World. Campsites include a picnic bench, grill, television, as well as electrical, water, and sewage hookups for RVs. The surrounding foliage is placed to give you extra privacy while you stay.

BOTTOM LINE
Affordable spacious cabins and campgrounds for those who like roughing it.

PROS
- Pool with Waterslide
- Quick-Service dining and BBQ available
- Spacious cabins sleep up to six
- Several Christmas events during the Holiday season including sleigh rides
- Boat to Magic Kingdom or bus to the other Parks
- Cook your own meals to save cash on your trip
- Each cabin has its own driveway for cars
- Unique activities from pony rides to archery
- See the Electric Water Pageant from the water
- Dogs are allowed in some of the campgrounds
- Complimentary parking for campsites (1 vehicle per reservation)

CONS
- Longer bus wait times and you have to walk far to the stops
- Smaller bed sizes in the cabins

DISNEY'S CARIBBEAN BEACH

Best for: Kids, Adults (especially pirate lovers)
Theme: Caribbean Resort
AAA Rating: 3-Diamond
Cost: Moderate
Location: Isolated, to the South of Epcot
Pool: Several, one with Waterslides
Transport to Parks: Skyliner Gondola to Epcot and Hollywood Studios, Busses to other parks
Amenities: Magical Express, Wi-Fi, Paid Laundry and Dry Cleaning, Multiple Pools, Jogging Trail, Bike Rentals, Volleyball Courts, Playgrounds, Fishing, Outdoor Movies, Campfires, and Arcade

OUR REVIEW
The Caribbean Beach Resort is an iconic Moderately priced set of Hotels to the southeast of Epcot. Set on a stunning lake, there are

several Caribbean-inspired lots with rooms throughout. It's one of the more popular of the Moderate Resorts because of its beautiful design, but the rooms aren't anything special. They are just standard painted walls, a bathroom, and a bed or two. Nothing about them feels like Disney unless you get a pirate-themed room. Though kids may love the pirate rooms, they are the furthest away from the amenities. Preferred Rooms are closer to the lobby and pool, otherwise the busses drop off at each of the different villages around the hotel. It may be tempting to stay at the Caribbean Beach Resort for the price, but as it's a bit far from the parks and Disney Springs, you may want to consider a Value Resort to save money or upgrade to the Wilderness Lodge and get better amenities. If you don't mind the distance, don't need the Disney theme, and want to get a great price, this Resort might work well.

BOTTOM LINE
A beautiful moderately priced Resort with simple rooms and a spread out feel.

PROS
- 45-acres of beautiful Caribbean vibes
- Gondola system to Epcot and Hollywood Studios
- Island with playgrounds
- Multiple Pools and beach areas
- Caribbean Pirate Adventure for Kids

CONS
- Standard rooms feel flat with a sparse theme
- Longer bus wait times
- Larger, spread out area that may require a lot of walking
- Not very close to any of the Parks or Disney Springs, so you have to take the bussing system

· **Magic Tips** ·
Kids ages 4-12 can join a pirate-themed adventure that sets sail from the Caribbean Beach daily from 9:30AM to 11:30AM! Kids hear pirate tales and also find treasure!
Cost: $40-$50 / child.

DISNEY'S RIVIERA RESORT

Best for: Teens, Adults
AAA Rating: TBA
Cost: Deluxe / Disney Vacation Club
Location: Next to the Caribbean Beach Resort, to the South of Epcot
Pool: Several, one with waterslide
Transport to Parks: Skyliner Gondola to Epcot and Hollywood Studios, Busses to other parks
Amenities: Magical Express, Rooftop Bar, Wi-Fi, Paid Laundry and Dry Cleaning, Multiple Pools, Jogging Trail, Volleyball Courts, Playgrounds, Outdoor Movies, Campfires, Spa and Fitness Center and Arcade

OUR REVIEW

While many other resorts don't exceed two-stories in height, the Riviera Resort offers spectacular views of Epcot and Hollywood Studios. The hotel is inspired by a trip Walt Disney took to the French Riviera in 1935. It also hosts a rooftop bar for watching Epcot's nightly fireworks, beautiful pools, and easy access to the Disney Skyliner gondolas.

BOTTOM LINE

A tower hotel near Epcot and Hollywood Studios with sweeping views of Walt Disney World.

PROS

- Some rooms have views of Epcot fireworks
- Gondola system to Epcot and Hollywood Studios

CONS

- Standard rooms don't have much of a view

DISNEY'S CORONADO SPRINGS

Best for: Adults
Theme: Latin American Resort
AAA Rating: 3-Diamond
Cost: Moderate
Location: Isolated, to the East of Animal Kingdom
Pool: Yes, with Waterslide

Transport to Parks: Busses
Amenities: Magical Express, Wi-Fi, Paid Laundry and Dry Cleaning, Multiple Pools, Jogging Trail, Volleyball Courts, Playgrounds, Outdoor Movies, Campfires, Spa and Fitness Center and Arcade

OUR REVIEW
Our favorite feature of Disney's Coronado Springs Resort is the Lost City of Cibola pool. There is a Mayan-style Pyramid with a waterfall next to a long waterslide and a large, beach-like swimming area. The rest of the Resort is very spread out. In fact, it can feel impossible to walk the entire thing in an afternoon. With several buildings located around a large lake, Coronado Springs brings a Latin flare to WDW.

The Gran Destino Tower has a stunning two-story lobby, new restaurants and sweeping views from its rooms. There is club access from the tower and most of the artwork was inspired by Walt Disney's love of Salvador Dali paintings (the hotel was named after one). The better dining options are also available in the Gran Destino Tower. If you're looking for a sophisticated style with a moderate price tag, book a room in the fabulous Gran Destino Tower at Coronado Springs.

> **· Magic Tips ·**
> Rooms with Cronos Club Level access in the Gran Destino Tower are about half as similar club level rooms in Disney Deluxe Resorts. Enjoy refreshments, snacks, and complimentary booze (like mimosas for guests 21). However, the Cronos Club has limited hours.

BOTTOM LINE
A moderate resort with a great pool and stylish Gran Destino tower.

PROS
- Beautiful Gran Destino Tower with sweeping resort views
- Top-notch dining in the Gran Destino Tower with lower price tags than many comparable restaurant options
- Fantastic pools
- Spa and Fitness Center at a moderate resort

CONS
- Standard rooms feel flat with a sparse theme
- Longer bus wait times for both leaving and returning
- Larger, spread out area that may require a lot of walking

- Not very close to any of the Parks or Disney Springs, so you have to take the bussing system

---

· Magic Tips ·

Keep in mind the Lyft is an inexpensive transport around Walt Disney World. At about $10-$15 each way, you may want this option instead of the complimentary bussing system.

DISNEY'S PORT ORLEANS
FRENCH QUARTER & RIVERSIDE

Best for: Everyone
Theme: New Orleans Hotel and Resort
AAA Rating: 3-Diamond
Cost: Moderate
Location: Isolated, to the north of Disney Springs
Pool: Multiple Pools, with Waterslides
Transport to Parks: Busses, Boat to Disney Springs
Amenities: Magical Express, Wi-Fi, Paid Laundry and Dry Cleaning, Multiple Pools, Jogging Paths, Playgrounds, Fishing, Bike Rentals, Horse-Drawn Carriage Rides, and Arcade

OUR REVIEW – FRENCH QUARTER
Out of all of the WDW Moderate hotels, we recommend the Port Orleans French Quarter. This part of the Port Orleans Resort is central to the lobby and features multi-story neighborhood-style housing. It's less spread out than the Riverside and has one large pool. The rooms have a distinct Louisiana plantation feel. Make sure to get a hot beignet at the Sassagoula Floatworks cafeteria!

OUR REVIEW – RIVERSIDE
The second gorgeous property in the Port Orleans Resort. The price is usually perfect to stay in this spacious ground with several pools and dining areas. The busses and boats also take you straight to the Parks from several parts of the Riverside. Kids will love the Royal Guest rooms that are spilling over with Disney-themed magic. The standard rooms are slightly less thrilling, but better for vacationing adults who may find the Royal Guest rooms a bit too themed. The touches on the standard room moldings and bathroom sink area are

very charming. Its pool is located on an island in the middle of the river.

BOTTOM LINE
Port Orleans is our favorite moderate resort with its stunning landscapes and well-designed rooms. The French Quarter is our top choice with great food and easy access to the bus stops to the Parks. Both hotel have access to a river boat ride to Disney Springs.

PROS
- Stunning landscapes and rivers
- Riverboat cruise to Disney Springs with a port in both Riverside and the French Quarter
- French Quarter requires less walking than Riverside
- Bussing system feels faster than other moderate resorts
- Several restaurants and the YeHaa Bob show

CONS
- Larger, spread out area that may require a lot of walking (Riverside)
- Not very close to any of the Parks, so you have to take the bussing system

DISNEY'S ALL-STAR RESORTS
ALL-STAR MUSIC, SPORTS, & MOVIES

Note: The Calypso Pool (All-Star Music) has scheduled closure in fall 2020.

Best for: Families with Young Kids and Kids
Themes: 3 Hotels with specially designed themed rooms and buildings
Music – Calypso, Jazz, Country Fair, Broadway, and Rock
Sports – Surfing, Baseball, Football, Tennis, and Basketball
Disney Movies – Toy Story, Fantasia, Love Bug, Mighty Ducks, and 101 Dalmatians
AAA Rating: 3-Diamond
Cost: Value
Location: Furthest south. Animal Kingdom is the nearest Park, but it's nowhere walkable. These Resort Hotels are also close to the ESPN Wide World of Sports Complex and Disney's Blizzard Beach.
Pool: Yes (no waterslides)

Transport to Parks: Bus only

Amenities: Magical Express, Wi-Fi, Paid Laundry, 2 Pools, Jogging Trail, Movie Nights, Playground, and Arcade

OUR REVIEW

These three Resort Hotels are clustered together at the very southern part of the WDW Resort. While its guests stay the furthest from the Magic Kingdom and the other 3 Parks, they still receive the promised Disney magic. The All-Star Resorts have the appeal of eye-popping Disney-themed buildings with bright character paintings on the walls. We recommend families on a tight budget with Young Kids to stay here. There are 2 pools in each Hotel and plenty of busses traveling to the Theme Parks. The hotels are broken up into themed hotel towers that spread around two pools.

BOTTOM LINE

These are a great place to stay if you want all of Disney's amenities for a much lower price. If you aren't traveling with children or a deluxe hotel isn't in your price range, we'd recommend other resort hotel properties as the dining and theming experiences tend to feel more mature. Of the three hotels, we'd likely go with Music or Movies for the décor.

PROS

- Inexpensive rooms
- 2 Pools in each Hotel
- Food Court and Pizza Delivery options
- Disney themes with large statues and decorative spaces that are perfect for Kids
- Family Suites sleep up to 6 at the All-Star Music Hotel

CONS

- Very far away from the theme parks
- Only transport option are the busses and every All-Star Resort Hotel shares the same bus line, so they can feel crowded
- Adults may find these rooms cheesy
- The Resorts cover a large area and may require some walking to your room from the bus stop, lobby, pools, and dining

> **· Magic Tips ·**
> Check the bed sizes before you book! Disney's All-Star Sports and All-Star Music have double beds in the standard rooms. All-Star Movies has been updated with king and queen options.

DISNEY'S POP CENTURY & ART OF ANIMATION

Best for: Families with Young Kids, Kids, and Tweens
Themes: Disney and Pixar Animated Movies (Finding Nemo, Cars, and The Little Mermaid) and 20th Century Pop Culture (50's, 60's, 70's, 80's, and 90's)
AAA Rating: 3-Diamond
Cost: Value
Location: South of Hollywood Studios and north of ESPN Wide World of Sports Complex
Pool: One in each themed area (except 70's in Pop Century), no waterslides
Transport to Parks: Skyliner Gondola, Bus
Amenities: Magical Express, Wi-Fi, Paid Laundry and Dry Cleaning Several Pools, Jogging Trail, Movie Nights by the Pool, Bike Rentals, Playground, and Arcade

---

Note: The Hippy Dippy Pool (Pop Century) will undergo refurbishment in early 2020. The Big Blue Pool (Art of Animation) has scheduled refurbishment in fall 2020.

OUR REVIEW
Disney's Art of Animation and Pop Century Resorts face one another over the Hourglass Lake (named for its shape). Depending on the room type you choose, you can stay in that themed part of the Resort. Most of the buildings have their own pool and unique theme. Most of the rooms in the Art of Animation are Family Suites and sleep up to 6 people. Pop Century has standard rooms with minimal décor. Of the two, we recommend the Art of Animation because of the unique Disney statues and the larger rooms. That is, if you can get a great price. The Art of Animation is popular and sometimes the

prices can skyrocket beyond what they are worth. If you're a family with 3-4 Kids, this might be your best and cheapest option to stay at the WDW Resort. Keep in mind that these are both family resorts and therefore the noise level can be high.

BOTTOM LINE
Perfect for families on a budget. Tons of Disney décor and statues, but we recommend Art of Animation for its larger rooms and theming.

PROS
- Inexpensive rooms
- Disney Skyliner Gondola access
- Multiple Pools
- Food Court and Pizza Delivery options
- Disney themes with large statues and decorative spaces that are perfect for Kids
- Family Suites sleep up to 6 at the Art of Animation
- Closer to the Parks than the All-Star Resorts

CONS
- Far away from the Parks
- Busses can become crowded quickly
- Adults may find the themed rooms in the Art of Animation cheesy
- The Resorts cover a large area and may require some walking to your room from the bus stop, lobby, pools, and dining areas
- Often noisy with kids

DISNEY'S OLD KEY WEST RESORT

Best for: Teens, Adults, Older Adults
Theme: Florida's Key West
AAA Rating: 3-Diamond
Cost: Disney Vacation Club
Location: Isolated, to the south of Epcot and west of Disney Springs.
Pool: Yes, with Waterslide
Transport to Parks: Busses to Parks, Boat to Disney Springs
Amenities: Magical Express, Wi-Fi, Paid Laundry and Dry Cleaning, Multiple Pools, Jogging Trail along a Golf Course and Canals, Tennis, Volleyball, Basketball, Fishing, Bike Rentals, Playgrounds, Outdoor

Movies by the Pool, Old Key West Campfires, Fitness Center and Arcade

OUR REVIEW

Disney's Old Key West Resort was the original Disney Vacation Club property and feels like a country club with a tranquil atmosphere. Guests who stay here are looking to get away from the bustle and noise of the Parks for a relaxing stay. While there are amenities for Kids, Old Key West has several tennis courts and serene pools that appeal mostly to an older crowd. The rooms are large and typically inexpensive for their size. There are also 2-bedroom villas with a full-sized kitchen that sleeps up to 9. There are also several restaurants here and a Riverboat to Disney Springs.

BOTTOM LINE

A tranquil Resort with a country club feel. Has some of the largest rooms in WDW.

PROS

- Quiet atmosphere with Beautiful scenery
- Huge rooms
- Several Basketball, Tennis, and Volleyball courts
- Gym
- Boat to Disney Springs

CONS

- Longer bus wait times for both leaving and returning
- Larger, spread out area that may require a lot of walking
- Not very close to any of the Parks, so you have to take the bussing system

DISNEY'S SARATOGA SPRINGS

Best for: Teens, Adults, Older Adults
Theme: 19th Century Upstate New York
AAA Rating: 3-Diamond
Cost: Disney Vacation Club
Location: Near Disney Springs
Pool: Multiple Pools, with Waterslide
Transport to Parks: Busses to Parks, Boat or Walking to Disney Springs

Amenities: Magical Express, Wi-Fi, Paid Laundry and Dry Cleaning, Multiple Pools, Jogging Trail along a Golf Course and Canals, Tennis, Basketball, Fishing, Bike Rentals, Playgrounds, Outdoor Movies by the Pool, Campfires, Full-service Spa, Fitness Center and Arcade

OUR REVIEW

Disney's Saratoga Springs Resort is similar to the Old Key West Resort as it feels like a country club with a peaceful environment. Older crowds will enjoy the lax pools, scenery, golf courses, spas, and quiet away from the Parks. The Resort is large and very spread out which can be both a good and bad thing. Shopping is also just a short walk or boat ride away at Disney Springs. The rooms are large and typically inexpensive for their size. The Treehouse Villas house up to 9 guests. The Congress Park area of Saratoga Springs is the closest to Disney Springs.

BOTTOM LINE

A peaceful Resort with an old country club feel. It's very spread out and often difficult to book rooms.

PROS
- Quiet atmosphere
- Walking distance or boat ride to Disney Springs
- Beautiful scenery
- Full-service Spa
- Gym

CONS
- Longer bus wait times for both leaving and returning
- Larger, spread out area that may require a lot of walking
- Not very close to any of the Parks, so you have to take the bussing system

SWAN & DOLPHIN

Best for: Tweens, Teens, Adults
Theme: Premium Hotel
AAA Rating: 4-Diamond
Location: Central, walking distance to Epcot and Disney's Hollywood Studios
Pool: Yes, with Waterslide
Transport to Parks: Boat, Walk, Busses

Amenities: Magical Express, Wi-Fi, Paid Laundry and Dry Cleaning, Pools with Waterslides and Waterfall, Jogging Paths, Movie Nights, Playground, Volleyball, Basketball, Tennis, Bike Rentals, Boat Rentals, Fishing, Club Access for Certain Rooms, Spa and Fitness Center, Child Care at Camp Dolphin, Mini Golf, and Arcade

Amenities Not Included: Magical Express doesn't run here and MagicBands can't charge to your Hotel room (but they can be linked with a credit card)

OUR REVIEW

The Swan and Dolphin are several-story tall hotel buildings designed by Disney to compete with the neighboring hotels. Located in prime spots between Epcot and Disney's Hollywood Studios, the Swan and Dolphin are beautiful sister hotels with their own subtle character. These hotels are not run by Disney. Instead, they are leased to another corporation and run by Starwood Hotels. While you may not receive the complete magic of staying at other Walt Disney World properties, you still get most of the benefits, which we list below. Staying at this hotel can be perfect for those who love Epcot and can find great deals. If we had to pick between the two, we'd go with the Swan because of the better amenities (though you can use them at both hotels). The convention centers can pack the Swan and Dolphin, and make them quite noisy.

BOTTOM LINE

Two beautiful resort hotels on the outside with slightly dated interiors. They are leased out by Disney to other companies so guests will not have access to the Magical Express or the ability to charge to the room using their MagicBand.

PROS

- Walking distance or boat ride to Hollywood Studios and Epcot
- Beautiful exterior
- 3-acre pool area
- Full-service spa (in Dolphin)
- Gym
- Great dining in the hotel and nearby hotels

CONS

° No Magical Express

- Typically booked 3rd party, so MagicBands wait for you at your hotel and sometimes you can't choose your design
- Very little Disney theming
- Rooms feel a little dated
- Parking costs more than other Hotels at $20/day or $30/day for valet

---

Extra Magic Hours: These hotels receive Walt Disney World's Extra Magic Hours benefit!

BOOKING

You'll have to book your Swan or Dolphin hotel room through a third party website. Though you won't get perks like the Magical Express and full use of the MagicBands, you may save on a "deluxe-style" hotel that's centrally located. Ask for a room with a view of Epcot or Hollywood Studios.

> **· Magic Tips ·**
>
> The sculpture atop of the Dolphin hotel looks more like a fish. This is because the design was created after nautical dolphin art which is very fishlike.

SHADES OF GREEN

Best for: Military Families
Theme: Golf Resort
Location: West of Magic Kingdom Park, near the golf courses
Pool: Yes, with Waterslide
Our Review: Shades of Green is a family resort with tennis courts, a pool, and is central to the golf courses. It's set up to give discounted vacations to those who serve in the military for the United States. Meals tend to be very inexpensive and the rooms are nice and big for the price. You might also want to use your military discount to stay closer to the Parks.

PROS
- Beautiful landscaping with golfing
- Large rooms for the price
- Inexpensive dining in the hotel

- Exclusive busses to the Parks and Disney Springs

CONS
- Far away from the theme parks
- Very little Disney theming

Extra Magic Hours: This hotel receives Walt Disney World's Extra Magic Hours benefit!

Book at www.shadesofgreen.org

MORE HOTEL TIPS

CHECKIN
You can easily checkin to your Walt Disney World Resort hotel room via the Walt Disney World application. You can also do this days before your arrival. Your room number will be displayed and MagicBand will become your hotel room key when it's time to checkin at 3PM and 4PM for Deluxe Villas.

CHECKOUT
The checkout process is automatic at the WDW Resort. You will be delivered an itemized final bill on the morning of your departure. You will not need to manually checkout, call, or visit the front desk. Checkout time is 11AM. For Late Checkout, call the front desk on the morning of your departure. If they have availability, you might be able to checkout as late as 1PM. If you need to store your belongings,

UPGRADING A ROOM
Based on availability, you may be able to upgrade your room. Most of the time, Disney will charge for this. If you checkin at the front desk, you can always ask for availability and an upgrade—it's worth a shot!

REQUESTING A ROOM
Some of the hotel rooms have better views than others. Some of the standard rooms (which normally have views of a parking lot or a rooftop) can have peaks at wilderness, bodies of water, and animals! To request a room type, it's best to call Disney and ask for specifics. If you need a room with better accessibility to the busses or dining areas, mention that. We don't recommend telling Disney which

specific room number you'd like because it may not be available. Instead, tell them what you are looking for and another room may suit your request.

TOP OFF-SITE HOTELS

Staying on property at the Walt Disney World Resort may be too expensive for your budget and needs. While we usually recommend staying on-property for all of Disney's benefits, there are several properties in and around WDW that make fantastic options. Here we list our most-recommended of these hotels.

> **Note:** Disney Springs hotels receive Extra Magic Hours and 60-Day Advanced FastPass+ booking.

DISNEY SPRINGS AREA HOTELS

If you're looking to stay close to the theme parks but in a deluxe or moderate-style hotel without the premium cost, Disney Springs houses several nearby hotels in its "Hotel Plaza" area. Each of these properties is endorsed by WDW and can often come with Disney-theming. At times, Disney Springs resorts will have Extra Magic House and 60-Day FastPass+ selection as a promotion.

B Resort & Spa
1905 Hotel Plaza Blvd., Lake Buena Vista, FL 32830
(888) 246-8357 / www.bhotelsandresorts.com/b-resort-and-spa

Star Rating	Our Rating	Price	Shuttle to Disney Parks	Pool
4	B+	Moderate	Yes	Yes

Pros: Affordable and stylish rooms. On-site spa with shuttle to and from Disney theme parks. You can also ask for a gaming console to play in your room.

Cons: Resort fee, inconsistent customer service

Best Western Lake Buena Vista

2000 Hotel Plaza Blvd., Lake Buena Vista, FL 32830
(407) 828-2424 / www.lakebuenavistaresorthotel.com

Star Rating	Our Rating	Price	Shuttle to Disney Parks	Pool
3	B	Economic	Yes	Yes

Pros: Affordable rooms with shuttle to and from Disney theme parks. There is also a fitness center. AAA discount available.
Cons: Further away from Disney Springs, Resort fee, hotel appears dated

---

DoubleTree Suites by Hilton Orlando

2305 Hotel Plaza Blvd., Lake Buena Vista, FL 32830
(407) 934-1000 / www.doubletree.com

Star Rating	Our Rating	Price	Shuttle to Disney Parks	Pool
3	B+	Economic	Yes	Yes

Pros: Affordable rooms with shuttle to and from Disney theme parks. There is also a fitness center and Hilton Honors members can get discounts on rooms and earn points.
Cons: Further away from Disney Springs, inconsistent customer service

---

Hilton Orlando Buena Vista Palace

1900 E. Buena Vista Dr, Lake Buena Vista, FL 32830
(407) 827-2727 / www.buenavistapalace.com

Star Rating	Our Rating	Price	Shuttle to Disney Parks	Pool
4	A	Moderate	Yes	Yes

Pros: Affordable and stylish 4-star rooms with a views. Offers shuttle to and from Disney theme parks, a fitness center, and Hilton Honors members can get discounts on rooms and earn points. Very close to Disney Springs.

Cons: May not live up to other Hilton hotels in terms of service and room style.

Hilton Orlando Lake Buena Vista
1751 Hotel Plaza Blvd, Lake Buena Vista, FL 32830
(407) 827-4000 / www.hilton.com

Star Rating	Our Rating	Price	Shuttle to Disney Parks	Pool
4	A-	Moderate	Yes	Yes

Pros: Affordable 4-star rooms with a views. Offers shuttle to and from Disney theme parks, a fitness center, and Hilton Honors members can get discounts on rooms and earn points. Very close to Disney Springs. Adults-only pool available.
Cons: May not live up to other Hilton hotels in terms of service and room style. High parking fees.

Holiday Inn Orlando
1805 Hotel Plaza Blvd, Lake Buena Vista, FL 32830
(407) 828-8888 / www.hiorlando.com

Star Rating	Our Rating	Price	Shuttle to Disney Parks	Pool
3	A	Economic	Yes	Yes

Pros: Very affordable and simple rooms. Offers shuttle to and from Disney theme parks and fitness center.
Cons: Parking costs extra and high resort fees. Rooms could use updating.

Wyndham Garden Lake Buena Vista
1850 Hotel Plaza Blvd, Lake Buena Vista, FL 32830
(407) 842-6644 /www.wyndhamlakebuenavista.com

Star Rating	Our Rating	Price	Shuttle to Disney Parks	Pool
3	B-	Economic	Yes	Yes

Pros: Very close to Disney Springs. Offers shuttle to and from Disney theme parks and fitness center. Rooms are clean and affordable.

Cons: Rooms are nothing special. Resort needs updating.

MORE OFF-SITE HOTELS

These hotel properties are bump up in price, but offer more amenities. Overall, they can still save you money in comparison to staying at a Disney Resort.

Margaritaville Resort Orlando

8000 Fins Up Circle, Kissimmee, FL 34747
(407) 479-0950 / www.margaritavilleresortorlando.com

Star Rating	Our Rating	Price	Shuttle to Disney Parks	Pool
4	A	Moderate	Yes	Yes

Pros: An island-themed resort hotel with "lagoon-style" sand pools, a luxury spa, signature dining, and a 14-acre Island H2O Live water park. Margaritaville is designed both for family fun and relaxation. Disney's Animal Kingdom theme park is only about 5 miles away. Larger groups may want to consider renting a cottage located on property.
Cons: Rates can skyrocket during the summer and holiday seasons. At times, the party scene near the pools can become noisy.

Hyatt Regency Grand Cypress

1 Grand Cypress Blvd, Orlando, FL 32836
(407) 239-1234 / www.hyatt.com

Star Rating	Our Rating	Price	Shuttle to Disney Parks	Pool
4	A	Deluxe	Yes	Yes

Pros: Beautiful property and rooms. Shuttle service to and from Disney theme parks, on-site spa, nearby golfing, rock climbing, and 24-hour fitness center. Pet accommodations available.
Cons: Can be expensive and have a very high resort fee. About a 5 to 10-minute drive to Disney Springs and 20-minute drive to the Magic Kingdom.

Waldorf Astoria Orlando

14200 Bonnet Creek Resort Ln, Orlando, FL 32821
(407) 597-5500 / www.waldorfastoriaorlando.com

Star Rating	Our Rating	Price	Shuttle to Disney Parks	Pool
5	A+	Luxury	Yes	Yes

Pros: Beautiful and affordable 5-star hotel property and rooms. Shuttle service to and from Disney theme parks, on-site spa, nearby golfing, and 24-hour fitness center. Hilton Honors members can get discounts on rooms and earn points. Excellent staff.
Cons: About a 10 to 15-minute drive to the Magic Kingdom.
Walt Disney World Benefits: This hotel receives Extra Magic Hours and 60-Day Advanced FastPass+ booking.

Gaylord Palms Resort

6000 W. Osceola Parkway, Orlando, FL 32821
(407) 586-0000 / www.gaylordpalms.com

Star Rating	Our Rating	Price	Shuttle to Disney Parks	Pool
4	A-	Luxury	Yes	Yes

Pros: Beautiful and affordable 4-star hotel property and rooms. Unique theming including an indoor restaurant on a boat. Shuttle service to Disney theme parks, on-site spa, pools with waterslides, wave pool, on-site alligators, nearby golfing, and 24-hour fitness center. Marriott Rewards members can get discounts on rooms and earn points. 10-minute drive to Epcot.
Cons: Hotel can sellout during popular months. Parking is expensive and can become backed up on busy weekends and holidays.

Hilton Orlando Bonnet Creek

14100 Bonnet Creek Resort Ln, Orlando, FL 32821-4023
(407) 597-3600 / www.hiltonbonnetcreek.com

Star Rating	Our Rating	Price	Shuttle to Disney Parks	Pool
4	A-	Deluxe	Yes	Yes

Pros: Clean and affordable 4-star hotel property and rooms. Oasis-like pool with lazy river, golf course, fitness center, jogging track, arcade, and bike rental. Shuttle service to Disney theme parks. Hilton

Honors members can get discounts on rooms and earn points. 10-minute drive to Epcot.

Cons: May not live up to typical Hilton hotel styles. Rooms by pools can become very noisy.

Walt Disney World Benefits: This hotel receives Extra Magic Hours and 60-Day Advanced FastPass+ booking.

Rosen Shingle Creek

9939 Universal Blvd, Orlando, FL 32819
(866) 996-9939 / www.rosenshinglecreek.com

Star Rating	Our Rating	Price	Shuttle to Disney Parks	Pool
4	A+	Luxury	Paid	Yes

Pros: We believe that the Rose Shingle Creek is one of the better deals for a luxury vacation stay outside of the Walt Disney World Resort. Beautiful and affordable 4-star hotel property and rooms. On-site spa, on-site golfing, and fitness center. Hilton Honors members can get discounts on rooms and earn points. Close to Universal Orlando (5-10 minute drive). Excellent staff.

Cons: Paid shuttle service through Mears to theme parks. A bit far from Walt Disney World (20-25 minute drive to the Magic Kingdom).

Walt Disney World Benefits: This hotel receives Extra Magic Hours and 60-Day Advanced FastPass+ booking.

Ritz-Carlton Grande Lakes

4012 Central Florida Pkwy, Orlando, FL 32837
(407) 206-2400 / www.ritzcarlton.com

Star Rating	Our Rating	Price	Shuttle to Disney Parks	Pool
5	A	Luxury	Yes	Yes

Pros: Elegant 5-star hotel property and stunning rooms. Shuttle service to and from Walt Disney World theme parks, Universal Orlando, and SeaWorld. On-site spa, butterfly garden, kids play area, bocce ball courts, 18-hole golfing, and fitness center. Superior service.

Cons: Expensive, so if you're looking for a bargain on a 5-star resort, you may want to try the Waldorf Astoria (though we prefer the Ritz Carlton or the Four Seasons). About 20 to 25-minute drive to the Magic Kingdom, Epcot, or Universal Orlando.

Four Seasons Resort Orlando

14200 Bonnet Creek Resort Ln, Orlando, FL 32821
(407) 597-5500 / www.fourseasons.com/orlando

Star Rating	Our Rating	Price	Shuttle to Disney Parks	Pool
5	A+	Luxury	Yes	Yes

Pros: Elegant 5-star hotel property and stunning rooms. Several pools with Lazy River, adults-only pool, splash zone, bocce ball, movies by the pool, and game room. Complimentary "luxury motor coach" to and from the Disney parks. Private car service available. Closer to the parks than the Ritz-Carlton (about 10 minutes to the Magic Kingdom or Epcot). Superior service.

Cons: Very expensive, so if you're looking for a bargain on a 5-star resort, you may want to try the Waldorf Astoria or the less-expensive Ritz Carlton (though we prefer the Four Seasons). About 20 to 25-minute drive to the Magic Kingdom, Epcot, or Universal Orlando.

Walt Disney World Benefits: This hotel receives Extra Magic Hours and 60-Day Advanced FastPass+ booking.

INTRODUCTION

Like many shopping locations in America, Disney Springs has gone through radical transformations. Originally known as Lake Buena Vista Shopping Village when it opened in 1975, this section of the Walt Disney World Resort has always focused heavily on dining and shopping experiences. Soon after its inception, the shopping area transformed into Walt Disney World Village, Disney Village Marketplace, and Downtown Disney before coming to its latest name in 2015.

Disney Springs is designed for wandering. Visitors will discover fun new shops, premium restaurants, and dazzling entertainment. Whether you're looking for a Disney-themed gift, a romantic dinner, or an unforgettable show, Disney Springs has it all.

For the most part, Disney Springs is a beautiful outdoor mall with chain stores as well as unique boutiques. Restaurants fill much of the area that's covered in waterways, bridges, and stunning Floridian scenes. The scene comes to life with beautifully paved walkways filled with music, glowing ponds, and spectacular banners. Here, we explore some of Disney Springs' unique shopping and dining experiences based on our top recommendations.

GETTING TO DISNEY SPRINGS

Disney Springs is located on property, but a bit far away from the Magic Kingdom and Animal Kingdom. If you're driving, parking at Disney Springs is free in any of their lots or garages. There are a few ways to travel there without a car:

- **Boat** – There is free water transport from the Disney's Port Orleans Resort (French Quarter and Riverside), Disney's Old Key West Resort, and Disney's Saratoga Springs Resort.

- **Bus** – Perhaps the least glamorous way, but it's efficient. Travel to Disney Springs from any of the Resort Parks or Hotels for free with the Disney Bus system.

- **Walk** – From Disney's Saratoga Springs Resort, you can walk directly to Disney Springs in about 15 minutes.

UNIQUE SHOPS

There are dozens of shops at Disney Springs—and still growing! Since many of them are found in retail locations around the world, we've just listed the unique shops dedicated to pleasing visitors of Walt Disney World:

THE ART OF DISNEY
Get Disney-themed gifts from art to fineries. You won't find anything like these pieces of art anywhere else!

BIBBIDI BOBBIDI BOUTIQUE
Perfect for Kids looking to get a makeover to look like their favorite Disney Princess. It's a replica of the one also offered in the Magic Kingdom Park. We recommend booking an appointment if you'd like a makeover. Otherwise, this Boutique gives free spritzes of pixie dust to any visitor!

BUILD A DINO
The makers of Build-A-Bear Workshop bring you a prehistoric version of the same concept. Make your own dinosaur toy or plush or build one as a gift. Kids will go crazy for this experience.

COCA-COLA STORE
Everything Coca-Cola from clothing to unique flavors in this impressive store.

DISNEY DESIGN-A-TEE
Looking for that perfect Disney gift but haven't quite found it? Design your own shirt instead here at this store. It's becoming even more popular now that families are getting matching shirts created for their stay in the Parks.

DISNEY'S CANDY CAULDRON
Discover an array of delicious Disney desserts including their famous hand-designed caramel apples.

DISNEY'S DAYS OF CHRISTMAS
A magic emporium where the holidays never end. Relive your Christmas spirit any day of the year in this stunning shop.

DISNEY'S PHOTOPASS STUDIOS
Looking for the perfect Disney photo experience? Search no further because you can have everything from classic Disney backdrops to *Frozen* wonderlands created in this professional photo studio.

DISNEY'S PIN TRADERS
Search through a seemingly endless supply of pins to buy and trade with people all over the WDW Resort. The largest Disney pin board is at the Disney Pin Trading Company Store in Disney Springs. While this board is only on display during part of each day, pin traders will drop their jaw after spotting it!

DISNEY'S WONDERFUL WORLD OF MEMORIES
If scrapbooking is your thing, then there is no better place in all of Walt Disney World. Commemorate your vacation with unique Disney-style stickers, pages, and more to complete your beautiful scrapbook.

GHIRARDELLI ICE CREAM & CHOCOLATE SHOP
Try world-famous chocolate, ice cream, and sodas in this classic chocolate shop. The smell of this shop is also heavenly! If you're just stopping by, you'll receive a free square of chocolate to sample.

GOOFY'S CANDY COMPANY

Love candy? This is where to get it! We highly recommend Goofy's Sour Gummy Worms as a perfect gift—or just for yourself. Guests can also stop by and try a free piece of candy here!

THE LEGO STORE

We can't think of a better way to bribe kids to go shopping than with the magic of LEGO! This store has it all from individual pieces to unique sets. You can also design your own figurines to buy. Even adults will be stunned by the amazing LEGO collections.

STAR WARS GALACTIC OUTPOST

The destination for Star Wars apparel! Buy everything from artwork to t-shirts and toys that range in theme from every *Star Wars* movie ever made.

SUPER HERO HEADQUARTERS

Power up with loads of Marvel merchandise in this specially themed store.

UNIQLO

This multi-level apparel destination will remind first-time visitors of retail giants like H&M. However, UNIQLO is also a fantastic place to purchase inexpensive Disney-branded clothing and accessories. They have everything from Mickey Mouse to Star Wars for kids and adults!

WORLD OF DISNEY

This may be the most popular store in all of the Walt Disney World Resort—and for a good reason. Pick from an overabundance of Disney merchandise from pins to toys to clothing and kitchenware. There's something for every Disney-lover in here and we highly recommend that you pay World of Disney a visit.

NOTE: There are dozens of more shops in Disney Springs. Many of them are often found in malls across the world, so we just opted to list the more unique locations.

GUEST SERVICES

The Guest Services booth at Disney Springs can be a lifesaver. If you have any issues with your MagicBand or vacation planning, head over there and a Disney Cast Member will take care of you.

> **· Magic Tips ·**
> Many of the shops in Disney Springs have hotel delivery free of charge for those staying on property! We love this feature and highly recommend using it.

ATTRACTIONS

THE VOID - VIRTUAL REALITY

We were skeptical about the VOID's boasted "hyper-realistic" virtual reality experience. It sounds like a great tagline to get visitors to buy tickets, but how real is it? The answer: very, *very* real! Its action-packed adventures have guests walking through tight corridors, battling enemies, and maneuvering over lava pits! There are thrilling moments, terrifying experiences, and iconic interactions (we won't spoil the "iconic" parts for you). You also *feel* it when an enemy blasts you with a laser! Luckily, it doesn't hurt, but your reaction will be real.

The VOID began its run at Walt Disney World with a *Star Wars*-inspired experience called Secrets of the Empire. If you're looking for more attractions outside of Star Wars: Galaxy's Edge and Star Tours, you're in luck! The VOID worked with Disney and Lucas Films to create one of the most amazing experiences at the WDW Resort. Star Wars: Secrets of the Empire will knock your socks off and make you feel like you've actually battled the Empire firsthand!

DETAILS

Tickets are about $30 per player and the VR runs for about 30 minutes. Guests must be 48" and 10 years of age to play. Groups can be no larger than 4 at a time; bigger groups will be split apart. The VOID also makes you sign a liability waiver. Ralphs Breaks VR and Secrets of the Empire switch off dates, so you won't be able to experience both on the same day.

TICKETS AND SCHEDULE:

https://www.thevoid.com/locations/orlando

NBA EXPERIENCE

The NBA Experience brings the technology from the pros to the fans in a set of attractions. Test your shot, play trivia, and see what its like to be a new recruit for the NBA! The NBA Experience is specifically tailored for basketball fans who dream of playing the sport for a living. It's great fun for all ages, though we recommend kids 8 and older for this experience.

DETAILS
Tickets are $34 (plus tax) for a day pass.

TICKETS:
https://disneyworld.disney.go.com/en_CA/entertainment/disney-springs/nba-experience/

CIRQUE DU SOLEI

Coming April 17, 2020!
Walt Disney Animation Studios and Cirque du Soleil have teamed up to bring a one-of-a-kind theatrical production to life! The Disney animated characters will interact with the performers to make this a touching and magical experience for all!
Tickets: https://disneyworld.disney.go.com/entertainment/disney-springs/cirque-du-soleil

AEROPHILE

Fly up to 400 feet into the air on a giant helium balloon, and get stunning views of the Walt Disney World Resort. Prices are $20 for adults and $15 for kids ages 3-9. Cloudy and foggy days may have limited viewing. Also weather can prevent the balloon from taking off. We also recommend booking a dinner somewhere at the Gran Destino Tower in Coronado Springs or the Riviera Resort's rooftop for amazing views and a delicious meal.

GO BOWLING

Splitsville has luxury bowling lanes that are fun for the entire family! Dine and bowl or just come for the bowling. Splitsville has extended hours usually from 10:30AM - 1AM.

INTRODUCTION

You may have come to the Walt Disney World Resort for the world-class attractions and themes. However, there's a hidden gem just awaiting you. The WDW Resort is home to some of the best food in the world with cuisine you'll be raving about well after your trip has come to an end. That is, *if* you know where to go. It's true that there are many quick-service stands with bland hamburgers and forgettable fries. There are places in the Resort with some of the best burgers, fries, and churros. You just need to know where these places are. In this chapter, we adventure through Walt Disney World eating spots. Whether it's hotel dining or Epcot cuisine, we review all that can tickle your tastebuds.

DINING TYPES

A listing of the different categories of restaurants. WDW keeps it simple by bringing you only a few types of eateries: Quick-Service, Table Service, and Fine Dining. It may be difficult to know the pricing based on their recommendations, so we've broken it down further here.

- **Quick-Service** – Meals that you can order and typically seat yourself soon after ordering.
- **Table Service** – Restaurants with a waiter. It is suggested that you tip based on the service you receive.

- **Fine Dining or Signature Dining** – The best that the WDW Resort has to offer with elegant décor and excellent, world-class courses. Fine Dining restaurants come with a premium price and often a dress code.
- **Snack Carts** – Carts, shacks, and huts serving snacks and drinks.
- **Bars and Lounges** – Calm areas with open seating and typically a full bar. Lounges typically have more seating than bars.

MOBILE ORDERING

The Walt Disney World App is your ticket to fast and easy ordering to some of the best dining locations in the parks! Not every restaurant has this option, but some with infamously long lines now have a way for you to cut ahead! We highly recommend mobile ordering instead of waiting. Disney has streamlined this system to make it quick and easy for your food availability.

Using Mobile Ordering:
1. Download the Walt Disney World App
2. Create a login (or login with your existing account)
3. Select "Order Food"
4. Choose your destination and arrival time
5. Select your items
6. Review the order and purchase with credit card
7. When your order is ready, head to the restaurant and alert a Cast Member that you have arrived for pickup!

We've marked all restaurants with mobile ordering using this icon: ‡ – Disney will likely add more restaurants and possibly change options, so use the app for a more up-to-date list.

Note: WDW's soda fountains and bottled waters are Coca-Cola products. The Resort's domestic beer is often Budweiser.

OUR RESTAURANT PRICING

WDW only has 3 tiers of pricing on their website. We don't think it's enough. To the savvy traveler, there is a big difference between something under $10 and something over $10. There's also a big difference between a table-service meal that will cost you $15-$25 versus well over $25 per person.

$ – Under $10 (typically snack carts)
$$ – $10 - $15 (typically Quick-Service Restaurants)
$$$ – $15 - $30 (Table Service Restaurants)
$$$$ – $30 - $60 (Dinner Buffets, Fine and Signature Dining)
$$$$$ – $60 or more (Dining experiences)

OUR FAVORITES
We list our favorites food items and locations from snacks to dining. Just look for the ❤ next to the item!

ALLERGY AND DINING REQUESTS

Disney is happy to accommodate special dining requests and wants to ensure that your food is safe for you to eat. If you have a dietary need or request, inform your waiter or the quick-service dining spot. Many times, the wait staff will ask before you're seated if you have any food allergies. To pre-plan, we recommend reviewing the menus of each dining spot before attending (these can be found on the Walt Disney World mobile app and WaltDisneyWorld.com). If Disney cannot meet your dietary needs, you may bring food with you to the parks. Your travel safety is important, so please reach out to Disney with any questions: special.diets@DisneyWorld.com

· **Magic Tips** ·
Disney's commitment to the environment has taken its theme parks away from using many plastics. This means that Quick-Service dining spots distribute soft drinks without a plastic lid or straw. If you'd like a paper straw, ask a Cast Member at your dining location.

BOOKING DINING

The popular restaurants fill up quickly, so don't forget to book in advance (up to 180 days). The easiest way to book dining is through the Walt Disney World mobile app or online on Disney World's website. If you need assistance, call **(714) 781-DINE** and book.

DISNEY DINING PLAN

INTRODUCTION

The Walt Disney World Resort offers special dining packages for guests staying on property. The Disney Dining Plans (DDP) are designed for guests to pre-pay for the food that they plan to enjoy during their vacation. While Disney touts DDP as ways to save money, for many guests, this simply isn't the case. So, think of DDP as more of an "all-inclusive" cost rather than a way to save money. We've discovered that DDP *can* save you a load of cash or end up costing you more, depending on your plan. Overall, we like DDP a lot, and with our tips, you can take maximum advance of this program.

HOW TO USE DDP

You may redeem your DDP points at one of 200 dining spots around Walt Disney World that take part of DDP. These include the four theme parks, water parks, Resort hotels, and Disney Springs (we noted most of their locations earlier in this chapter). Each meal or snack becomes 1 credit on your reservation. A Table Service credit and a Quick-Service credit are separate points. Snack credits are also separate points. Signature Dining restaurants require 2 Table Service credits to dine. Your MagicBand can be scanned to use your credits.

Quick-Service meals come with an entree and a drink. Table Service Meals come with 1 entree, 1 dessert, and 1 beverage—or you can use 1 Table Service credit toward a buffet. Snack credits can be used toward items like popcorn, ice cream, chips, coffee, and drinks. Different snack locations will offer various items. For Table Service and Quick-Service, adults ages 21 and older can use their drink credit for an alcoholic beverage.

All credits of one party are linked to a single account, therefore someone in your group can borrow from the entire pool. This can be a bit tricky for those with large groups, so it's important to keep this in mind before purchasing DDP. Guests will not be able to break up these dining credits across multiple locations. Meaning, you cannot redeem 1 Quick-Service credit for an entree at one restaurant and a drink at another.

Additionally, the Walt Disney World mobile app keeps track of your used and remaining dining credits. After using a credit, you receipt will also show your party's remaining credits. If you have trouble accessing this information, you can also receive a breakdown from your hotel concierge.

QUALIFICATIONS
To buy one of the Disney Dining Plans, you'll need to book a package through Disney with a room and theme park tickets. Those staying with Disney Vacation Club may not have to purchase the theme park tickets to buy a DDP.

DINING PLAN TYPES
There are three types of Disney Dining Plans and each offer different meals depending on your needs. If you tend to eat a Quick-Service burger and sandwich places, you might want to skip the more expensive meals. If you enjoy eating at several of Disney's themed Table Service dining experiences, you may want an upgraded plan.

ALL PLANS
All dining and snack credits and other perks are valid midnight of the day you checkout. Each Dining Plan comes with a refillable mug per person that can be used for fountain drinks at Resort hotels.

DISNEY QUICK SERVICE PLAN
2 Quick-Service Meals and 2 Snacks per person, per night. Quick-Service meals are spots without a waiter and are scattered around the WDW Resort. These are also the least expensive meals. You will not be able to use this plan at Table Service, Character Dining experiences, or Signature restaurants.
Cost per day: $52.50/adult (ages 10+) and $23.78/child (ages 3-9)

DISNEY DINING PLAN
1 Quick-Service Meal, 1 Table Service Meal, and 2 Snacks per person, per night. Table Service meals are restaurants with a waiter or a buffet. You can also use 2 of your Table Service credits for a Signature Dining experience like the California Grill or the Yachtsman Steakhouse.
Cost per day: $75.49/adult (ages 10+) and $43.49/child (ages 3-9)

DISNEY DELUXE DINING PLAN
3 Meals (either Table Service or Quick-Service), and 2 Snacks per person, per night. If you are planning on dining at table service restaurants more than once a day, we recommend this package. Or,

if you plan on dining at several Signature Dining locations, we also recommend this package.

Cost per day: $116.25/adult (ages 10+) and $43.49/child (ages 3-9)

MORE TIPS

DDP is relatively flexible. Each night you stay gives you dining credits. So, you can use as many or as little of your credits each day. For example, you can choose to use one Quick-Service credit and one Table Service credit per day, or use two Quick-Service one day and two Table Service another. You can also use two Table Service and one Quick-Service meal in a day. Really, the choice is yours. If you run out of credits, you will be billed. Tip is also not included with DDP, so we recommend bringing cash or charging your room or credit card upon receipt.

> · **Magic Tips** ·
>
> If you're traveling with a group, the Disney Dining Plans make paying easy! You won't have to worry about splitting bills since you're using one credit per person.

DINING PLAN CONS

As we've said before, depending on your needs, the Dining Disney Plan may not save you money. It may also cost you more than just paying out of pocket for your meals. If you're not interested in planning all of your dining before you head to the parks, we don't recommend DDP. It might feel overwhelming to pre-plan your vacation, meal by meal for each day. The Quick-Service DDP may work for your needs in this occasion. That way, you can grab food when you're hungry.

Children ten and older with smaller appetites may end up costing you more than they'll eat. While some ten-year-olds eat as much as an adult, many do not. Nonetheless, you'll pay the same for a ten-year-old boy as you would an adult man. Children who are picky and inconsistent eaters may not benefit from DDP. Make sure you review kids' menus before booking.

Furthermore, the reliable drink mug that comes with each dining plan is very, very small. They hold about one can of Coke, which is fine for children and those who don't drink very many liquids. Most guests wishing to fill their mugs, even with filtered drinking water, will find themselves bouncing back and forth between their hotel room and the refill station near the lobbies.

We also wish that the table service credits could have a choice of appetizer instead of dessert. Most guests don't feel like eating 2-3 desserts a day. Some restaurants will allow those with the Deluxe Dining Plan to get both an appetizer and a dessert with each meal at no additional cost.

Overall, the Disney Dining Plan comes with *a lot* of food. Will you want to eat an entree, dessert, and specialty beverage more than once a day? If the answer is yes, then we highly recommend DDP for you.

DINING PLAN TIPS

1. Book your restaurant reservations well in advance to secure your top dining choices.
2. Snack credits can be used in a variety of ways, including for a Starbucks coffee or pastry.
3. Snack credits can be redeemed at many locations at Epcot's famous Food & Wine Festival. You can also use 1 Quick-Service credit as 3 snack credits at participating locations!
4. At Table Service locations, you can always ask your waiter to substitute your food. It's not a guarantee, but if you don't feel up for dessert, you may ask to change it for an appetizer.
5. Dinner buffets are always a great idea to get your money's worth. These usually cost about $60 per adult for a dinner buffet. 1 Table Service credit is all that you need to redeem at   most of these locations!
6. When dining for dinner, order a steak; it's the best value for an entree that you can find.
7. Snacks credits are the biggest items that go to waste while using DDP. I you don't use all of them, you can redeem Snack credits at most hotel shops. These can be used for candy bars and other to-go items.
8. Snacks can be used for specialty drinks and desserts. This includes popular items like Dole Whips and LeFou's Brew at Gaston's Tavern in Fantasyland (Magic Kingdom)!
9. Watch your credits! Since you pay with DDP at the end of your meal, you may find yourself with a surprise bill if you've run out of dining credits (keep track on the Walt Disney World app).

FREE DINING PLAN DEAL

Almost every year, Walt Disney World releases a very limited discount where guests staying at select Disney resort properties get a Disney Dining Plan for free! Of course, there are limitations. Often these include a minimum of a four-night stay and park hopper tickets for each person in your group. These deals are often released in April for travel in August through December (with October, Thanksgiving, and Christmas weeks usually excluded). We've done the math and it usually saves hundreds of dollars for a family of four, even in contrast with booking a discounted room.

Most of the time, Pop Century or Old Key West are the best options for this dining deal. Pop Century is centrally located to many of the attractions and comes with the Quick-Service Dining Plan. Old Key West is also centrally located and comes with the Disney Dining Plan (with table service) at a much lower rate. Disney's Boardwalk Inn comes at a closer second to Old Key West.

> **· Magic Tips ·**
> We update our free e-mail newsletter when the free dining deal becomes available. Haven't joined our list yet? Subscribe at: **www.magicguidebooks.com/list**

TABLES IN WONDERLAND

Florida residents, Walt Disney World Passholders, and Disney Vacation Club Members can join a unique discounted dining program called Tables in Wonderland. Save 20% on food *and* alcohol for your party at over 100 Walt Disney World restaurants. This is a great option for guests with larger groups who might consume alcohol as Passholder and DVC discounts don't cover adult beverages. One Tables in Wonderland pass works for up to 10 guests or you can combine two passes for up to 20 guests in one bill.

Tables in Wonderland is $175 for Florida Residents and $150 for Passholders and DVC members.

Booking: **http://tablesinwonderland.com**

MAGIC KINGDOM DINING

‡ ALOHA ISLE ❤

Adventureland

Description: Grab a famous Dole Whip here. One of the best treats in all of WDW.

Type: Snack Cart

Price: $ / **Dining Plan:** Yes

Menu Items: Dole Whip, Juice, Water, Pineapple

Recommendation: Pineapple Float ❤

AUNTIE POLLY'S

Frontierland

Description: This seasonal stack stand rarely opens in Frontierland, but serves delicious biscuit sliders, rooter floats, and other snacks.

AUNTIE GRAVITY'S GALACTIC GOODIES

Tomorrowland

Description: Ice cream stand

Type: Snack Cart

Price: $ / **Dining Plan:** No

Menu Items: Ice cream, floats, muffins, fruit, smoothies, soda pop

Recommendation: Hot Fudge Sundae

> **· Magic Tips ·**
> WDW has a strict no-sad-faces policy—we're not kidding! If your child spills an ice cream cone, tell a Cast Member at the point of purchase and they will happily replace it for free.

BE OUR GUEST RESTAURANT ❤

Fantasyland

Description: Not to be missed! A dazzling restaurant with three main dining areas: the dark west wing, the ballroom, and the rose gallery. It has some of the best food in the Magic Kingdom.

Type: Quick-Service (breakfast and lunch) / Table Service (dinner)

Price: $$$-$$$$ / **Dining Plan:** Yes

Menu Items:
Breakfast: eggs, bacon, croissant doughnut, ham, breakfast sandwiches, vegetable quiche, fries, soda pop, coffee, milk
Kids: crepes, French toast, eggs, cereal
Lunch: soups, sandwiches, salad, desserts, soda pop, coffee, tea, beer, wine
Kids Lunch: sandwiches, shrimp, pasta, chicken, grilled cheese
Dinner (3-course, prix fixe meal): escargot, French onion soup, lobster bisque, salad, filet mignon, lamb chops, ricotta tortellini, chicken, roasted pork, seafood bouillabaisse, desserts, wines, beers
Kids Dinner: chicken, beef tenderloin, shrimp skewer, macaroni and cheese
Recommendations: Get a reservation! You won't be able to dine here without one. Eat in the west wing of the Be Our Guest Restaurant—it's dark and beautifully decorated. Thunder and lightning clash every few minutes near the red rose with the wilting petals. For dinner, we recommend the Center-Cut Filet Mignon.

‡ CASEY'S CORNER ❤
Main Street, U.S.A.
Description: Quick grab hot dogs and drinks
Type: Quick-Service
Price: $$ / **Dining Plan:** Yes
Menu Items: hot dogs, pulled pork, brownie, soda pop, lemonade, juice, hot chocolate, coffee, iced tea
Recommendation: Corn Dog Nuggets ❤

· **Magic Tips** ·
Looking for a spot to eat? Eat on the grass near the hub in front of the castle. It's comfortable place to rest.

CHESHIRE CAFE
Fantasyland
Description: *Alice in Wonderland*-themed snacks and treats
Type: Snacks
Price: $ / **Dining Plan:** No
Menu Items: cereal, muffin, fruit, soda pop, lemonade, juice, hot chocolate, coffee, iced tea
Recommendation: Cheshire Cat Tail

CINDERELLA'S ROYAL TABLE
Fantasyland
Description: A fanciful castle feast with Disney Princesses
Type: Character Dining
Price: $$$-$$$$ / **Dining Plan:** Yes
Menu Items:
Breakfast: eggs, bacon, ham, beef, French toast, shrimp and grits, quiche, soda pop, coffee, milk, juice
Kids Breakfast: eggs, bacon, waffle
Lunch & Dinner: pork, chicken, vegetable couscous, fish, beef and shrimp, salad, desserts, soda pop, coffee, milk, juice, various desserts
Kids Lunch & Dinner: salad, turkey pot pie, chicken nuggets, chicken leg, beef tenderloin
Recommendation: Chef's Tasting Platter

‡ COLUMBIA HARBOUR HOUSE ♥
Liberty Square
Description: The best place for American-style seafood in the Magic Kingdom
Type: Quick-Service
Price: $$ / **Dining Plan:** Yes
Menu Items: lobster roll, sandwiches, chicken nuggets, fried shrimp, chicken pot pie, salad, battered fish, grilled salmon, clam chowder, french fries, chili, vegetables, various desserts, soda pop, iced tea, juices, coffee
Kids Menu: sandwiches, salad, chicken nuggets, fish
Recommendations: Lobster Roll ♥ and Slushy Lemonade

COOL SHIP
Tomorrowland
Description: Snack cart
Type: Snacks
Price: $ / **Dining Plan:** No
Menu Items: Mickey pretzel, soda pop, lemonade, juice, hot chocolate, coffee, iced tea

‡ COSMIC RAY'S STARLIGHT CAFE
Tomorrowland
Description: Futuristic hamburger fast-food joint
Type: Quick-Service
Price: $$ / **Dining Plan:** Yes
Menu Items:

Lunch & Dinner: burgers, chicken, hot dog, sandwiches, french fries, vegetables, cheese dip, various desserts, soda pop, iced tea, juices, coffee

Kids Lunch & Dinner: sandwiches, salad, macaroni and cheese, chicken nuggets

Recommendation: Bland food, try another spot

THE CRYSTAL PALACE
Main Street, U.S.A.
Description: Beautiful, Victorian-style character buffet with Winnie the Pooh and friends
Type: Character Buffet
Price: $$$ / **Dining Plan:** Yes
Menu Items:
Breakfast: fruit, cereals, pastries, custom scrambled eggs and omelets, potatoes, other changing breakfast choices
Lunch & Dinner: salad, carved meats, shrimp, chicken, beef, fish, vegetables, pastas, various desserts, wine, beer, hard cider
Drinks: soda pop, lemonade, juice, hot chocolate, coffee, tea, wine, beer, hard cider

THE DIAMOND HORSESHOE
Liberty Square
Description: Old West dining and music hall with American eats
Type: Quick-Service
Price: $$ / **Dining Plan:** Yes
Menu Items:
Lunch & Dinner: salad, carved meats, corn, beans, sausage, pulled pork, macaroni and cheese, braised beef, brownie
Drinks: soda pop, lemonade, juice, hot chocolate, coffee, tea
Recommendation: Barbecue Pulled Pork

THE FRIAR'S NOOK
Fantasyland
Description: Mac and cheese and more American bites to eat
Type: Quick-Service
Price: $ / **Dining Plan:** Yes
Menu Items: macaroni and cheese, hot dogs, various desserts, soda pop, lemonade, juice, hot chocolate, coffee, iced tea, milk
Recommendation: Macaroni and Cheese

GASTON'S TAVERN
Fantasyland

Description: Beauty and the Beast-inspired tavern where you can meet Gaston and try snacks
Type: Quick-Service
Price: $ / **Dining Plan:** No
Menu Items: cinnamon rolls, pretzels, chocolate croissant, specialty drinks, soda pop, lemonade, juice, hot chocolate, coffee, iced tea, milk
Recommendations: Mac and Cheese-stuffed Pretzel and Warm Cinnamon Roll
Skip: LeFou's Brew unless you really like very sweet apple juice. If you just want to try it, there's enough to share.

GOLDEN OAK OUTPOST
Frontierland
Description: Old West quick-service with American eats
Type: Quick-Service
Price: $ / **Dining Plan:** Yes
Menu Items: chicken nuggets, waffle fries, chocolate chip cookies, soda pop, lemonade, juice, hot chocolate, coffee, iced tea, milk

JUNGLE NAVIGATION CO. LTD. SKIPPER CANTEEN
Adventureland
Description: Food inspired by Asia, South America, and Africa in a jungle outpost setting
Type: Quick-Service
Price: $$$ / **Dining Plan:** Yes
Menu Items: pot stickers, salad, falafel, soup, beef, fried fish, steak, shrimp, noodle bowls, pasta, fried chicken, vegetable stew, various desserts, specialty drinks, soda pop, lemonade, juice, hot chocolate, coffee, iced tea, milk
Kids Menu: fish, chicken noodle soup, steak, salad, macaroni and cheese, crispy chicken
Recommendation: Gyoza pot stickers for an appetizer

LIBERTY SQUARE MARKET
Liberty Square
Description: American Snacks
Type: Snacks
Price: $ / **Dining Plan:** No
Menu Items: hot dogs, turkey leg, fruit, soda pop, lemonade, juice, hot chocolate, coffee, iced tea, milk

LIBERTY TREE TAVERN ❤
Liberty Square

Description: Colonial style dining area with New England eats
Type: Table Service
Price: $$$ / **Dining Plan:** Yes
Menu Items: clam chowder, soups, corn fritters, salad, pot roast, cheeseburger, grilled chicken, turkey, pork sandwich, pastas, various desserts, specialty drinks, soda pop, lemonade, juice, hot chocolate, coffee, iced tea, milk, beer, cider, wines
Kids Menu: pot roast, turkey, pasta, macaroni and cheese
Recommendation: Patriot's Platter (a delicious all-you-can-eat Thanksgiving turkey dinner)

‡ THE LUNCHING PAD
Tomorrowland
Description: Futuristic fast-food snacks
Type: Quick-Service
Price: $$ / **Dining Plan:** Yes
Menu Items: hot dog, pretzels, chips, soda pop, lemonade, juice, hot chocolate, coffee, iced tea, milk
Recommendation: Ham and Cheese-stuffed Pretzel

MAIN STREET BAKERY (STARBUCKS)
Main Street, U.S.A.
Description: Starbucks coffee and pastries
Type: Quick-Service
Price: $ / **Dining Plan:** Yes
Menu Items: Starbucks-brand coffees and specialty drinks, smoothies, Teavana Iced teas, hot chocolate

‡ PECOS BILL TALL TALE INN AND CAFE
Frontierland
Description: Old West saloon with Southwest flavors
Type: Quick-Service
Price: $$ / **Dining Plan:** Yes
Menu Items: nachos, burgers, fajitas, burrito, salad, desserts, soda pop, lemonade, juice, hot chocolate, coffee, iced tea, milk
Kids Menu: macaroni and cheese, mini corn dogs, sandwich
Recommendation: Beef nachos

> **· Magic Tips ·**
> Pecos Bill Tall Tale Inn & Cafe has a secret menu item. Between 3PM and 6PM, guests can order a giant, $85 plate of Rio Grande Nachos that feeds up to six people!

‡ PINOCCHIO VILLAGE HAUS
Fantasyland
Description: Dining inspired by Disney's Pinocchio
Type: Quick-Service
Price: $ / **Dining Plan:** Yes
Menu Items: flatbreads, chicken parmesan, pasta, chicken nuggets, salad, fries, tomato soup, breadsticks, various desserts, soda pop, lemonade, juice, hot chocolate, coffee, iced tea, milk – *Kids Menu*: macaroni and cheese, pizza, chicken nuggets, sandwich
Recommendation: Village Haus is notoriously bland. The Sausage and Pepper Flatbread is okay.

PLAZA ICE CREAM PARLOR
Main Street, U.S.A.
Description: Classic American ice cream shop
Type: Quick-Service
Price: $ / **Dining Plan:** No
Menu Items: various ice cream flavors, sundaes, kids' ice cream cone, floats, toppings, bottled water

THE PLAZA RESTAURANT
Main Street, U.S.A.
Description: Classic American dining
Type: Table Service
Price: $$ / **Dining Plan:** Yes
Menu Items:
Breakfast: steak and eggs, Mickey waffles, eggs benedict, omelets, bacon, eggs, sausage, fruit, oatmeal, grits, cocktails, juice, coffee, tea, soda
Lunch & Dinner: steak, salad, fries, fried green tomatoes, sandwiches, pork chop, meatloaf, salad, vegetarian bangers and mash, desserts, sundaes, soda, beer, wine,
Kids Lunch & Dinner Menu: sandwiches, burgers, chicken strips
Recommendations: All-American Breakfast Platter (breakfast), Baked Honey-Barbecued Brisket Macaroni & Cheese

PRINCE ERIC'S VILLAGE MARKET
Fantasyland
Description: Fruit cart
Type: Snack Cart
Price: $ / **Dining Plan:** No
Menu Items: fruit, hummus, chips, lemonade, bottled water

SLEEPY HOLLOW ❤

Liberty Square
Description: Waffle sandwich house
Type: Snacks
Price: $ / **Dining Plan:** No
Menu Items: waffle sandwiches, funnel cake, ice cream sandwiches, cookies, soda pop, lemonade, juice, hot chocolate, coffee, iced tea, milk
Recommendation: Fruit Waffle Sandwich ❤

· **Magic Tips** ·

The Spring Roll Cart in Adventureland (near the Enchanted Tiki Room) offers delicious new twists on the classic egg roll. Rotating egg roll flavors include bacon mac n cheese, cheeseburger, Philly cheesesteak, and buffalo chicken!

STORYBOOK TREATS

Fantasyland
Description: Ice cream and floats
Type: Snacks
Price: $ / **Dining Plan:** No
Menu Items: sundaes, floats, soft-serve ice cream, soda pop, hot chocolate, coffee, iced tea, milk.
Recommendation: Peter Pan Float (key lime ice cream and Sprite)

SUNSHINE TREE TERRACE

Adventureland
Description: Ice cream and slushies
Type: Snacks
Price: $ / **Dining Plan:** No
Menu Items: slushies, soft-serve ice cream in a cup, soda pop, hot chocolate, coffee, iced tea, milk

‡ TOMORROWLAND TERRACE RESTAURANT

Tomorrowland
Description: Futuristic fast food dining
Type: Quick-Service
Price: $$ / **Dining Plan:** Yes
Menu Items: burgers, chicken strips, sandwiches, lettuce wraps, salads, soda pop, coffee, iced tea, milk
Kids Menu: macaroni and cheese, chicken strips

Recommendation: Kids may like it, but adults will likely find the food bland

TONY'S TOWN SQUARE RESTAURANT
Main Street, U.S.A.
Description: Lady and the Tramp-inspired Italian Restaurant
Type: Table Service
Price: $$ / **Dining Plan:** Yes
Menu Items: steak, spaghetti, shrimp scampi, pizza, pasta, salads, soda pop, hot chocolate, coffee, iced tea, milk
Kids Menu: macaroni and cheese, chicken strips, sandwich
Recommendation: It's fun for the Lady and the Tramp feel, but the food isn't as great as you'd hope.

TORTUGA TAVERN
Adventureland
Description: Pirate-themed American eats
Type: Quick-Service
Price: $$ / **Dining Plan:** Yes
Menu Items: sandwiches, salads, soda pop, hot chocolate, coffee, iced tea, milk
Kids Menu: macaroni and cheese
Recommendation: The brisket

WESTWARD HO
Frontierland
Description: Snack cart
Type: Snacks
Price: $$ / **Dining Plan:** No
Menu Items: corn dog, chips, chocolate chip cookie, soda pop, hot chocolate, coffee, iced tea, milk
Kids Menu: macaroni and cheese
Recommendation: Good if you want a bag of chips or a drink, but the corn dog is forgettable.

EPCOT DINING

AKERSHUS ROYAL BANQUET HALL
World Showcase – Norway
Description: Dine while you meet your favorite Disney princesses in this Norwegian castle. The food has a Norwegian flare.
Type: Character Dining
Price: $$$$ / **Dining Plan:** Yes
Menu Items:
Breakfast: eggs, sausage, bacon, potato casserole, salami, turkey, corn, fish, cheeses, punch
Lunch & Dinner: salmon, chicken, pork, pasta, meatballs, shrimp, assorted desserts, punch, specialty cocktails, wine
Kids Lunch & Dinner: macaroni and cheese, meatballs, pizza, chicken, salmon, beef
Recommendation: Traditional Kjottkake (meatballs, gravy, and mashed potatoes)

> **· Magic Tips ·**
> If you are looking to meet and take photos with several Disney princesses without the line, make a reservation for a character dining experience at Akershus Royal Banquet Hall!

BIERGARTEN RESTAURANT ❤
World Showcase – Germany
Description: German feasts in a nighttime village
Type: Character Dining
Price: $$$$ / **Dining Plan:** Yes
Menu Items: schnitzel, salad, sausage, greens, soup, chicken, potato, macaroni and cheese, cheese platter, meatballs, spätzle, ham, meat loaf, assorted desserts, beer, wine, schnapps
Recommendation: Pork Schnitzel ❤

BLOCK AND HANS
World Showcase – America
Description: American beer stand
Type: Quick-Service
Price: $$ / **Dining Plan:** Yes

Menu Items: beer, pretzels, bottled water
Recommendation: Order a beer with a Mickey-shaped Pretzel and cheese sauce

CHEFS DE FRANCE ❤

World Showcase – France
Description: French cuisine restaurant
Type: Fine Dining
Dress Code: Park attire
Price: $$$ / **Dining Plan:** Yes
Menu Items: French onion soup, escargot, salad, flatbread, lasagna, baked macaroni,
Recommendations: Everything here is great, and we recommend the Gratin de Macaroni (Baked Macaroni and Cheese), Boeuf Bourguignon (Beef Short Ribs), or Filet de Boeuf Grille (Grilled Tenderloin) ❤

CHOZA DE MARGARITA

World Showcase – Mexico
Description: Outdoor margarita hut
Type: Snack
Price: $-$$ / **Dining Plan:** No
Menu Items: margaritas, beer, Mexican fruit punch, empanadas, pork tacos
Recommendation: Any flavor of Signature Margarita

CORAL REEF RESTAURANT

Future World
Description: Restaurant with a massive aquarium wall filled with exotic fish and other sea life
Type: Table Service
Price: $$$ / **Dining Plan:** Yes
Menu Items: salad, octopus, calamari, fondue, soups, pork, chicken, fish, shellfish, steak, assorted desserts, beer, wine, specialty cocktails
Kids Menu: macaroni and cheese, steak, fish and chips, pork, chicken tenders
Recommendation: This spot is fantastic for unique dining. We recommend the Crispy Rhode Island Calamari

CREPES DES CHEFS DE FRANCE

World Showcase – France
Description: Crepe hut
Type: Quick-Service

Price: $ / **Dining Plan:** No
Menu Items: crepes, ice cream, soda pop, bottled water, coffee, beer
Recommendation: Chocolate Crepe

‡ ELECTRIC UMBRELLA
Future World
Description: Futuristic fast food
Type: Quick-Service
Price: $ / **Dining Plan:** Yes
Menu Items: burgers, sandwiches, chicken nuggets, flatbread, salad, beer, margarita, slushies, coffee, hot tea, hot chocolate, soda pop, assorted desserts
Kids Menu: flatbread, cheeseburger, macaroni and cheese, chicken wrap
Recommendation: This is typical WDW bland quick-service dining spot. We recommend skipping it and heading to one of the choices in the World Showcase.

Note: The Electric Umbrella is scheduled for an extensive refurbishment in 2020 and may be closed for most of the year.

FIFE AND DRUM TAVERN
World Showcase – America
Description: American favorite snacks
Type: Snack cart
Price: $ / **Dining Plan:** Yes
Menu Items: turkey leg, popcorn, soft-serve ice cream, soda pop, slushies, beer, wine, hard root beer
Recommendations: Disney has some delicious popcorn! The American Dream slushy is a good one, too.

· **Magic Tips** ·

Disney's snack stands sell souvenir popcorn buckets in the shape of popular characters. While these buckets can cost more than $20 each, they usually come with inexpensive refills and a lid to protect kids from spilling.

FUNNEL CAKE ❤

World Showcase – America

Description: American desserts

Type: Snack cart

Price: $ / **Dining Plan:** No

Menu Items: funnel cake, bottled water

Recommendation: Funnel cake with sugar ❤

THE GARDEN GRILL ❤

Future World

Description: Rotating restaurant serving freshly picked food while overlooking Living with the Land

Type: Character Dining

Price: $$$ / **Dining Plan:** Yes

Menu Items:

Breakfast Buffet: sticky buns, fruit, potatoes, scrambled eggs, bacon, ham, Mickey waffles, juices, coffee, tea

Lunch & Dinner Buffet: salad, turkey, beef, macaroni and cheese, fries, vegetables, stuffing, sausage, short cake, punch, beer, wine

Recommendation: All of the buffets are delicious ❤

GELATI

World Showcase – Italy

Description: Gelato stand

Type: Snack shack

Price: $ / **Dining Plan:** No

Menu Items: gelato, tiramisu, cannoli, margarita, wine, Italian soda, iced tea, soda pop, sparkling water, bottled water

Recommendation: Gelato sandwich

JOY OF TEA

World Showcase – Japan

Description: Tea hut

Type: Snack hut

Price: $ / **Dining Plan:** No

Menu Items: Pork buns, egg rolls, curry chicken pockets, tea, slushies, ice cream, wine, beer, mixed drinks

Recommendations: Pork and Vegetable Egg Rolls

KABUKI CAFE

World Showcase – Japan

Description: Japanese sushi and soda bar

Type: Snack hut

Price: $ / **Dining Plan:** No
Menu Items: sushi, edamame, shaved ice, bottled soda, hot chocolate, bottled water
Recommendation: Try a shaved ice—adults might like the Sake Mist, an alcoholic shaved ice.

KATSURA GRILL
World Showcase – Japan
Description: Japanese restaurant in a tranquil garden
Type: Quick-Service
Price: $ / **Dining Plan:** Yes
Menu Items: sushi, noodles, miso soup, edamame, rice, teriyaki, chicken, shrimp, bottled soda, hot chocolate, bottled water, beer, wine, juice, tea, various desserts
Kids Menu: chicken, beef, or shrimp teriyaki
Recommendations: Chicken and Beef Teriyaki

KRINGLA BAKERI OG KAFE
World Showcase – Norway
Description: Norwegian cafeteria-style cuisine
Type: Quick-Service
Price: $$ / **Dining Plan:** Yes
Menu Items: sandwiches, meatballs, biscuit, pastries, salad, fish, soda pop, hot chocolate, bottled water, beer, wine, juice, tea, various desserts – Kids: sandwich
Recommendation: Norwegian Club

LA CANTINA DE SAN ANGEL
World Showcase – Mexico
Description: Mexican cafeteria-style cuisine
Type: Quick-Service
Price: $$ / **Dining Plan:** Yes
Menu Items: tacos, nachos, salad, churro, juices, coffee, various desserts, beer, margarita – *Kids Menu*: empanadas, chicken tenders
Recommendations: Tacos de Barbacoa, Churros with Caramel Sauce

LA CAVA DEL TEQUILA
World Showcase – Mexico
Description: Underground tequila bar
Type: Lounge
Price: $$ / **Dining Plan:** No
Menu Items: tequila
Recommendation: Hibiscus tequila

LA HACIENDA DE SAN ANGEL
World Showcase – Mexico
Description: Mexican restaurant
Type: Table Service
Price: $$ / **Dining Plan:** Yes
Menu Items: gorditas, empanada, steak, short ribs, fried shrimp, chicken, pork confit, tacos, fish, margaritas, tequila, beer, wine, various desserts
Kids Menu: salad, fruit cup, grilled chicken, tacos, quesadilla, fish, churros, ice cream
Recommendation: Taquiza taco sampler

THE LAND CART
Future World
Description: Fruit cart
Type: Snack Cart
Price: $ / **Dining Plan:** No
Menu Items: fruit, cheese plate, vegetable plate, pretzels, hummus, soda pop, juice, beer

L'ARTISAN DES GLACES
World Showcase – France
Description: Ice cream parlor
Type: Ice Cream Shop
Price: $ / **Dining Plan:** No
Menu Items: ice cream, macaron, bottled water

LE CELLIER STEAKHOUSE ❤
World Showcase – Canada
Description: French Canadian restaurant
Type: Fine Dining
Dress Code: Business Causal, though the dress code is not always enforced; don't wear tank tops, hats, cut off clothes, or sports clothing
Price: $$$$ / **Dining Plan:** Yes

Menu Items: cheeses, steak, pork rib, chicken breast, tofu, halibut, fries, mashed potatoes, macaroni and cheese, scallops, poutine, various desserts, wine, teas

Kids Menu: cheddar soup, salad, grilled chicken, salmon, pasta, sirloin with french fries, chocolate "moose" ice cream

Recommendations: Le Cellier is known for its poutine and steaks. We highly recommend the Signature Poutine ❤, french fries with cheese, truffles, and a red wine sauce and Le Cellier Filet Mignon

LES HALLES BOULANGERIE-PATISSERIE
World Showcase – France
Description: Fast French Favorites
Type: Quick-Service
Price: $$ / **Dining Plan:** Yes
Menu Items: French sandwiches, salad, croissant, quiche, lobster bisque, pastries, various desserts, soda pop, champagne, mimosa, beer, wine, coffees, milk, smoothies, teas
Recommendations: Croque Monsieur, crème brulee

LOTUS BLOSSOM CAFE
World Showcase – China
Description: American takes on Chinese Favorites
Type: Quick-Service
Price: $$ / **Dining Plan:** Yes
Menu Items: egg rolls, pot stickers, orange chicken, shrimp fried rice, salad, ice cream, soda pop, beer, coffees, milk, hot chocolate – *Kids Menu:* pot stickers and spring rolls, sweet-and-sour chicken
Recommendation: Pork and Vegetable Egg Rolls
Skip: The Orange Chicken, especially if you like the one at Panda Express. You'll be disappointed.

NINE DRAGONS RESTAURANT ❤
World Showcase – China
Description: Chinese Dining
Type: Table Service
Price: $$$ / **Dining Plan:** Yes
Menu Items: spring rolls, pot stickers, dumplings, Asian chicken, fried rice, Asian beef, lo mein, tofu stir fry, salad, various desserts, soda pop, specialty cocktails, smoothie, beer, wine, teas
Recommendation: Pork Belly Bao Buns (appetizer), Honey Crispy Chicken (entree), Banana Cheesecake Eggrolls (dessert)

> **· Magic Tips ·**
> Nine Dragons offers partial views of the Epcot nighttime show. Request a table near the windows for 30-45 minutes before showtime. The lights will dim and a soundtrack for the show will play as you watch the fireworks from your table.

POPCORN IN CANADA
World Showcase – Canada
Description: Popcorn cart
Type: Snack cart
Price: $ / **Dining Plan:** No
Menu Items: popcorn, beer, whisky, bottled water
Recommendation: WDW has great popcorn!

PROMENADE REFRESHMENTS
World Showcase – Canada
Description: Snack House / **Type:** Snack cart
Price: $ / **Dining Plan:** Yes
Menu Items: hot dogs, chips, ice cream, beer, soda pop,
Recommendation: Chili Hot Dog

REGAL EAGLE
Opening in 2020
Description: Quick-Service American Barbecue
Type: Snack Cart
Price: TBA / **Dining Plan:** TBA
Menu Items: American barbecue favorites, beer

REFRESHMENT OUTPOST
World Showcase – America
Description: Snack Cart
Type: Snack Cart
Price: $ / **Dining Plan:** Yes
Menu Items: hot dogs, chips, ice cream, beer, soda pop, slushy, hot chocolate, bottled water

REFRESHMENT PORT
World Showcase – Canada
Description: Snack House
Type: Snack Shack
Price: $ / **Dining Plan:** Yes

Menu Items: croissant doughnut, chicken nuggets, ice cream, french fries, beer, soda pop, slushy, hot chocolate, bottled water
Recommendation: Croissant Doughnut 💜

RESTAURANT MARRAKESH
World Showcase – Morocco
Description: Moroccan dining experience with belly dancers
Type: Table Service
Price: $$$ / **Dining Plan:** Yes
Menu Items: chicken skewers, beef rolls, salad, roast lamb, lemon chicken, couscous, kebab, beer, mixed drinks, soda pop, various desserts
Kids Menu: chicken tenders, hamburger, pasta
Skip: The food here isn't very impressive, though it does feel healthier than a lot of other choices in Epcot. Also, the promised belly dancing is short-lived and unimpressive.

ROSE AND CROWN DINING ROOM 💜
World Showcase – United Kingdom
Description: Authentic British restaurant with excellent food and beer
Type: Table Service
Price: $$$ / **Dining Plan:** Yes
Menu Items: soup, salad, fish and chips, shepherd's pie, burger, corn beef and cabbage, bangers and mash, beer, mixed drinks, soda pop, various desserts
Kids Menu: fish and chips, bangers and mash, steak and chips, turkey meatballs, grilled chicken, baked fish
Recommendations: Fish and Chips, Bangers and Mash

· **Magic Tips** ·
The Rose and Crown has an excellent view of the Epcot fireworks. Book a dining reservation just before showtime to have an awesome view while you dine!

ROSE AND CROWN PUB
World Showcase – United Kingdom
Description: Authentic British pub with a wide variety of beers /
Type: Lounge
Price: $$ / **Dining Plan:** No
Menu Items: scotch egg, fish and chips, beer, mixed drinks, soda pop, wine, whiskey

Recommendation: Fish and Chips

SAN ANGEL INN RESTAURANTE
World Showcase – Mexico
Description: Indoor Mexican dining
Type: Table Service
Price: $$$ / **Dining Plan:** Yes
Menu Items: soup, queso, quesadilla, steak, tacos, chicken, various desserts, margarita, soda pop
Kids Menu: tacos, grilled tilapia, cheese quesadilla
Recommendation: Skip this one. The atmosphere is fun but the food is bland and inauthentic. You can walk inside here to check out the scenery and shops without dining.

SOMMERFEST
World Showcase – Germany
Description: Fast German Favorites
Type: Quick-Service
Price: $$ / **Dining Plan:** Yes
Menu Items: bratwurst, frankfurter, potato salad, pretzel, baked macaroni, various German desserts, beer, wine, soda pop, bottled water

SPACE 220
Future World
Description: A themed restaurant aboard an intergalactic space station!
Type: Table Service
Price: TBA / **Dining Plan:** TBA
Details: At the time of this guide's publication, we have few details about this outer space dining experience. However, Disney has announced that guests will board an elevator that transports them high into the Earth's orbit. There, they will board a space station with sweeping views of the Earth and the stars!

SPICE ROAD TABLE
World Showcase – Morocco
Description: Mediterranean Restaurant
Type: Table Service
Price: $$$ / **Dining Plan:** Yes
Menu Items: calamari, shrimp, skewers, fondue, lamb, chicken, vegetable platter, fish, various desserts, cappuccino, espresso, soda pop, sparkling water, beer, specialty drinks
Recommendation: Lamb Slider

SUNSHINE SEASONS
Future World
Description: Indoor fresh, yet fast, food
Type: Quick-Service
Price: $$ / **Dining Plan:** Yes
Menu Items: chicken, fish, soups, salad, fish tacos, flatbread, stir-fry, various desserts, cappuccino, espresso, soda pop, bottled beer
Kids Menu: Mongolian beef, salmon, chicken, macaroni and cheese, cheese panini, sandwich
Recommendation: Fish tacos—fresh and delicious

TANGIERINE CAFÉ
World Showcase – Morocco
Description: Mediterranean Restaurant
Type: Quick-Service
Price: $$$ / **Dining Plan:** Yes
Menu Items: salad, falafel, shawarma, hummus, pastries, soda pop
Kids Menu: hamburger, chicken tenders
Recommendation: Mediterranean Falafel Wrap

TAKUMI-TEI
World Showcase – Japan
Description: Takumi-Tei is a unique and authentic dining experience for Epcot. Styled after traditional Japanese tea-service meals, this restaurant delivers exquisite food. Each room of the restaurant is based around an element like water, wood, stone, or earth. The rooms also have accompanying features like an actual waterfall in the water room! If you're looking for an unforgettable Disney dining experience, we highly recommend Takumi-Tei.
Type: Signature Dining / Table Service
Price: $$$$-$$$$$ / **Dining Plan:** No
Menu Items: wagyu beef, roasted duck, sushi, desserts, teas, cocktails, wines, Japanese beer, soda pop,
Kids Menu: shrimp, steak, chicken
Recommendations: Takumi-Tei is best for adults looking for an adventurous dining option. We recommend the Chef's Table in the Water Room. It's a 3-hour dining event with a wide range of Japanese bites from seafood to wagyu beef. The bites become more flavorful throughout the meal and is best enjoyed with a beverage pairing. Of course, an exquisite meal like this comes at a cost: $180 per person with beverage pairing at an additional I $100 per person. For a less expensive Japanese dining option, try Teppan Edo or Tokyo Dining.

TOKYO DINING
World Showcase – Japan
Description: Traditional Japanese
Type: Table Service
Price: $$$ / **Dining Plan:** Yes
Menu Items: sushi, tempura, teriyaki chicken, noodles, desserts, tea, Japanese beer, wine, cocktails, soda pop
Kids Menu: shrimp, steak, chicken
Recommendations: The Chef's Creation Bento Box comes with an assortment of sushi, tempura, and steak

TEPPAN EDO ❤
World Showcase – Japan
Description: Authentic Japanese cuisine with amazing chefs that perform in front of you
Type: Table Service
Price: $$$ / **Dining Plan:** Yes
Menu Items: chicken, sushi, steak, seafood, sake, beer, various desserts, soda pop, tea, milk
Kids Menu: shrimp, steak, chicken
Recommendations: Teppan Edo is a must if you've never done Teppan-style Japanese dining before. These authentic Japanese chefs are incredible and put on a show like no other. Try the Filet Mignon and lobster tail. The green tea ice cream is also incredible.

TEST TRACK COOL WASH
Future World
Description: Slushy Station
Type: Snack Cart
Price: $ / **Dining Plan:** No
Menu Items: slushies, chips, alcoholic floats, soda pop, water

TUTTO GUSTO WINE CELLAR
World Showcase – Italy
Description: Italian wine cellar that showcases over 200 bottles
Type: Lounge
Price: $$ / **Dining Plan:** No
Menu Items: wine, cheeses, bread, small plates, pasta, sliders, paninis, various desserts
Recommendation: Meatball sliders

TUTTO ITALIA RISTORANTE
World Showcase – Italy

Description: Authentic Italian Restaurant
Type: Table Service
Price: $$$ / **Dining Plan:** Yes
Menu Items: salad, calamari, chicken, pasta, seafood, various desserts, beer, cocktails, soda pop
Kids Menu: spaghetti, pizza, mozzarella sticks, chicken tenders
Recommendation: Meatball sliders

UK BEER CART
World Showcase – United Kingdom
Description: Beer Cart
Type: Snack Cart
Price: $ / **Dining Plan:** Yes
Menu Items: beer, pear cider, bottled water

VIA NAPOLI RISTORANTE E PIZZERIA ❤
World Showcase – Italy
Description: Authentic Italian Pizzeria
Type: Table Service
Price: $$$ / **Dining Plan:** Yes
Menu Items: pizza, calamari, small plates, pasta, various desserts, beer, cocktails, soda pop
Kids Menu: spaghetti, pizza, salad
Recommendation: Their pizzas are amazing and authentic. We love creating our own Margherita pizza with meatball ❤

> **· Magic Tips ·**
> Seasonally, Disney will open Pizza al Taglio, a quick-service pizza window next to Via Napoli. Get a delicious slice of pizza to go when this window is available!

YORKSHIRE COUNTY FISH SHOP
World Showcase – United Kingdom
Description: British quick-service
Type: Quick-Service
Price: $ / **Dining Plan:** Yes
Menu Items: fish and chips, sponge cake, soda pop, beer
Recommendation: Fish and chips

HOLLYWOOD STUDIOS DINING

50'S PRIME TIME CAFÉ ♥
Echo Lake
Description: Swanky mid-century American dining
Type: Table Service
Price: $$$ / **Dining Plan:** Yes
Menu Items: pot pie, pork chops, lasagna, pot roast, salad, fried chicken, fish, meatloaf, fries, onion rings, shakes, ice cream, various desserts, soda pop, hot chocolate, coffee, iced tea, milk, wine, beer, specialty cocktails
Kids Menu: salad, soup, salmon, spaghetti, meatloaf, chicken
Recommendations: Onion Rings, Aunt Liz's Golden Fried Chicken ♥, Peanut Butter and Jelly Milk Shake

‡ ABC COMMISSARY
Commissary Lane
Description: Fast dining with indoor seating
Type: Quick-Service
Price: $$ / **Dining Plan:** Yes
Menu Items: BBQ ribs, burgers, sandwiches, salad, chicken strips, desserts, soda pop, sangria
Kids Menu: cheeseburger, sandwich

ANAHEIM PRODUCE
Sunset Boulevard
Description: Snacks
Type: Snack cart
Price: $ / **Dining Plan:** No
Menu Items: fruit, chips, snack bars, pretzels, granola, lemonade, soda pop, beer, margarita, hard cider, bottled water

‡ BACKLOT EXPRESS
Echo Lake
Description: Star Wars-themed fast food
Type: Quick-Service
Price: $$ / **Dining Plan:** Yes
Menu Items: burgers, sandwiches, chicken and biscuits, chicken tenders, salad, french fries, buttermilk biscuits, desserts soda, margaritas, mixed drinks – *Kids Menu*: chicken tenders, macaroni and cheese

Recommendation: The food here is impressively decorative, though much of the flavor is fairly bland.

BASELINE TAPHOUSE ❤

Grand Avenue
Description: American Gastropub / Lounge
Type: Quick-Service
Price: $-$$ / **Dining Plan:** No
Menu Items: pretzel, cheese plates, other small bites, beers and wines on tap, cocktails and ciders on tap, non-alcoholic specialty drinks
Recommendations: If you're looking for a stylish, new experience at the WDW Resort, look no further than the BaseLine Tap House. With excellent artisan cheeses and craft beers, it's the perfect hangout for adults. Try the California Cheese and Charcuterie Plate and the Blue Sky Black Cherry Soda on Tap is delicious!

‡ CATALINA EDDIE'S

Sunset Boulevard
Description: Pizza shack
Type: Quick-Service
Price: $$ / **Dining Plan:** Yes
Menu Items: pizza, Caesar salad, various desserts, soda pop, hot chocolate, coffee, iced tea, milk, beer, sangria
Kids Menu: cheese pizza, sandwiches
Recommendation: Any of the pizzas

‡ DOCKING BAY 7 FOOD AND CARGO ❤

Star Wars: Galaxy's Edge
Description: An intergalactic canteen in a rustic, Star Wars-inspired building. The food here is a mix of flavors that will tickle the tastebuds of adventurous eaters.
Type: Quick-Service
Price: $$ / **Dining Plan:** Yes

Menu: breakfast items, ribs, salads, air-fried chicken, noodles, juice soda, coffee, tea, desserts
Kids: air-fried chicken
Recommendation: Smoked Kaadu Ribs ❤, Oi-oi Puff (dessert) ❤, Moof Juice (sweet drink)

DOCKSIDE DINER
Echo Lake
Description: Fast food from a boat
Type: Quick-Service
Price: $$ / **Dining Plan:** Yes
Menu Items: wraps, chili-cheese hot dog, macaroni and cheese, various desserts, soda pop, hot chocolate, coffee, iced tea, beer, wine
Kids Menu: turkey sandwich
Recommendations: Seasonal Milkshake

‡ FAIRFAX FARE
Sunset Boulevard
Description: American favorites shack
Type: Quick-Service
Price: $$ / **Dining Plan:** Yes
Menu Items: ribs, sandwiches, salads, chicken, chili-cheese dog, baked potatoes, various desserts, soda pop, hot chocolate, coffee, iced tea, milk, beer – Kids: sandwiches
Recommendation: ½ Slab of Spareribs

THE HOLLYWOOD BROWN DERBY
Hollywood Boulevard
Description: Replica of the Brown Derby restaurant in the Golden Age of Hollywood
Type: Signature Dining / Table Service
Dress Code: Park attire
Price: $$$$ / **Dining Plan:** Yes
Menu Items: steak, lamb, pork chops, pho, salmon, chicken, salad, fish, burger, lobster, various desserts, soda pop, hot chocolate, coffee, iced tea, milk, beer, wine
Kids Menu: sandwiches, chicken noodle soup, chicken, fish, pasta
Recommendations: Premium American Kobe Beef and Double Vanilla Bean Crème Brulee
Why We Skip It: The Hollywood Brown Derby is a top choice for many fine-diners at WDW. The food isn't that remarkable for the price you're paying. We'd much rather go to the 50's Prime Time Café.

THE HOLLYWOOD BROWN DERBY LOUNGE
Hollywood Boulevard
Description: Lounge in the iconic Brown Derby
Type: Lounge Dining
Dress Code: Park attire
Price: $$ / **Dining Plan:** Yes
Menu Items: shrimp, corn bisque, cheese boards, sliders, salad, various desserts, soda pop, hot chocolate, coffee, iced tea, milk, beer, extensive wine list, specialty cocktails
Recommendations: Artisanal Cheeses and Charcuterie Board

HOLLYWOOD SCOOPS
Sunset Boulevard
Description: Ice Cream Parlor
Type: Lounge Dining
Price: $ / **Dining Plan:** No
Menu Items: ice cream, sundaes, apple crisp, root beer float
Recommendations: Brownie Sundae, Hard Root Beer Float

HOLLYWOOD & VINE
Echo Lake
Description: Character Breakfast / Lunch & Dinner Diner
Type: Character Dining / Table Service
Price: $$$ / **Dining Plan:** Yes
Menu Items:
Breakfast Buffet: Mickey waffles, pancakes, "potato" tots, custom omelets, fruit, cereal, pastries, scrambled eggs, bacon, sausage
Lunch & Dinner Buffet: salad, baked chicken, pork, pasta, lobster and shrimp macaroni and cheese, vegetables, desserts, ice cream
Recommendation: If your young kids are early risers, book breakfast for Disney Junior Play 'n Dine. They can meet their favorite Disney characters before heading into the park.

> **· Magic Tips ·**
> Hollywood & Vine has reservations well before normal park hours. If you finish eating before park guests arrive, you can be one of the first into Toy Story Land and Star Wars: Galaxy's Edge!

KAT SAKA'S KETTLE ❤

Description: Sweet and spicy kettle-cooked popcorn
Type: Snack
Price: $ / **Dining Plan:** Yes
Menu Items: mixed drinks, bar snacks
Recommendations: Outpost Popcorn Mix. We recommend eating the many flavors of popcorn together for the best taste!

> **· Magic Tips ·**
> Kat Saka's Kettle and several soda carts around Black Spire Outpost sell specially designed Orb bottles. These spherical soda bottles are unique to Galaxy's Edge!

KRNR THE ROCK STATION

Sunset Boulevard
Description: Concert-style Food Truck
Type: Quick-Service
Price: $ / **Dining Plan:** Yes
Menu Items: chili-cheese hot dog, all-beef hot dogs, nachos, chips, cookies, soda floats, soda pop, Jack 'N' Coke (adult beverage)
Recommendations: Chili-Cheese Beef Hot Dog

MAMA MELROSE'S RISTORANTE ITALIANO

Grand Avenue
Description: Italian Restaurant
Type: Table Service
Price: $$$ / **Dining Plan:** Yes
Menu Items: steak, calamari, mussels, salad, flatbread, pasta, chicken, fish, lasagna, gelato, various desserts, soda pop, hot chocolate, coffee, iced tea, milk, beer, wine
Kids Menu: sandwiches, spaghetti, chicken, fish, penne pasta
Recommendation: Flatbreads

‡ MILK STAND
Star Wars: Galaxy's Edge
Description: Plant-based smoothies
Type: Snack
Price: $ / **Dining Plan:** No
Menu Items: Blue Milk (berry smoothie), Green Milk (melon smoothie), Alcoholic Blue Milk (rum), Alcoholic Green Milk (tequila)
Recommendations: Blue Milk

EPIC EATS
Echo Lake
Description: Indiana Jones-themed dessert outpost
Type: Quick-Service
Price: $ / **Dining Plan:** No
Menu Items: funnel cakes, soda floats, beer
Recommendation: Funnel cake with Strawberry Topping and Soft-serve Vanilla Ice Cream (and drizzled with chocolate sauce)

OGA'S CANTINA ❤
Star Wars: Galaxy's Edge
Description: A lively Star Wars-themed bar
Type: Lounge
Price: $$ / **Dining Plan:** Yes
Menu Items: mixed drinks, bar snacks
Recommendations: T-16 Skyhopper (vodka, melon, and kiwi blend) and the non-alcoholic Hyperdrive (Punch It!), a blend of berry flavors and Sprite.

‡ PIZZERIZZO
Grand Avenue (may only run seasonally)
Description: *Muppets*-themed Pizza Diner
Type: Quick-Service
Price: $$ / **Dining Plan:** Yes
Menu Items: pizzas, pasta salad, cannoli, tiramisu, soda pop
Kids Menu: kid-sized pizzas, macaroni and cheese
Skip: The burgers and nuggets are bland.

‡ RONTO ROASTERS
Star Wars: Galaxy's Edge
Description: Star Wars-themed snacks
Type: Quick-Service
Price: $$ / **Dining Plan:** Yes
Menu Items: sausage wraps, turkey jerky, mixed drinks, sodas

Recommendations: Ronto Wrap and the Coruscant Cooler (fruit juices and bourbon)

‡ ROSIE'S ALL-AMERICAN CAFE
Sunset Boulevard
Description: American favorites shack
Type: Quick-Service
Price: $$ / **Dining Plan:** Yes
Menu Items: burgers, chicken nuggets, sandwiches, various desserts, soda pop, hot chocolate, coffee, iced tea, beer, sangria – Kids: chicken nuggets, sandwich
Skip: The burgers and nuggets are bland.

· Magic Tips ·

Outside of Ronto Roster, cranking the spit of meat, is a lesser known droid named 8D-J8. In the folklore of Galaxy's Edge, this bot was once a smelter droid who has been reprogrammed for his meat-cooking post. The simulated roaster he's cranking under is a podracer engine reworked into a grill!

SCI-FI DINE-IN THEATER RESTAURANT ❤
Commissary Lane
Description: Drive-in theater
Type: Table Service
Price: $$ / **Dining Plan:** Yes
Menu Items: steak, pasta, shepherd's pie, burgers, chicken nuggets, sandwiches, ribs, salad, various desserts, soda pop, hot chocolate, coffee, iced tea, beer, sangria
Kids Menu: penne pasta, chicken breast, salmon, salad, chicken noodle soup
Recommendation: We love this place! Sit in cars while you watch classic cheesy sci-fi film clips and eat 50's style diner food! Try any of their burgers.

· Magic Tips ·

The Sci-Fi Dine-In Theater has a complimentary popcorn machine for waiting guests—just like at the movies!

THE TROLLEY CAR CAFE (STARBUCKS)
Hollywood Boulevard
Description: Starbucks coffee and pastries
Type: Quick-Service
Price: $ / **Dining Plan:** Yes
Menu Items: Starbucks brand coffees and specialty drinks, smoothies, Teavana iced teas, hot chocolate

TUNE-IN LOUNGE ❤
Echo Lake
Description: Swanky 50's lounge
Type: Snacks
Price: $$ / **Dining Plan:** No
Menu Items: pot pie, pork chops, lasagna, pot roast, salad, fried chicken, fish, meatloaf, fries, onion rings, shakes, ice cream, various desserts, soda pop, hot chocolate, coffee, iced tea, milk, wine, beer, specialty cocktails
Kids Menu: salad, soup, salmon, spaghetti, meatloaf, chicken
Recommendation: Beer-battered Onion Rings, Aunt Liz's Golden Fried Chicken ❤, Dad's Electric Lemonade ❤

‡ WOODY'S LUNCH BOX ❤
Toy Story Land
Description: Toy Story-themed dining
Type: Quick-Service
Price: $$ / **Dining Plan:** Yes
Menu Items:
Breakfast: specialty pastries, breakfast sandwiches, specialty drinks, soda pop, adult mixed drinks, beer, and hard cider
Lunch & Dinner: specialty pastries, sandwiches, specialty drinks, potato barrels, soda pop, adult mixed drinks, beer, and hard cider
Kids Lunch & Dinner: Grilled cheese sandwich, turkey sandwich
Recommendation: S'more French Toast Sandwich for breakfast, and a Grilled Three-Cheese Sandwich with a side of tomato-basil soup for lunch. The "Totchos" are great to try, too (nachos made with fried potato barrels instead of chips).

ANIMAL KINGDOM DINING

ANANDAPUR ICE CREAM TRUCK
Asia
Description: Decorative ice cream truck
Type: Snacks
Price: $ / **Dining Plan:** No
Menu Items: ice cream, float, bottled water, soda pop
Recommendations: Float

CARAVAN ROAD
Asia
Description: Asian snack hut
Type: Snacks
Price: $ / **Dining Plan:** No
Menu Items: Teriyaki beef sliders, edamame, soda pop, water

CREATURE COMFORTS (STARBUCKS)
Discovery Island
Description: Starbucks coffee and pastries
Type: Quick-Service
Price: $ / **Dining Plan:** Yes
Menu Items: Starbucks brand coffees and specialty drinks, smoothies, Teavana iced teas, hot chocolate

DAWA BAR ❤
Africa
Description: African outdoor wine bar
Type: Lounge
Price: $ / **Dining Plan:** No
Menu Items: margarita, mojito, alcoholic punch, domestic and specialty beer, wines
Recommendation: Lost on Safari ❤

> **· Magic Tips ·**
> Not many guests realized that Animal Kingdom has full bars in nearly every themed land! Those 21+ can enjoy cocktails, beers, or their own requested creation from the bartender.

DINO-BITE SNACK
DinoLand U.S.A.
Description: Dinosaur-themed Ice Cream Parlor
Type: Ice Cream Shack
Price: $ / **Dining Plan:** No
Menu Items: ice cream, floats, sundaes, pretzels, cheese dip, chips, cookies, beer, coffee, hot chocolate
Recommendations: Bugs Sundae

DINO DINER
DinoLand U.S.A.
Description: Dinosaur-themed snack and treat truck
Type: Snacks
Price: $ / **Dining Plan:** Yes
Menu Items: sausage hoagie, churros, cupcakes, soda pop, beer, frozen lemonade with rum
Recommendations: Churro with Chocolate Sauce

DRINKWALLAH
Asia
Description: To-go snack shack
Type: Snacks
Price: $ / **Dining Plan:** No
Menu Items: chips, nuts, soda pop, and rum cocktails

EIGHT SPOON CAFE
Discovery Island
Description: Snack shack
Type: Quick-Service
Price: $ / **Dining Plan:** Yes
Menu Items: Mac and Cheese, Mickey pretzel, cheese dip, chips, soda pop, bottled water
Recommendation: Macaroni and Cheese with Pulled Pork

‡ FLAME TREE BARBECUE ❤
Discovery Island
Description: Barbecue
Type: Quick-Service
Price: $$ / **Dining Plan:** Yes
Menu Items: ribs, chicken, sandwiches, salad, french fries, mousse desserts, soda pop, coffee, hot chocolate, hot tea, iced tea, beer, wine
Kids Menu: hot dog, drumstick, sandwiches

Recommendations: Ribs and Chicken Combo ❤, french fries with Pulled Pork and Cheese

HARAMBE FRUIT MARKET
Africa
Description: Fruit Cart
Type: Quick-Service
Price: $ / **Dining Plan:** No
Menu Items: fruit, yogurt, crackers, chips, soda pop, coffee

‡ HARAMBE MARKET
Africa
Description: African-themed worldly cuisine
Type: Quick-Service
Price: $$ / **Dining Plan:** Yes
Menu Items: ribs, skewers, sausage, soda pop, coffee, hot chocolate, iced tea, beer, wine, sangria, bottled water
Recommendation: Grilled Chicken Skewer

ISLE OF JAVA
Discovery Island
Description: Coffee shack
Type: Quick-Service
Price: $ / **Dining Plan:** No
Menu Items: cappuccino, espresso, pastries, coffee, hot chocolate, iced tea, beer, rum and Coke
Recommendation: Island Cappuccino

KUSAFIRI COFFEE SHOP AND BAKERY
Africa
Description: Coffee shack
Type: Quick-Service
Price: $ / **Dining Plan:** No
Menu Items:
Breakfast: breakfast wrap, cinnamon roll, pastries, yogurt, fruit, cappuccino, espresso, coffee, iced coffee, hot chocolate, tea
Lunch: panini, sandwiches, cinnamon roll, pastries, yogurt, fruit, cappuccino, espresso, coffee, iced coffee, hot chocolate, tea
Recommendation: Ham and Cheese Panini

MAHINDI
Africa
Description: Popcorn Hut
Type: Quick-Service

Price: $ / **Dining Plan:** No
Menu Items: popcorn, nuts, chips, slushy, soda pop, beer
Recommendation: Jungle Juice Slushy

MR. KAMAL'S ❤
Asia
Description: A snack cart with some tasty bites
Type: Quick-Service
Price: $ / **Dining Plan:** Yes
Menu Items: dumplings, hummus, fries, soda pop
Recommendation: Chicken Dumplings ❤

NOMAD LOUNGE ❤
Africa
Description: African Safari lounge
Type: Lounge
Price: $$ / **Dining Plan:** No
Menu Items: chicken wings, tapas, ribs, specialty non-alcoholic and alcoholic drinks, domestic and specialty beer, wines
Recommendation: Indian Butter Chicken Wings ❤

‡ PIZZAFARI
Africa
Description: Pizza Restaurant
Type: Quick-Service
Price: $$ / **Dining Plan:** Yes

Menu Items: flatbread, pizza, salad, subs, pasta, soups, various desserts, hot tea, cold tea, coffee, hot chocolate, beer, vodka lemonade
Kids Menu: cheese pizza, macaroni and cheese, sandwich, pasta with marinara
Recommendation: Mediterranean Flatbread

PONGU PONGU
Pandora—The World of Avatar
Description: Lounge Bar
Type: Lounge
Price: $$ / **Dining Plan:** Yes
Menu Items: specialty beverages, dessert lumpia
Recommendations: The Night Blossom drink ❤

RAINFOREST CAFE
Main Entrance
Description: Jungle-themed restaurant

Type: Table Service
Price: $$ / **Dining Plan:** Yes
Menu Items:
Breakfast: omelets, bacon, sausage, eggs benedict, French toast, waffle, breakfast pizza, breakfast slider, specialty drinks
Kids Menu: waffle, oatmeal, toast, cereal
Lunch & Dinner: burgers, sandwiches, soup, salad, steak, chicken, shrimp, pasta, french fries, onion rings, various desserts, beer, wine, hard cider, specialty cocktails
Kids Menu: chicken, popcorn shrimp, cheese pizza, macaroni and cheese, sandwich, grilled cheese
Recommendation: The Rainforest Cafe is great for families because of the wide variety of options for Kids. Adults will likely find the food forgettable—though not bad. Still, the theme is so well done, especially with the décor, that it's worth a stop with Kids.

‡ RESTAURANTOSAURUS
DinoLand U.S.A.
Description: Archeological dig restaurant
Type: Quick-Service
Price: $$ / **Dining Plan:** Yes
Menu Items: burgers, salad, sandwiches, soups, chicken nuggets, various desserts, soda pop, hot chocolate, coffee, iced tea, beer
Kids Menu: cheeseburger, sandwich, corn dog nuggets
Recommendations: Another one of WDW's typical fast food. It's not very flavorful so we recommend trying another spot.

‡ SATU'LI CANTEEN ❤
Pandora—The World of Avatar
Description: Asian fusion Lunch & Dinner bowls
Type: Quick-Service
Price: $$ / **Dining Plan:** Yes
Menu Items: rice bowls, bao buns, specialty beverages
Recommendations: Cheeseburger Steamed Pods (Bao Buns Kids Menu) ❤ and Blueberry Cream Cheese Mousse ❤

THE SMILING CROCODILE
Asia
Description: Snack Shack
Type: Quick-Service
Price: $$ / **Dining Plan:** No
Menu Items: grits, drumstick, soda pop, beer, bottled water

TAMU TAMU REFRESHMENTS ❤

Africa
Description: Dessert Hut serving Dole Whips
Type: Quick-Service
Price: $$ / **Dining Plan:** No
Menu Items: Dole whip, sundae, chocolate waffle, ice cream sandwich, soda pop, bottled water
Recommendations: Dole Whip ❤, Dole Whip Cup with Coconut Rum ❤

TERRA TREATS
Discovery Island
Description: Healthy Snack Shack
Type: Quick-Service
Price: $ / **Dining Plan:** No
Menu Items: Hummus, gluten-free snacks and desserts, soda pop, bottled water, soy milk, gluten-free beer

THIRSTY RIVER BAR AND TRIK SNACKS
Asia
Description: Specialty Drink Hut
Type: Quick-Service
Price: $$ / **Dining Plan:** No
Menu Items: pastries, juice, fruit, chocolate twist, soda pop, bottled water, milk, hot chocolate, iced coffee

TIFFINS ❤
Discovery Island
Description: International cuisine fine dining
Type: Fine Dining
Dress Code: Park attire
Price: $$$$ / **Dining Plan:** Yes
Menu Items: chicken, lamb chop, pork tenderloin, prawns, fish, short rib, vegetable curry, duck, seafood, salad, various desserts, specialty cocktails, soda pop, beer, iced tea
Kids Menu: salad, soup, chicken, fish, pasta, short ribs
Recommendations: Just about everything you get at Tiffins is absolutely delicious. Order the Wagyu Strip Loin and Braised Short Rib ❤

TRILO-BITES
Discovery Island
Description: Dinosaur outpost shack
Type: Snacks
Price: $ / **Dining Plan:** Yes

Menu Items: chicken and waffles, waffle sundae, float, soda pop, beer, bottled water
Recommendation: Buffalo Chicken Waffle Slider

TUSKER HOUSE RESTAURANT ❤

Africa
Description: American Buffet in Africa with Donald Duck and friends
Type: Character Dining
Price: $$$ / **Dining Plan:** Yes
Menu Items:
Breakfast Buffet: Mickey waffles, pancakes, potato tots, custom omelets, fruit, cereal, pastries, scrambled eggs, bacon, sausage, ham, apple turnovers
Lunch & Dinner Buffet: BBQ pork loin, chutney, salad, chicken, pork, pasta, lobster and shrimp macaroni and cheese, vegetables, corn dog nuggets, desserts, ice cream, mojito, beer

WARUNG OUTPOST

Asia
Description: Asian outdoor bar
Type: Walk-up Bar
Price: $ / **Dining Plan:** No
Menu Items: margaritas, beer, Mickey pretzel, chips, smoothies

YAK & YETI LOCAL FOODS CAFES
Asia
Description: Asian street food
Type: Quick-Service
Price: $ / **Dining Plan:** Yes
Menu Items:
Breakfast: breakfast sandwiches, breakfast burritos, hash brown bites, fruit salad, juice, coffee
Kids Breakfast: pancake and sausage stick, french toast sticks
Lunch & Dinner: teriyaki bowl, Asian honey chicken, Asian chicken wrap, ginger chicken salad, tikka masala, egg rolls, Kobe beef hot dog, mango pie, soda pop, beer
Kids Lunch & Dinner: cheeseburger, chicken strips

YAK AND YETI ❤

Asia
Description: Asian-style eatery at the base of the Himalayas
Type: Bar, Quick-Service, and Table Service Restaurant
Price: $ – $$$ / **Dining Plan:** Yes (but not for Quality Beverages bar)

Local Food Cafes Menu: beef bowl, cheeseburger, chicken, sandwich, hot dog, wrap, salad, egg rolls, various desserts, soda pop, juice, milk, beer

Kids Menu: cheeseburger, sandwich, chicken strips

Quality Beverages Menu: chicken sandwich, salad, turkey leg, egg rolls, frozen lemonade, soda pop, juice, bottled water, draft beer, sangria, margarita

Restaurant: chicken wings, egg rolls, pot stickers, lettuce cups, lo mein noodles, seafood curry, tempura shrimp, Mahi Mahi, fish, salad, tikka masala, wok dishes, BBQ ribs, kabobs, fried rice, bok choy, various desserts, specialty drinks, beer, wine, sake

Kids Menu: burger, sandwich, egg roll, mac and cheese, chicken tenders, corn dogs, teriyaki chicken breast

Recommendations: Pork Pot Stickers, Pork Egg Rolls ♥, Tempura Shrimp ♥, Chicken Tikka Masala

DISNEY WATER PARKS DINING

TYPHOON LAGOON EATS

HAPPY LANDINGS ICE CREAM
Description: Snack Shack
Type: Snacks
Price: $ / **Dining Plan:** No
Menu Items: ice cream, sundae, bottled water, soda pop, all-day refillable mug for soda pop

LEANING PALMS
Description: American dining beach house
Type: Quick-Service
Price: $$ / **Dining Plan:** Yes
Menu Items: burgers, chicken nuggets, wraps, sandwiches, pizzas, hot dogs, assorted desserts, soda pop, beer, wine, sangria, hot chocolate, coffee, milk, frozen lemonade
Kids Menu: chicken nuggets, turkey sandwich

LET'S GO SLURPIN'
Description: Beach bar
Type: Lounge Bar
Price: $$ / **Dining Plan:** No
Menu Items: margarita, mai tai, rum, cocktails, beer, wine

LOWTIDE LOU'S
Description: Beach Sandwich Bar
Type: Snacks and drinks
Price: $ / **Dining Plan:** Yes
Menu Items: turkey pesto, sandwiches, wraps, nachos, soda pop, bottled water, margarita, pina colada, vodka mixed drinks, beer, wine, sangria
Kids Menu: sandwiches

SNACK SHACK
Description: Dining Hut
Type: Quick-Service
Price: $$ / **Dining Plan:** Yes
Menu Items: turkey pesto, sandwiches, wraps, salads, soda pop, bottled water, margarita, pina colada, refillable fountain beverage mug
Kids Menu: sandwiches

TYPHOON TILLY'S
Description: Barbecue Shack
Type: Quick-Service
Price: $$ / **Dining Plan:** Yes
Menu Items: sandwiches, wraps, salads, shrimp, fish, soda pop, bottled water, beer, wine, sangria
Kids Menu: turkey sandwich, corn dog nuggets

BLIZZARD BEACH EATS

ARCTIC EXPEDITIONS
Description: Food Truck
Type: Snacks
Price: $$ / **Dining Plan:** No
Menu Items: gyro, cheese steak, salad, turkey leg, various desserts, beer, lemonade, bottled water

AVALUNCH
Description: Dining Hut
Type: Quick-Service
Price: $$ / **Dining Plan:** Yes
Menu Items: brisket, specialty hot dogs, pretzels, various desserts, beer, sangria, soda pop, bottled water

COOLING HUT
Description: Dining Hut
Type: Quick-Service
Price: $ / **Dining Plan:** Yes
Menu Items: tuna sandwich, chicken wrap, popcorn, hummus, fruit cup, pretzels, chips, yogurt, various desserts, beer, hard cider, soda pop, bottled water

FROSTBITE FREDDY'S FROZEN FRESHMENTS
Description: Snack and Frozen Drink Shack
Type: Snacks
Price: $ / **Dining Plan:** No
Menu Items: brisket nachos, turkey leg, orange swirl cone, soda pop, beer, mixed adult beverages
Recommendation: barbecue brisket nachos

I.C. EXPEDITIONS
Description: Ice Cream Truck
Type: Snacks
Price: $ / **Dining Plan:** No
Menu Items: sundaes, floats, ice cream bars, bottled water

LOTTAWATTA LODGE
Description: Ski Lodge Restaurant
Type: Quick-Service
Price: $$ / **Dining Plan:** Yes
Menu Items: burgers, fries, wraps, rolls, hot dog, flatbread, various desserts, ice cream, sundaes, all-day refillable mug, frozen lemonade, hot chocolate, coffee, beer, sangria, wine

MINI DONUTS ❤
Description: Donut Cart
Type: Snacks
Price: $ / **Dining Plan:** No
Menu Items: mini donuts and dipping sauces, coffee, hot chocolate, hot tea, frozen lemonade
Recommendation: Mini Donuts ❤

POLAR PUB
Description: Outdoor Bar
Type: Lounge
Price: $$ / **Dining Plan:** No
Menu Items: margarita, daiquiri, specialty drinks, beer, wine, bottled water, chips

WARMING HUT
Description: International Food Hut
Type: Quick-Service
Price: $$ / **Dining Plan:** Yes
Menu Items: teriyaki rice bowl, egg roll, empanada, chicken wrap, various desserts, soda pop, beer, all-day refillable mug, hard cider

HOTEL DINING

The WDW hotels have some of the best dining choices around. If you're not staying at that particular Resort hotel, you can still wander in and dine at a restaurant. The Quick-Service locations are often just hamburgers, sandwiches, hot dogs, and soda. These aren't that special, unfortunately, so we haven't detailed them much in this section.

ALL-STAR RESORTS
These Resorts have their own themed quick-service restaurants. The breakfasts here are pretty good!

> **· Magic Tips ·**
> The World Premiere Food Court at Disney's All-Star Movie Resort has a secret menu! You can try poutine, a bacon mac 'n' cheese dog, and also a burger made with cinnamon buns (it's aptly named the Cinnamon Bun Burger)! Just ask when you order.

ALL-STAR MOVIE RESORT
Silver Screen Spirits Pool Bar – $$ / **Dining Plan:** Yes / Quick-Service
‡ **World Premiere Food Court** – $$ / **Dining Plan:** Yes / Quick-Service Breakfast, Lunch, and Dinner

ALL-STAR MUSIC RESORT
‡ **Intermission Food Court** – $$ / **Dining Plan:** Yes / Quick-Service Breakfast, Lunch, and Dinner
Singing Spirits Pool Bar – $$ / **Dining Plan:** Yes / Quick-Service

ALL-STAR SPORTS RESORT
‡ **End Zone Food Court** – $$ / **Dining Plan:** Yes / Quick-Service Breakfast, Lunch, and Dinner
Grandstand Spirits – $$ / **Dining Plan:** Yes / Quick-Service Pool Bar

ANIMAL KINGDOM LODGE

BOMA – FLAVORS OF AFRICA
Jambo House
Description: African cuisine in a safari setting
Type: Table Service
Price: $$$ / **Dining Plan:** Yes
Menu Items:
Breakfast: fruit, salad, yogurt, salmon, cheeses, omelets, pancakes, bread pudding, oatmeal, ham, turkey, waffles, corned beef hash, potatoes, vegetables, coffee, tea, lemonade, juices, soda pop, milk
Dinner: soups, stews, salads, salmon, pork ribs, chicken, beef sirloin, vegetables, soda pop, coffee, tea, milk
Recommendation: Come for breakfast. The dinner is pricey, so we'd recommend just dining at Jiko instead.

JIKO – THE COOKIE PLACE ❤
Jambo House
Description: African cuisine with an extensive wine selection
Type: Fine Dining
Dress Code: Business casual / cocktail attire – though we've seen plenty of men in shorts here
Price: $$$$ / **Dining Plan:** Yes
Menu Items: steak, wild boar tenderloin, halibut, vegetables, pork shank, seafood, short rib, macaroni and cheese, lamb shank,

assorted desserts, teas, liqueurs, wines, specialty cocktails, soda pop, coffee, tea, milk

Kids Menu: cheese pizza, macaroni and cheese, chicken, steak, fish, scallops

Recommendations: Crispy Bobotie Roll for the appetizer ❤, Grilled Buffalo Rib-Eye or Botswana-style Seswaa Beef Short Rib for the entrée ❤, Braai Macaroni and Cheese enhancement

‡ THE MARA ❤

Jambo House

Description: African- and American-inspired fast food

Type: Table Service

Price: $-$$ / **Dining Plan:** Yes

Menu Items:

Breakfast: scrambled eggs, breakfast potatoes, Mickey-shaped waffles, breakfast sandwiches, oatmeal, bacon, sausage, pastries, coffee

Kids Breakfast: cereal, waffles, breakfast platter with eggs and bacon or sausage

Lunch: burger, flatbreads, salads, sandwiches, soup, cupcakes, coffee, soda pop

Dinner: ribs, burger, lamb stew, chicken nuggets, flatbreads, falafel, salads, chili-cheese hot dog, soup, soda pop, coffee

Kids Lunch & Dinner: turkey sandwich, cheeseburger, chicken nuggets, salad with chicken

Late-Night Dining: flatbreads, kids cheese pizza, desserts, soda pop, coffee

Recommendation: We like The Mara for its inexpensive, but tasty entrees. It's a great place to stop by for breakfast before heading to the parks or late-night after you play.

SANAA

Kidani Village

Description: American and African dining with an Indian flare overlooking an animal-filled Savanna

Type: Table Service

Price: $$$ / **Dining Plan:** Yes

Menu Items: lamb sliders, shrimp, salad, tandoori chicken, burger, fish, chicken sandwich, steak, assorted desserts, teas, liqueurs, margarita, specialty cocktails, soda pop, coffee, tea, milk – *Kids Menu*: cheese pizza, macaroni and cheese, chicken, cheeseburger, fish, shrimp

Recommendation: If you want to dine and see the animals at the same time, this is the place to do it. Sanaa is better for those not looking for African flares.

UNIQUE DINING EXPERIENCES

Reservations required and Dining Plan Not Accepted
- **Dine with Animal Specialist** – $$$ Dine with an animal specialist at Sanaa. You'll learn a lot about the many species of African Animals while dining on a 4-course meal of bread, salad, meat, and a dessert.
- **Wanyama Safari** – $$$$ Board a caravan safari and meet several of the Animal Kingdom Lodge's African animals like giraffes and zebras. Afterward, you'll dine at Jiko.

LOUNGES AND BARS

- **CAPE TOWN LOUNGE AND WINE BAR** (*Jambo House*) – $-$$ / Dining: No / Lounge
- **MAJI POOL BAR** (*Jambo House*) – $$ / Dining: Yes / Quick-Service
- **UZIMA SPRINGS POOL BAR** (*Jambo House*) – $$ / Dining: No / Quick-Service Pool Bar

ART OF ANIMATION

- **THE DROP OFF POOL BAR** – $$ / **Dining Plan:** No / Quick-Service
- **LANDSCAPE OF FLAVORS** – $$ / Dining Plan: Yes / Quick-Service Breakfast, Lunch, and Dinner / Recommendations: breakfast or build-your-own-burger for lunch or dinner.

BEACH CLUB AND YACHT CLUB

ALE & COMPASS LOUNGE
Description: New England-style restaurant
Type: Table Service
Price: $$-$$$ / **Dining Plan:** Yes

Menu Items: American breakfast buffet, salad, flatbreads, burgers, sandwiches, lobster roll, desserts, soda, wines, cocktails, beers
Kids Menu: cheeseburger, grilled chicken, pasta bolognese, fish
Recommendation: Breakfast buffet, Applewood-smoked Bacon Flatbread, Cabernet-braise Short Ribs

BEACHES & CREAM SODA SHOP ❤
Description: Seaside soda parlor and diner
Type: Table Service
Price: $$ / **Dining Plan:** Yes
Menu Items: steak, lobster, chicken, pork chop, desserts, wines, soda, juices
Kids Menu: chicken breast, fish, steak skewers, mac n cheese
Recommendations: Get a reservation because this cool little diner is popular! The food here is good, but the beach-style ambience and dessert are even better. Try a sandwich and get the huge (and delicious) Kitchen Sink dessert (a mix of ice creams and toppings served in a small kitchen sink) ❤

> **· Magic Tips ·**
> Some items on the Disney Dining Plan can be combined to purchase items. For example, 4 people can combine their desserts to get the Kitchen Sink at Beaches & Cream Soda (it's more than enough for four adults to share)!

CAPE MAY CAFE ❤
Description: New England-style beach buffet
Type: Character Dining
Price: $$$ / **Dining Plan:** Yes
Menu Items:
Breakfast and Brunch: Mickey waffles, cheeses, cereals, pastries, yogurt, fruit, meats, coffee, mimosas, espresso, teas
Lunch & Dinner: pasta, carving station, seafood, soup, salad, cheese, bread, desserts
Recommendation: Character breakfast or brunch buffet ❤

YACHTSMAN STEAKHOUSE ❤
Description: New England-style steakhouse
Type: Signature Dining
Price: $$$$ / **Dining Plan:** Yes
Menu Items: steak, lobster, chicken, pork chop, desserts, wines, soda, juices

Kids Menu: chicken breast, fish, steak skewers, mac n cheese
Recommendations: Any of their steaks ❤
Dress Code: Business casual / cocktail attire

MORE DINING

- **Ale & Compass Lounge** – $$ / Dining Plan: No / Type: Lounge / Description: seafood appetizers, wines, cocktails, beers
- **Beach Club Marketplace** – $ / Dining Plan: Yes / Description: Get American breakfast, lunch, and dinner at this Quick-Service location / Type: Quick-Service
- **Crew's Cup Lounge** – $$ / Dining Plan: No / Type: Lounge / Description: Seafood, spirits, and American favorites served until 10PM!
- **Hurricane Hanna's Waterside Bar and Grill** – $-$$ / Dining Plan: Yes / Description: Poolside drinks / Type: Quick-Service / Recommendation: Great for an adult beverage and fine for a bite to eat poolside.
- **Martha's Vineyard** – $$ / Dining Plan: No / Description: Bar with seafood bites / Type: Lounge / Recommendation: Martha's Vineyard offers a full bar for alcoholic drinks. Try the Sautéed Mussels or Salt and Pepper Calamari

BOARDWALK INN & DISNEY'S BOARDWALK

TRATTORIA AL FORNO
Description: Old World Italian
Type: Table Service and Character Breakfast
Price: $$$ / **Dining Plan:** Yes
Menu Items:
Breakfast: Buffet with breakfast calzone, eggs, pastries, pancakes, frittata, cheese torte, omelets, and kids' items
Dinner: pizza, steak, gnocchi, pasta, salad, calamari, mussels
Kids Menu: pasta with meatballs, pizza, and steak
Recommendation: Character dining at the Bon Voyage Adventure Breakfast to meet Rapunzel!

MORE DINING

- **AbracadaBar** – $$ / Dining Plan: No / Lounge / Recommendation: Try one of several delicious mixed drinks, beers, or wines. There are also non-alcoholic choices for kids.
- **Ample Hills Creamery** – $$ / Dining Plan: Yes / Quick-Service Ice Cream

- **Belle Vue Lounge** – $$ / Dining Plan: Yes / Quick-Service
- **Leaping Horse Libations** – $$ / Dining Plan: Yes / Quick-Service
- **Pizza Window** – $ / Dining Plan: Yes / Quick-Service / Recommendation: Grab a full-sized pizza here

CARIBBEAN BEACH RESORT

SEBASTIAN'S BISTRO
Description: *The Little Mermaid*-inspired dining
Type: Table Service
Price: $$$ / **Dining Plan:** Yes
Menu Items:
Lunch: burgers, sandwiches, steak, grilled fish, vegetarian sandwich, jerk chicken, crab cake, rolls, chicken wings, salads, desserts, cocktails, wines, beer, coffee, soda
Dinner: pork shoulder, shrimp and tamales, fish, jerk chicken, curry, jerk butternut squash, steak, crab cake, rolls, chicken wings, salads, desserts, cocktails, wines, beer, coffee, soda
Kids Lunch/Dinner: pasta, jerk chicken, shrimp, burger, meat pie, pork shoulder
Recommendations: Caribbean Pull-Apart Rolls for appetizer and Jerk Chicken for lunch or dinner

‡ SPYGLASS GRILL
Description: Caribbean walkup counter
Type: Quick-Service
Price: $$ / **Dining Plan:** Yes
Menu Items:
Breakfast: sandwiches, breakfast wrap, oatmeal, scrambled eggs, fruit plate, cream cheese guava-stuffed French toast, coffee, tea
Lunch & Dinner: bacon cheeseburger, chorizo burger, Cuban sandwich, Caribbean tacos, turkey sandwich, vegan taco, smoothies
Recommendations: Caribbean Tacos and a Lava Smoothie

MORE DINING
- **Banana Cabana Pool Bar** – $$ / Dining Plan: No / Pool Bar
- **‡ Centertown Market** – $$ / Dining Plan: Yes / Quick-Service for Breakfast, Lunch, and Dinner / Recommendation: Strawberry-Guava French Toast (breakfast) or to-go wrap (lunch)

CONTEMPORARY & BAY LAKE TOWER

CALIFORNIA GRILL ❤

Description: American and Seafood Restaurant that overlooks the Magic Kingdom and Seven Seas Lagoon
Type: Fine Dining
Dress Code: Business casual / cocktail attire
Price: $$$$ / **Dining Plan:** Yes
Menu Items:
Brunch: pastries, salad, greek yogurt, fish, shrimp tempura, sushi, pancakes, chicken, grits, eggs benedict, assorted desserts, wine, cocktails
Dinner: sausage, flatbread, cheese boards, charcuteries, sushi, soup, salad, steak, pork, fish, chicken, vegetable curry, seafood ramen, various desserts, wine, cocktails, beer, ciders
Kids Dinner: chicken breast, salmon, beef tenderloin, cheese pizza, macaroni and cheese
Recommendation: Go for brunch! ❤

CHEF MICKEY'S

Description: Buffet with Mickey and friends
Type: Character Dining
Price: $$$ / **Dining Plan:** Yes
Menu Items:
Breakfast: bagels, croissants, pastries, biscuits and gravy, pancakes, potato casserole, shrimp, frittatas, tofu scramble, oatmeal, fruit, yogurts, soda pop, coffee, tea
Brunch: fruit, salad, yogurts, soup, frittatas, pork ribs, assorted desserts
Kids Breakfast: scrambled eggs, tater tots, macaroni and cheese, chicken nuggets, mini waffles, soda pop
Dinner: mixed fruit, salad, shrimp, seafood, pasta, beef, turkey, soup, salmon, macaroni and cheese, mashed potatoes, vegetables, pastries, assorted desserts, specialty cocktails, lemonade, soda pop – *Kids Dinner*: chicken nuggets, mini corn dogs, vegetables, macaroni and cheese

Recommendations: Because of its lively environment and central location near the monorail, Chef Mickey's can get a bit noisy. If you're looking for a character dining experience with Mr. Mouse himself, there's no better place! Go for the breakfast buffet.

THE WAVE... OF AMERICAN FLAVORS
Description: American Buffet Favorites / **Type:** Buffet
Price: $$$ / **Dining Plan:** Yes
Menu Items:
Breakfast: omelets, French toast, frittata, continental breakfast, pancakes, eggs benedict, juices, soda pop
Brunch: fruit, salad, yogurts, soup, frittatas, pork ribs, assorted desserts, soda pop, breakfast specialty cocktails, teas, coffee
Kids Breakfast: cereals, eggs, waffles, pancakes, fruit
Lunch: salads, soup, burgers, sandwiches, fish, fried rice, assorted desserts
Kids Lunch: pork tenderloin, penne pasta, chicken strips, grilled fish, cheeseburger, grilled cheese, beef kabob, cheese pizza
Dinner: steak, salads, soup, gnocchi, seafood, pork chop, fried rice, assorted desserts
Kids Dinner: pork tenderloin, penne pasta, chicken strips, grilled fish, cheeseburger, grilled cheese, beef kabob, cheese pizza
Recommendations: Sweet Potato Pancakes for breakfast, The Wave Bison Burger for lunch

MORE DINING

- **CALIFORNIA GRILL LOUNGE** – $$ / Dining Plan: No / Lounge
- ‡ **CONTEMPO CAFE** – $$ / Dining Plan: Yes / Quick-Service American breakfast, lunch, and dinner
- **CONTEMPORARY GROUNDS** – $ / Dining Plan: No / Snacks and Coffee
- **COVE BAR** – $$ / Dining Plan: No / Lounge
- **OUTER RIM** – $$ / Dining Plan: No / Lounge
- **THE SAND BAR** – $ / Dining Plan: Yes / Quick-Service
- **THE WAVE LOUNGE** – $$ / Dining Plan: No / Lounge

CORONADO SPRINGS

EL MERCADO DE CORONADO
Description: American / **Type:** Quick-Service
Price: $-$$ / **Dining Plan:** Yes
Menu Items: American breakfast items, nachos, rice bowls, burgers, sandwiches, pizza, paninis, salads, beer, wine, margaritas, coffee, tea, soda pop
Kids – cheeseburger, pizza, macaroni n cheese, chicken tenders
Recommendations: Maya Grill's Signature Fajita Skillet

MAYA GRILL

Description: Mexican and American Cuisine / **Type:** Table Service
Price: $$$ / **Dining Plan:** Yes
Menu Items: queso, calamari, tacos, tomatillos, pork, short ribs, fish, Cornish hen, fajita, steak, assorted desserts, specialty drinks, beer, wine, margaritas, coffee, tea, soda pop
Recommendations: Maya Grill's Signature Fajita Skillet

THREE BRIDGES BAR & GRILL ❤

Description: Outdoor Spanish-American dining spot in the center of the resort's lake / **Type:** Table Service
Price: $$-$$$ / **Dining Plan:** Yes
Menu Items: sandwiches, salads, steak, burgers, tacos, churros, cocktails, beer, wine, hard cider, soda pop, tea, coffee
Recommendations: Come here for shareable appetizers and drinks. Try the Warm Manchego with Oaxaca Cheese and Fried Shrimp Corn Dogs

TOLEDO — TAPAS, STEAK, & SEAFOOD

Description: Spanish-inspired rooftop dining / **Type:** Table Service
Price: $$$ / **Dining Plan:** Yes
Menu Items: tapas, steak, chicken, seafood, desserts, cocktails, beer, wine, margaritas, coffee, tea, soda pop
Recommendations: Best for adults who might enjoy rooftop dining with sweeping views of the Walt Disney World Resort. We recommend small bites like Savory Churros (deep-fried cheese), and 'Bravas' Potatoes. For a finer tapas experience, visit Jaleo in Disney Springs.

MORE DINING

- **Barcelona Lounge** – $ / Dining Plan: No / Espresso bar
- **Cafe Rix** – $ / Dining Plan: Yes / Dessert Bar
- **Dahlia Lounge** – $ / Dining Plan: No / Drinks and snacks
- **Rix Sports Bar & Grill** – $-$$ / Dining Plan: Yes / Quick-Service   Spanish-American breakfast, lunch, and dinner
- **Laguna Bar** – $ / Dining Plan: No / Outdoor bar
- **Siestas Cantina** – $$ / Dining Plan: Yes / Pool bar

FORT WILDERNESS

TRAIL'S END RESTAURANT
Description: American Dining / **Type:** Table Service
Price: $$$ / **Dining Plan:** Yes
Menu Items:
Breakfast and Brunch: fruit, pastries, eggs, breakfast pizza, Mickey waffles, cheese grits, carving station, soup, chili, fried chicken, desserts, bacon, sausage, coffee, tea, milk, juices
Lunch & Dinner: chicken breast, shrimp, salad, flatbread, sandwiches, chicken and waffles, steak, grits, assorted desserts, beer
Kids Lunch & Dinner: baked chicken, grilled salmon, cheeseburger, macaroni and cheese, chicken nuggets, grilled cheese
Recommendations: Breakfast or Brunch Buffet, Chicken and Waffles

HOOP-DEE_DOO MUSICAL REVUE ❤
Description: Back country BBQ dinner show
Price: $$$$ / **Dining Plan:** Yes
Menu Items: "All-you-can-eat" fried chicken, BBQ ribs, salad, beans, cornbread, and a dessert
Recommendations: This dining experience works more like a concert with three levels of seating. Filled with show-stopping numbers and loads of humor, this show is highly recommended for the entire family! We recommend sitting in levels 1 or 2 since level 3 can often have obstructed views with your back to the stage. If you use the Disney Dining Plan, you will only have the choice between levels 2 and 3. this will count as two table service meals.

MORE DINING

- **Crockett's Tavern** – $ / Dining Plan: No / Quick-Service pizzas, wings, nachos and Lounge
- **Mickey's Backyard BBQ** – $$$ / Dining Plan: Yes / Character BBQ Buffet
- **P and J's Southern Takeout** – $$ / Dining Plan: Yes / Quick-Service Western favorites

GRAND FLORIDIAN

1900 PARK FARE
Description: American Buffet and Tea Party

Type: Character Dining Buffet
Price: $$$ / **Dining Plan:** Yes
Menu Items:
Brunch: salads, bacon, bagels, soup, rice, potato puffs, sausage, eggs, French toast, shrimp, fruit, croissants, Mickey waffles, assorted pastries, tea, coffee, soda pop
Dinner: salad, greens, soup, chicken, salmon, fried catfish, stir fry, shrimp, mashed potatoes, pork, ravioli, assorted desserts, tea, coffee, soda pop
Kids Dinner: macaroni and cheese, cheese ravioli, hot dog, pizza, chicken tenders, vegetables, taco bar
Recommendation: Dine any time for delicious meals and many characters.

CITRICOS
Description: American and Mediterranean dining
Type: Table Service
Price: $$$-$$$$ / **Dining Plan:** Yes
Menu Items: cheese board, meat board, salad, flatbread, pork, shrimp, soup, short ribs, fish, tofu ratatouille, chicken, beef, vegetables, mashed potatoes, assorted desserts, mixed drinks, wines, beer, soda pop, tea
Kids Menu: chicken, pasta with marinara, shrimp, pork tenderloin, macaroni and cheese, cheese pizza, macaroni and meat sauce
Recommendations: Slow-Roasted Pork Belly, Red Wine-braised Beef Short Ribs

GRAND FLORIDIAN CAFE
Description: American dining
Type: Table Service
Price: $$$ / **Dining Plan:** Yes
Menu Items:
Breakfast: omelets, eggs, steak, bacon, sausage, breakfast potatoes, French toast, pancakes, Mickey waffles, salads, yogurt, oatmeal, pastries, morning mixed drinks, wines, beer, soda pop, tea
Kids Breakfast: omelet, eggs, Mickey waffles, pancakes with sprinkles
Lunch: shrimp, soup, salad, sandwiches, fish, chicken, wraps, burgers, assorted desserts, mixed drinks, wines, beer, soda pop, tea
Kids: chicken, salmon, chicken wrap, meaty macaroni, cheese pizza, chicken nuggets
Dinner: salad, soup, shrimp, chicken, fish, steak, pork chops, burgers, grits, ravioli, assorted desserts, mixed drinks, wines, beer, soda pop, tea

Kids Dinner: chicken, salmon, chicken wrap, meaty macaroni, cheese pizza, chicken nuggets

Recommendations: Artisan-made Spinach-Ricotta Ravioli, The Café Sandwich (open faced with ham, turkey, bacon, cheese, and fried onion), or the Lobster 'Thermidor' Burger

NARCOOSSEE'S ❤

Description: American and Seafood Restaurant
Type: Fine Dining
Dress Code: Business Casual
Price: $$$-$$$$ / **Dining Plan:** Yes
Menu Items: soups, salads, shellfish, fish, cheeses, pasta, steak, chicken, pork, lobster, vegetables, assorted desserts, wines, soda pop, tea
Kids Menu: steak, cheeseburger, hamburger, mac and cheese, fried chicken tenders, shrimp, pasta, veggie burger
Recommendations: St. Augustine Soft-shell Crab, Grass Fed Filet Mignon ❤, Chocolate Crème Brulee ❤

VICTORIA & ALBERT'S ❤

Description: Victorian dining
Type: Fine Dining
Dress Code: Men: dinner jackets and slacks with shoes / Women: dress, pant suit, or skirt and blouse. This dress code is strictly enforced.
Price: $$$$-$$$$$ / **Dining Plan:** Yes
Menu Items: caviar, shrimp, fish, scallops, duck, pork, lasagna, lamb, beef, cheeses, various desserts, soda pop, coffee, tea, wines
Recommendation: The finest dining in all of WDW with perfect Victorian décor and service. There are options for Kids, but this is mostly an adult affair. Note that the menu changes from time to time, so we don't provide recommendations other than the food here is exquisite.

MORE DINING

- **Beaches Pool Bar and Grill** – $$ / Dining Plan: Yes / Pool Bar
- **Citricos Lounge** – $$ / Dining Plan: No / Lounge
- **Courtyard Pool Bar** – $$ / Dining Plan: No / Pool Bar
- **Garden View Tea Room** – $$ / Dining Plan: No / Tea Lounge

- **Gasparilla Island Grill** – $$ / Dining Plan: Yes / American Quick-Service Pool Bar
- **Enchanted Rose** – Set to open sometime in 2020, this new lounge will have decor and drinks themed after Disney's *Beauty and the Beast*.

OLD KEY WEST

OLIVIA'S CAFE
Description: American Cuisine
Type: Table Service
Price: $$$ / **Dining Plan:** Yes
Menu Items:
Breakfast: biscuits and gravy, omelets, eggs, chorizo, French toast, pancakes, waffles, cereal, bacon, sausage, ham, potatoes, coffee, tea, milk, morning cocktails, bottled water
Kids Breakfast: mini pancakes, waffles, eggs and breakfast potatoes
Lunch & Dinner: corn fritters, onion rings, crab cakes, soup, salads, burger, pork ribs, chicken, pasta, sandwiches, chicken, fish, assorted desserts, specialty drinks, beer, coffee, tea, soda pop
Kids Lunch & Dinner: chicken, grilled cheese
Recommendations: Island Barbecue Pork Ribs, Olivia's Potatoes for a side

MORE DINING

- **Good's Food to Go** – $ / Dining Plan: Yes / Burger and Hot Dog Quick-Service
- **Gurgling Suitcase** – $ / Dining Plan: No / Pool Bar
- **Turtle Shack Poolside** – $ / Dining Plan: Yes / Pool Bar

POLYNESIAN VILLAGE

KONA CAFE
Description: American and Seafood Restaurant / **Type:** Table Service
Price: $$ / **Dining Plan:** Yes
Menu Items:
Breakfast: French toast, steak and eggs, ham, bacon, sausage, pancakes, omelets, eggs, fruit, oatmeal, assorted pastries, tea, coffee, soda pop, juices
Kids Breakfast: oatmeal, fruit, eggs, pancakes, French toast, toast

Lunch: crab cakes, beef, pork, pot stickers, salad, soup, tacos, Asian noodles, sandwiches, burgers, assorted desserts, tea, coffee, soda pop, milk

Kids Lunch: salad, chicken, shrimp skewers, cheeseburger, cheese tortellini, hot dog

Dinner: crab cakes, beef, pork, pot stickers, sushi, salad, soup, duck, pork, lamb, assorted desserts, tea, coffee, soda pop, milk

Kids Dinner: salad, chicken, shrimp skewers, cheeseburger, cheese tortellini

Recommendations: Big Kahuna for breakfast, fish tacos for lunch, any of the pan noodles for dinner

'OHANA ❤

Description: Polynesian Character Dining
Type: Character Dining / Buffet
Price: $$$-$$$$ / **Dining Plan:** Yes
Menu Items:
Breakfast Buffet: scrambled eggs, fried potatoes, pork, Mickey-shaped waffles, assorted pastries, tea, coffee, soda pop, juices, milk
Dinner Buffet: breads, salads, dumplings, chicken wings, Asian chicken, steak, shrimp, stir fry, desserts, tea, coffee, soda pop, milk
Recommendations: We recommend coming for dinner for some unique dishes served family style (shareable plates). 'Ohana is also very popular, so book your reservation as far in advance as possible!

> · **Magic Tips** ·
> 'Ohana offers a little-know Twilight Feast room service option. Get several plates delivered to your room for around $50/person. Adults with small to moderate appetites may find that splitting this meal is a great option, too. It's cheaper than the dinner price tag of 'Ohana and you can order late into the night!

TRADER SAM'S GROG GROTTO ❤

Description: Island Dive Bar
Type: Lounge
Price: $$ / **Dining Plan:** No
Menu Items: mixed drinks, wines, beer, sushi, lettuce cups, tacos, fish, sliders, sausages, dumplings, soda pop

Recommendation: Disney fans love Trader Sam's! The room is a bit secret and stored away behind a metal door. Open it to discover a hidden gem in the WDW Resort. The room and the waiters react to different ordered drinks. Watch the volcanoes erupt, room storm, and bartenders transform to zombies looking for brains! Okay, it's more funny than scary, but Trader Sam's is not to be missed! Order any of their delicious mixed drinks and Kalua Pork Tacos. After 8pm, it's 21+ only.

MORE DINING

- **Barefoot Pool Bar** – $ / Dining Plan: No / Pool Bar
- **Capt. Cook's** – $$ / Dining Plan: Yes / Quick-Service Breakfast, Lunch, and Dinner
- **Kona Island** – $ / Dining Plan: No / Quick-Service treats and drinks
- **Oasis Bar and Grill** – $$ / Dining Plan: Yes / Quick-Service and Pool Bar
- **Pineapple Lanai** ❤ – $$ / Dining Plan: Yes / Dole Whip Station.
- **Tambu Lounge** – $$ / Dining Plan: No / Lounge
- **Trader Sam's Tiki Terrace** – $$ / Dining Plan: No / Lounge / Go to Trader Sam's Grog Grotto instead for a better theme and experience

POP CENTURY

- **‡ Everything POP Shopping and Dining** – $$ / Dining Plan: Yes / Quick-Service
- **Pedals Pool Bar** – $$ / Dining Plan: No / Pool Bar

PORT ORLEANS - FRENCH QUARTER

‡ SASSAGOULA FLOATWORKS & FOOD FACTORY ❤
Description: Southern American Boat Restaurant
Type: Quick-Service
Price: $$ / **Dining Plan:** Yes
Menu Items:
Breakfast: buttermilk pancakes, blueberry pancakes, chocolate chip pancakes, grilled steak, scrambled eggs, croissant breakfast sandwich, fried chicken and biscuit

Lunch & Dinner: bacon cheeseburger, BBQ burger, cheese steak, chicken sandwich
Kids: chicken nuggets, grilled cheese, burgers (with or without cheese)
Dessert: Beignets
Recommendations: All of the food here is delicious, but we love their beignets. ♥ Sassagoula also serves a Beignet Cheeseburger that uses beignets as the buns!

MORE DINING

- **Mardi Grogs** – $ / Dining Plan: No / Quick-Service Bar
- **Scat Cat's Club** – $$ / Dining Plan: No / Lounge

· **Magic Tips** ·
Scat Cat's Club is known for its Baton Rouge Beignets—with your choice of alcohol (Baileys, Kahlua, or RumChata). You can also ask for the secret menu item: Chocolate Baton Rouge Beignets (we recommend these with Kahlua)!

PORT ORLEANS - RIVERSIDE

BOATWRIGHT'S DINING HALL
Description: Southern American Boat Restaurant
Type: Table Service
Price: $$$ / **Dining Plan:** Yes
Menu Items: seafood, salad, fritters, gumbo, meat and cheese board, prime rib, steak, catfish, pork chop, pasta, jambalaya, chicken, vegetables, assorted desserts, tea, coffee, soda pop, juices, beer, mixed drinks
Kids Menu: turkey, pasta, fish, beef skewers, macaroni and cheese, cheeseburger, cheese pizza, jambalaya
Recommendations: Cajun Bayou Catfish, Crawfish Mac and Cheese, Red Velvet Cheesecake

MORE DINING

- **Muddy Rivers** – $ / Dining Plan: No / Bar
- **River Roost** – $$ / Dining Plan: No / Lounge with live entertainment
- **Riverside Mill Food Court** – $$ / Dining Plan: Yes / New Orleans-style Quick-Service

RIVIERA RESORT

TOPOLINO'S TERRACE
Description: French and Italian dining
Type: Character Dining / Buffet
Price: $$$-$$$$ / **Dining Plan:** Yes
Menu Items:
Breakfast: character buffet with omelets, smoked salmons, steak, waffles, quiche, pastries, cocktails, juice, tea, coffee
Dinner: pasta, seafood, steak, cocktails, wines, European beers, soda pop, juice
Recommendations: This restaurant has a fantastic rooftop views while you dine!

MORE DINING
- **Bar Riviera** – Poolside bar
- **Le Petit Cafe** – Coffee and wine bar in the lobby
- **Primo Piatoo** – A quick-service dining spot

SARATOGA SPRINGS

THE TURF CLUB BAR AND GRILL
Description: American Dining
Type: Table Service
Price: $$$ / **Dining Plan:** Yes
Menu Items: calamari, mussels, soups, onion rings, salad, shrimp, prime rib, lamb chops, pasta, fish, chicken, steak, vegetables, assorted desserts, tea, coffee, soda pop, juices, beer, mixed drinks, soda pop
Kids Menu: grilled fish, pasta, chicken breasts, cheeseburger, hot dog, pizza
Recommendations: Onion Rings with dips, Grilled New York Strip

MORE DINING
- **The Artist's Palette** – $ / Dining Plan: Yes / Quick-Service Sandwiches while painting
- **Backstretch Pool Bar** – $$ / Dining Plan: Yes / Pool Bar
- **On the Rocks** – $ / Dining Plan: Yes / Lounge
- **The Paddock Grill** – $ / Dining Plan: Yes / Lounge
- **The Turf Club Lounge** – $ / Dining Plan: No / Lounge

WILDERNESS LODGE

STORY BOOK DINING AT ARTIST POINT ❤

Description: *Snow White*-themed dinner event
Type: Character Dining
Price: $$$$ / **Dining Plan:** Yes—a great value!
Menu Items: prime rib roast, chicken, gnocchi, snapper, veal shank, desserts, cocktails
Kids Menu: grilled chicken, pasta, prim rib, chicken tenders
Recommendations: Dine with characters from *Snow White and the Seven Dwarfs* in an enchanted setting! This fun-filled evening has characters from the classic animated film including Snow White, some of the Seven Dwarfs (usually Dopey and another), and the Evil Queen! Guests interact with these characters while they dine under twinkling indoor trees. The meal is served in courses and we recommend the entree, Brother's Grimm Roasted Chicken (served with herb-crusted potatoes and squash).

WHISPERING CANYON CAFE

Description: American Dining with rowdy waiters! The Whispering Canyon Cafe has quieted down in contrast to its early years.
Type: Table Service
Price: $$$ / **Dining Plan:** Yes
Menu Items:
Breakfast: all-you-can-eat skillets, omelets, benedicts, eggs, waffles, pancakes, breakfast sides, juice, tea, coffee
Kids Breakfast: all-you-can-at skillets, omelets, Mickey waffles, breakfast sides
Lunch & Dinner: nachos, all-you-can-eat skillets, sandwiches, burgers, salad, desserts, cocktails, wines, beers, soda pop, juice
Kids Lunch & Dinner: all-you-can-at skillets, quesadilla, cheeseburger, chicken nuggets, mac n cheese, fish
Recommendation: All-You-Care-To-Enjoy Skillet

MORE DINING

- **‡ Roaring Fork** – $ / Dining Plan: Yes / Quick-Service breakfast and sandwiches
- **Territory Lounge** – $$ / Dining Plan: No / Bar and Lounge / Recommendation: Great for adults
- **Trout Pass Pool Bar** – $ / Dining Plan: No / Pool Bar

DOLPHIN AND SWAN

Note: Disney Dining Plans are not accepted at these hotels.

THE FOUNTAIN
Description: American Dining
Type: Table Service
Price: $$$ / **Location:** Dolphin
Menu Items:
Breakfast and Brunch: fruit, pastries, eggs, breakfast pizza, Mickey waffles, cheese grits, carving station, soup, chili, fried chicken, desserts, bacon, sausage, coffee, tea, milk, juices
Lunch & Dinner: chicken breast, shrimp, salad, flatbread, sandwiches, chicken and waffles, steak, grits, assorted desserts, beer
Kids Lunch & Dinner: baked chicken, grilled salmon, cheeseburger, macaroni and cheese, chicken nuggets, grilled cheese
Recommendations: We're not very impressed with this menu. For the price, you may as well boat over to Disney's Boardwalk.

FRESH MEDITERRANEAN MARKET
Description: American and Mediterranean Dining
Type: Table Service / **Location:** Dolphin
Price: $$$
Menu Items:
Breakfast and Brunch: French toast, grits, eggs, cereal, yogurt, pancakes, omelets, bacon, sausage, coffee, tea, milk, juices, breakfast mixed drinks
Lunch: salads, wine
Recommendations: "Monkey Puzzle" French Toast

GARDEN GROVE
Description: American and Seafood Dining
Type: Character Dining
Price: $$$ / **Location:** Swan
Menu Items: clam chowder, soups, salads, meat and seafood buffet, assorted desserts, soda pop, wine, sangria, beer
Kids Menu: pasta, fish tacos, chicken fingers, turkey sliders, tuna salad sandwich, Margherita pizza
Recommendation: Dinner Buffet

IL MULINO

Description: Italian Restaurant / **Type:** Table Service
Price: $$$ / **Location:** Swan
Menu Items: shrimp, calamari, steaks, mussels, clams, insalate, beef, soup, pizza, risotto, pasta, fish, assorted desserts, soda pop, wine, sangria, beer
Kids Menu: pizzas, fettuccini alfredo
Recommendation: Rustica Pizza

KIMONOS ❤

Description: Sushi Bar with Karaoke / **Type:** Table Service
Price: $$$ / **Location:** Swan
Menu Items: sushi, salad, kimchee, tempura, miso soup
Recommendations: The best sushi in Orlando—and a great place to sing some karaoke in the evenings. Try the Gyoza or Tempura Platter and a Shrimp Tempura Roll for the entrée ❤

SHULA'S STEAK HOUSE

Description: American Steakhouse designed to celebrate the Miami Dolphins football team.
Type: Fine Dining
Price: $$$$ / **Location:** Dolphin
Menu Items: steak, seafood, soup, salad, mashed potatoes, vegetables, assorted desserts, wines, soda pop
Kids Menu: chicken, cheeseburger
Recommendation: Try any of their savory steaks.

TODD ENGLISH'S BLUEZOO

Description: Stylish Seafood Restaurant
Type: Fine Dining
Price: $$$$ / **Location:** Dolphin
Menu Items: fish, steak, chicken, lobster, Bolognese, fries, vegetables, assorted desserts, soda pop, cocktails, wines, cider, beer
Kids Menu: beef tenderloin, chicken, fish fillets, spaghetti, cheese pizza, clam chowder, shrimp
Recommendations: Maine Lobster Pot Pie, Lobster Broccoli Stuffed Cheddar Potato

MORE DINING (SWAN)
- **Il Mulino Lounge** – $$$ / Type: Lounge
- **Java Bar** – $$ / Type: Lounge
- **Kimonos Lounge** – $$ / Type: Lounge

- **Splash** – $$ / Type: Quick-Service / Menu: wraps, burgers, and pizza

MORE DINING (DOLPHIN)
- **Todd English bluezoo Lounge** – $$ / Type: Lounge / Menu: burgers and nachos
- **Cabana Bar and Beach Club** – $ / Type: Poolside fish tacos and salads
- **Lobby Lounge** – $ / Type: Lounge
- **Picabu** – $$ / Type: Quick-Service / Menu: American Favorites
- **Shula's Lounge** – $$ / Type: Lounge

> **· Magic Tips ·**
> Guests can order pizza to their resort from popular chains like Pizza Hut and Dominos. However, you'll need to meet the delivery person in the lobby.

DINING OUT

Disney Springs and Disney's Boardwalk have several delicious dining options. Their spaces are ever-evolving, so we've included the best choices.

DISNEY SPRINGS

THE BOATHOUSE ❤
Description: American Seafood Dining
Type: Table Service
Price: $$$ / **Dining Plan:** Yes
Menu Items: steak, fish, lobster, shrimp, salad, burger, sandwiches, seafood small plates, fries, macaroni and cheese, cocktails, wines, beer, assorted desserts, soda pop
Kids Menu: fish, chicken, popcorn shrimp, pig in a blanket, cheese burger, macaroni and cheese, chicken tenders **Recommendations:** We love the presentation of this restaurant. It's classy but fun and the

food is fantastic. Their steaks are great and you can make a surf and turf combo by adding Main Lobster.

CHEF ART SMITH'S HOMECOMIN' ❤

Description: Southern Florida comfort food
Type: Table Service
Price: $$-$$$ / **Dining Plan:** Yes
Menu Items:
Brunch: biscuits, eggs, doughnuts, hush puppies, breakfast cocktails, bacon, coffee, tea, juice
Lunch/Dinner: fried chicken, fried catfish, pork chop, seafood, short rib, burgers, sandwiches, biscuits, moonshine, beers, cocktails, wines, soda pop, sweet tea
Kids Menu: quesadillas, tacos, enchiladas
Recommendations: One of the best restaurants in Walt Disney World! Come for lunch or dinner and try Art's Famous Fried Chicken (comes with the restaurant's signature cheddar drop biscuit) or the Fried Chicken & Doughnuts ❤

‡ D-LUXE BURGER ❤

Description: Burger Joint
Type: Quick-Service
Price: $ / **Dining Plan:** Yes
Menu Items: Burgers, fries, macaron, soda pop, beer, wine, alcoholic sodas, shakes, floats
Kids Menu: cheeseburger, chicken burger
Recommendations: The burgers are the best in all of WDW, but the fries are nothing to remember. Try the Barbecue Classic Burger and a Red Velvet Burger Macaron for dessert.

EARL OF SANDWICH ❤

Description: Sandwich Shop
Type: Quick-Service
Price: $ / **Dining Plan:** Yes
Menu Items: hot sandwiches, soups, wraps, macaroni and cheese, salad, various desserts, soda pop, hot tea, coffee, wine, beer, hot chocolate, milk
Recommendation: The best hot sandwiches in all of WDW! We recommend The Holiday Turkey (tastes like Thanksgiving!) ❤

FRONTERA COCINA

Description: Mexican dishes crafted by celebrity chef, Rick Bayless
Type: Table Service
Price: $$ / **Dining Plan:** Yes

Menu Items: tacos, carnitas, carne asada, enchiladas, tortas, queso, chips and guacamole, desserts, soda pop, margaritas, cocktails, sangria, tequila flights, wines, beer
Kids Menu: quesadillas, tacos, enchiladas
Recommendations: The Southern Pig (pulled pork sandwich) or the Smoked & Fried Chicken sandwich

---

· Magic Tips ·

Many restaurants in Disney Springs also use the Open Table app for reservations. Sometimes Open Table will have availability for seating when DisneyWorld.com does not. Cancellation policies are also more lenient with this app.

JALEO
Description: Tapas Restaurant and Lounge
Type: Signature Dining / Table Service
Price: $$$-$$$$ / **Dining Plan:** Yes
Menu Items: Spanish-style tapas, queso, cocktails, beers, wines, juice, tea, coffee, desserts
Kids Menu: tapas including chicken, fish, and pork
Recommendations: Jaleo is ideal for large parties, dates, and foodies. We highly recommend ordering off of the Chef's Tasting Menu for the full experience. These come with a series of tapas perfect for sharing!

MARIA & ENZO'S RISTORANTE
Description: Southern Italian Cuisine / **Type:** Table Service
Price: $ **Dining Plan:** Yes
Menu Items: pasta, salad, ricotta, parmigiana, steak, ahi tuna, Italian desserts
Kids Menu: pasta, chicken finger parmesan
Recommendations: Come hungry and order a three-course meal! Perfect for date nights. Try the Sicilian lasagna.
Hideaway: Check out Enzo's Hideaway, a Prohibition-style speakeasy next to the restaurant. Adults can score some tasty drinks here!

MORIMOTO ASIA
Description: Modern Asian Cuisine
Type: Signature Dining / Table Service
Price: $$$ / **Dining Plan:** Yes

Menu Items: sushi, shrimp tempura, edamame, miso soup, salad, calamari, dumplings, egg rolls, noodles, fried rice, fish, vegetable dishes, assorted desserts, sake, cocktails, beer, wine
Kids Menu: macaroni and cheese, lo mein, orange chicken, menchi katsu, hot dogs, fried chicken
Recommendations: The sushi is great! We recommend the Shrimp Tempura roll and the Sake Sangria (21+). There are also a less-expensive, to-go options at Morimoto Asia Street Food next door.

· **Magic Tips** ·
Signature dining restaurants cost 2 Disney Dining Plan table service credits, but don't always deliver the best deal for entrees. For example, diners at Morimoto Asia will only be able to select one sushi roll as part of their meal with the Disney Dining Plan.

POLITE PIG
Description: New American BBQ favorites and beer
Type: Quick-Service
Price: $$ / **Dining Plan:** Yes
Menu Items: baby back ribs, chicken, salmon, sausage, brisket, sandwiches, salads, fries, macaroni and cheese, soda pop, beer, wine, bourbon
Kids Menu: chicken tenders, macaroni and cheese, pork slider, smoked chicken
Recommendations: The Southern Pig (pulled pork sandwich) or the Smoked & Fried Chicken sandwich

T-REX
Description: Dinosaur-themed Restaurant
Type: Table Service
Price: $$$ / **Dining Plan:** Yes
Menu Items: nachos, quesadilla, salad, soup, burgers, sandwiches, shrimp, fish, fries, pasta, chicken, steak, various desserts, cocktails, beer, wine, soda pop
Kids Menu: grilled chicken, corn dog, sliders, popcorn shrimp, chicken nuggets, pork ribs, pasta, pizza, macaroni and cheese
Recommendations: Like the Rainforest Café, T-REX is more about the theme than the food. Kids will love it, but adults will find it just okay, but nothing to write home about. Still, it's worth seeing the enormous dinosaurs and prehistoric scenery while you eat. Order a burger.

TERRALINA CRAFTED ITALIAN
Description: Home-cooked Italian
Type: Table Service
Price: $$$ / **Dining Plan:** No
Menu Items: antipasta, calamari, meatballs, salad, wood-fired pizza, sandwiches (crispy chicken, roasted pork, grilled vegetable), chicken, beef short rib, porchetta, pasta (wide variety), parmesan burger, swordfish peperonatta, ribeye, pork chop, gelato, wines
Kids Menue: spaghetti, mac & cheese, chicken fingers, grilled chicken, hamburger, hot dog, grilled fish

MORE DINING

Sprinkles ($) – Delicious cupcakes! Get their famous Red Velvet Cupcake. No dining plan.
Pizza Point ($-$$) – Delicious slices-to-order pizza and sandwiches.
Paradiso 37 ($$) – While the outside looks fun and inviting, the Latin American food is less than savory and the seating is very close together.

DISNEY'S BOARDWALK

FLYING FISH ❤
Description: American Seafood Dining
Type: Fine Dining
Dress Code: Business casual / cocktail attire
Price: $$$$ / **Dining Plan:** Yes
Menu Items: fish, crab, salad, steak, chicken, shellfish, assorted desserts, specialty cocktails, wine, beer, cider
Kids Menu: fish, chicken breast, pasta
Recommendations: Easily one of the Walt Disney World Resort's best and well-themed dining experiences. There aren't as many options for Kids, but adults will love this seafood culinary experience. Try the Tour of the Coast for a seafood appetizer and Wagyu Filet Mignon for a savory entrée.

MORE DINING

- **Boardwalk Joe's Marvelous Margaritas** ($-$$) – Delicious margaritas and other tropical drinks.
- **Funnel Cake Cart** ($) – Try one of WDW's famous funnel cakes. They are fried and dusted with powdered sugar to perfection.

> **· Magic Tips ·**
> While many restaurants prohibit adults from ordering off of the kids menu, Disney doesn't have such rules! Order from any part of the menu, no matter your age! Certain Disney Springs restaurants and all buffets do limit by age group.

FOUR SEASONS ORLANDO

FLYING FISH
Description: Stylish steakhouse and bar
Type: Fine Dining / lounge
Dress Code: Business casual / cocktail attire
Price: $$$$ / **Dining Plan:** No
Menu Items: steak, tapas, sushi, pork chip, lobster, seafood, cocktails, beer, wine, soda, juice, desserts
Kids Menu: chicken fingers, steak, mac and cheese, grilled cheese
Recommendations: You don't need to be a guest at the Four Seasons to enjoy this fine dining experience. Plate prices are comparable to most Disney Resort hotel Signature Restaurants. The steaks and seafood at Capa are highly recommended.

> **· Magic Tips ·**
> Capa has a great view of the Magic Kingdom fireworks! They are a bit far away, but you'll have an excellent view of the resort from the rooftop.

CHAPTER FIFTEEN

VISITING WITH KIDS

INTRODUCTION

If you're planning a vacation to Walt Disney World, there's a huge chance that you'll be visiting with children (if not, you might want to skip this chapter and head straight to the next one). Walt Disney World feels like a haven for families with kids—and, for the most part, it is! There are hundreds of attractions, dozens of Disney-themed places to stay, pools with waterslides, and, of course, the enchanting magic of the Parks.

If your kids know that they're visiting Disney World, they are likely bursting at the seams and counting down the days. After all, it's one of the happiest places they can be! That's not to assume there won't be a snag or two... or *six* on your vacation. Kids have their limitations, even on fun. Unfortunately for adults, the not-so-fun times can be difficult to deal with outside of the home. Fortunately, however, there are ways that you can limit the problems and also cut them short when they arise.

We haven't forgotten the tweens and teens! This chapter covers their favorites as well. Maybe you're looking for the best places to stay, eat, or play—we've got it covered. Now we'll review the best of everything designed for kids of all ages at Walt Disney World.

TIPS FOR VISITING WITH KIDS

1. **Get to the Theme Parks Early –** This may be the most valuable piece of information that we can give you when traveling to the Walt Disney World Theme Parks. Kids aren't fans of long lines (but who is?), and the best way to keep them happy is to avoid waiting. Getting to the Parks early on will help you. We recommend riding an attraction you didn't receive a FastPass+ selection for at the start of your day.

2. **Don't Over-Do It –** Kids get tired. Ride after ride. Show after show. From morning until night. The Young Kids likely won't make it and also the Teens will be groaning for some pool time. Plan for about 4-5 hours on the rides with Kids and Young Kids (Tweens and Teens can generally last longer). After that, take a break and see what everyone is in the mood for afterward. We also recommend spacing out your days. If you know that everyone loves the Magic Kingdom Park and Epcot is not as important, get a Park Hopper and return to the Magic Kingdom later in your trip for more of what they love.

3. **Take Breaks –** In order to not "over-do it" you'll need to take breaks. Plan to head back to the Hotel for lunch or right after. Keep them cool, hydrated, and ready for more once their batteries have charged. It's common to walk up to 12 miles a day in a single park! After all that walking, both you and the kids might be craving naps.

4. **Have Backup Plans –** Bad weather or tantrums can wreck an otherwise perfect day. Plan to have something else fun to do. Maybe bring a board game for the hotel room or change your time slot for lunch or dinner. Like temper tantrums, Florida showers tend to last under a half hour, but if you're faced with longer poor weather or fits, having a backup is a lifesaver.

5. **Consider Giving *Yourself* a Break –** In a perfect world, being around our kids 24/7 would bring us endless joy. However, this is not a perfect world. We invite you to review our next chapter that's all about adults. It'll give you tips on what to do with your kids while you save some time for the spa, dining out, or just visiting the Parks without them.

BABIES & TODDLERS

We hear a lot of parents asking if they should bring their baby to Walt Disney World. The answer is YES! Many parents love bringing their babies to the parks! If you decide to bring your baby to the resort, here is a list of what to bring, do, and all about the Baby Care Centers.

WHAT TO BRING

- **Stroller** – Kids can get tired and Walt Disney World has zones to park strollers with attendants that watch them while you ride. All strollers must be within the limits of 31" (79cm) wide and 52" (132cm) long. Rental locations are near the entrance of the theme parks and start at $15 a day ($13/day for longer stays). Double Strollers are also available for $31 a day or $27 for multi-day lengths. Stroller parks are located around many of the kid-friendly areas. Cast Members patrol these areas for safety.
- **Protection from the Sun** – We recommend sunscreen, hats, blankets, and a covered stroller to keep your little one comfortable.
- **Blankets and Warm Clothes** – These items are essential for cooler days (or at night when the temperatures drop).
- **Diapers, Wipes, and a Change of Clothes** – Just in case of a mess, a change of clothes can be a lifesaver.
- **Bottles and Formula** – Don't forget the liners!
- **Baby Food** – WDW will allow small glass jars as long as they contain baby food.
- **Backpack** – Carry your baby's necessities in the bag. We also recommend a backpack that you can easily hook onto a stroller.

> **· Magic Tips ·**
>
> If you're unable to travel with a stroller or other items, it may be best to order them. Target and Amazon sells single and double strollers at a fraction of the rental cost. Have one delivered to your hotel room or purchase one at a nearby Target store. You can get other necessary supplies this way, too!

BABY CARE CENTERS

Just in case you forget something, the WDW Resort Parks are equipped with nannies that are there to help. They offer nursing rooms, rocking chairs, changing tables, highchairs for feeding, a microwave, and fresh water. You can also purchase items like clothing, medications (over-the-counter), formula, baby food, diapers, and wipes.

LOCATIONS
Magic Kingdom Park – Next to First Aid, between Main Street, U.S.A. and Adventureland

Epcot – In the World Showcase, at the Odyssey Center building, next to the Mexican Pavilion

Disney's Hollywood Studios – Hollywood Boulevard, to the left as you enter through the main gate

Disney's Animal Kingdom – Discovery Island, near the bridge to Africa

Changing Rooms – These are found in most restrooms (men and women)

Breast Feeding – Feeding your baby is a top priority and you shouldn't be nervous to do so at WDW. If you want privacy (or quiet), head to the Baby Care Centers in the parks.

First Aid – Located next to the Baby Care Center in the Magic Kingdom on Main Street, U.S.A.

ATTRACTIONS WITH BABIES & TODDLERS

- **See a Show or Parade** – With wonderful music and dancing characters, your baby or toddler will be delighted. Check the map for a schedule of shows and parades.
- **Space Out Rides** – Space out rides and times waiting in line for simple joys like looking at the baby ducks in the many ponds or eat a snack under some shade.
- **Don't Forget FastPass+** – These reservations save everyone waiting in line. The less time waiting, the happier the kid!

RIDER SWITCH

Do you have a Young Kid with you, but all of the adults in your party want to ride? Many WDW Resort rides give you the option to wait and switch places when finished. This especially helps when a kid turns out not to be tall enough to ride or he/she becomes too scared. To use the Rider Switch, ask a Cast Member at the start of the queue. You will be assigned a Rider Switch pass and moved to a special area as people from your party ride the attraction.

ATTRACTIONS WITH RIDER SWITCH

Magic Kingdom Park
- The Barnstormer
- Big Thunder Mountain Railroad
- Space Mountain
- Splash Mountain
- Tomorrowland Speedway

Epcot
- Frozen Ever After
- Mission: SPACE
- Soarin'
- Test Track

Disney's Hollywood Studios
- Rock 'n' Roller Coaster Starring Aerosmith
- Star Tours – The Adventures Continue
- The Twilight Zone Tower of Terror
- Millennium Falcon: Smuggler's Run
- Star Wars: Rise of the Resistance (expected, unconfirmed)

Disney's Animal Kingdom Park
- Avatar Flight of Passage
- DINOSAUR
- Expedition Everest
- Kali River Rapids
- Primeval Whirl

KIDS AGES 3-9

Taking Kids this age is fun because their excitement is unparalleled. They will be *itching* to ride attractions, see parades, and meet their favorite characters. You'll be busy keeping them busy, but planning everything ahead is what makes things go a lot smoother. As far as Kids go, you'll want to also take time for these activities:

1. **Make Time for the Pool** – One of the best vacation memories for kids will likely be the hotel pool. The WDW Resort pools all have waterslides and so do many located off-property. A couple of hours in the pool can be the recharge that everyone needs. If you're staying for a while, you may want to reserve an entire day for the pool.

2. **Budget to Shop** – Kids love to buy things at the Parks. Disney knows this so they place gift shops with dazzling trinkets *everywhere*. Kids will likely want to avoid strolling through Disney Springs, but getting a Buzz Lightyear, Elsa, or Stitch toy can be unforgettable. Sometimes getting pre-filled Disney gift cards is the best way to go. Your Kids can manage their own budget without expecting you to fork out more money. This will save you a lot of *no's* and negotiating.

3. **Book Character Dining** – If your kids are going to want to meet characters, there's no better way. These are buffets where characters hang out, take pictures, sign autographs, and joke around with your family. A dozen characters can show up to a Character breakfast. We recommend booking one of these experiences early in your trip so that the kids are burnt out on attempting to get autographs. This will save you *tons* of time waiting in long lines for character meetups in the Parks.

> **· Magic Tips ·**
> If you're staying at a Walt Disney World Resort hotel, select a character wake up call! These are phone calls by Disney characters (usually Mickey) that kids will love to hear from in the morning. Character calls are free and can be accessed from a button on hotel room phones.

TWEENS AGES 10-12

Tweens can be both a very fun and very challenging group to visit WDW with. They call them "Tweens" because they're in between being a Kid and a Teen. Because of this, you might be dealing with an array of emotions. They might want to be a diehard *Frozen* fan with you as well as be in a "leave me alone" mood, all at the same time. There are ways to avoid the latter. Here are a few tips to planning a trip with Tweens:

1. **Plan with Them** – You'll need to make the final choices, but ask your Tween what their interests are. Which Parks are most important? What rides are they itching to jump on? Do the water parks sound fun to them? If you're having trouble picking a hotel, you might also narrow it down to a few and have your Tween help you decide. They are often very good at expressing themselves emotionally and logically. That's the perfect combination for planning a trip to Walt Disney World!

2. **Tween-Only Time** – It's completely up to you, but you might opt to let your Tween explore in a group. A group of responsible thirteen year olds can often explore the water parks and some of the Parks by themselves. You're the adult, so you set the rules. Maybe give them a few hours alone. Check in with them on a phone. Have them meet you promptly at a certain location. They'll be happy they had their independence and extremely excited to share their experiences with you. Also keep in mind that not every Tween will want to go off on his or her own. Sometimes you are their comfort zone. In that case, embrace it, and take turns picking the rides.

3. **Try Something New** – If you've been to the Parks before with your Tweens, maybe it's time for them to try something you like. Have them explore the foods of Epcot with you or sit and watch a fireworks display. They'll appreciate you treating them as older, even though you also allow them to be a kid at the Resort.

TEENS AGES 13-17

We recommend all of the Tween activities for Teens as well. Because Teens are much more decisive and independent, they'll often want more wiggle room to be themselves. There are a few other options that Teens will crave:

1. **Get Some Sleep** – Don't plan early with Teens. Most of the time, they'd rather be at the theme parks until closing and not have a bright and early agenda. Book your FastPass+ reservations for the early afternoon and mosey into the parks when everyone is refreshed and comfortable.

2. **Disney Springs** – Shopping at Disney Springs is a blast for Teens. There are so many amazing stores for them to look at, clothes to try on, and unique items to buy. Teens will also love the movie theatre with dine-in seating.

3. **Star Wars: Secrets of the Empire** – Video game-loving teens will go crazy for this unique Star Wars-themed VR experience. Knock their socks off by taking them out of reality and into the VOID to battle the Empire! Located in Disney Springs, advanced tickets required (about $30 / person):
   www.thevoid.com/locations/orlando

4. **The Spa** – Perhaps have a mother/daughter or father/son spa day. Take them out for their first bit of relaxation at the spa. Being pampered can sometimes feel very adult and like a rite of passage. Let them indulge with you! The Grand Floridian and Saratoga Springs resorts both have spas. You don't need to stay there to book.

5. **Caring for Giants** (Animal Kingdom admission required) – Go beyond the atmosphere of a zoo with this up-close encounter with elephants at Animal Kingdom! This 1-hour shows you how the elephants are cared for at the park. It's an unforgettable and breathtaking experience that animal-loving teens will never forget. Reserve over the phone for $30 / person: (407) 939-7529

6. **Star Wars Guided Tour** (Hollywood Studios admission required) – Take the ultimate tour specially designed for the biggest Star Wars fans! This 7-hour tour gives you VIP access to all of the Star Wars-themed action in Hollywood Studios. On the tour you'll have reserved seating to watch *Star Wars: Path of the Jedi*, two stage shows including March of the First Order, and the kids (4-12) get priority enrollment for Jedi training! You'll also cut ahead to ride Star Tours and meet with Chewbacca and Kylo Ren! Afterward, you'll certainly work up an appetite, and this tour comes with a very delicious Star Wars-themed dinner and dessert party during the nighttime Galactic Spectacular show. Tours begin at 3PM on select dates. Reserve over the phone for $92.95 / person: (407) 939-7529

7. **Time for Selfies** – While vacations are a great time for families to relax and enjoy each other's company, individual expression shouldn't be ignored. If your teen wants to take a selfie—or *ten*—we recommend being supportive of this. For many teens, sharing their vacation updates with friends is all part of the fun! Of course, while excessive selfies are never a healthy choice, the right amount of sharing will make your teen feel more appreciative of the trip.

CHAPTER SIXTEEN

WALT DISNEY WORLD FOR ADULTS

INTRODUCTION

The Walt Disney World Resort may have been originally built with families in mind, but that doesn't mean it hasn't also become an adult retreat. After all, Walt Disney himself was an adult when he came up with the idea for the Parks, and he knew that also the kids at heart would come there for enjoyment.

Over the decades, WDW has done a fantastic job catering to adults. With the previous Pleasure Island in the former Downtown Disney, they created an adult playground with sweeping sights and delicious food and beverages. They've since revamped it with Disney Springs, and the adult-aimed entertainment has never been better. With bountiful places to shop and eat all around the Resort, adults have an abundance of choices. From dive bars to thrill rides to fine-dining and golf courses, the WDW Resort has something for every grown-up. In this section, we outline adult activities from the best places to drink to avoiding families with children.

PARENTS' EVENING OUT

If you're an adult with children, part of your perfect WDW Resort vacation might be a night without them. If you're interested in heading back to the Parks, many are often open until midnight. Our top choice is Epcot for its beautiful views, fine dining, and variety of adult beverages. Then again, you might just feel like hitting the Parks late at night, utilizing those Extra Magic Hours at the Magic Kingdom or Hollywood Studios. At times, some of these Parks are open as late as 2AM!

Whatever you choose to do with your time, there are great options for kids without their parents inside the resort. We recommend planning the night ahead of time to ensure you can have an easy transition into your night alone.

CHILDREN'S CENTERS

A place just for kids—without the parents! Kids make arts and crafts, watch movies, and eat while parents can enjoy an evening at the Resort. This is a perfect time for your kids to make new friends as they enjoy Disney-themed fun under the supervision of Disney's professional caregivers. Guests don't have to stay at that particular hotel to book:

REQUIREMENTS:
1. Make a reservation in advance.
2. Your child must be potty trained (without using pull-up diapers)

BEACH CLUB RESORT
Captain Hook's Pirate Crew
A dinner event for kids with Captain Hook! They'll learn to act like a pirate before dining on pasta and dessert.
Location & Hours: Seaside Retreat in Beach Club / 5:00pm – 8:30pm
Cost: $55 flat rate per child (must be 4-12 years old). Dinner is included with this cost.
Reservation Number: (407) 824-5437

DOLPHIN HOTEL
Camp Dolphin
This might be our least favorite because of the fewer activities, but older kids might enjoy their Xbox 360. For just a couple of hours, it's perfect for any kid.
Location: On the first floor of the Dolphin Hotel
Hours: 5pm – Midnight
Ages: 4 - 12
Cost: $12/hour per child. You can get 2 hours free if you book a spa package at the Mandara Spa or a dining reservation at Shula's Steak House, Todd English's bluezoo, or Mulino New York Trattoria. Dinner is an additional $10 per child.

Reservations (required): (407) 934-4241 – Book up to 180 days in advance and call during business hours.

BABYSITTERS

The Walt Disney World works with a third-party service for babysitting. This service is call Kid's Nite Out and it's perfect if you'd rather have a babysitter in the room than take your child to an Activity Center.

SERVICES

- Professional assistance in-room.
- Professional assistance at the Parks. If you desire, the babysitter will accompany your family around the Resort.
- Provides for Kids ages 6 months to 12 years old.
- Offers arts and crafts, bedtime reading, and games to play.

RATES

- Per hour: 1 Child - $18 / 2 Children - $21 / 3 Children - $24 / 4 Children - $26
- An extra $2 per hour charge occurs for every hour after 9PM.
- $10 babysitter travel fee (one-time only)

Reservations: (800) 696-8105
Website: http://www.kidsniteout.com

TOP ADULT DINING & BARS

If you're looking for an evening out, there are plenty of choices around the Walt Disney World Resort. However, you might have a difficult choice deciding. Should you just stay at your Hotel? Should you go off-property? Maybe you just want to try something different, but don't know where to begin. In this section, we review all of the best bars, restaurants, and activities that we highly recommend for adults looking for a delicious evening by themselves.

1. TRADER SAM'S GROG GROTTO – Polynesian Village Hotel
Theme: Island-themed tiki bar inspired by the character in the Jungle Cruise ride
Price: $$ / **Disney Dining Plan:** No
Why We Recommend It: Dim lighting, air conditioning, and scraggly bartenders serve excellent drinks and bar food in this unique setting. Try a specialty cocktail or order a beer on draft. Certain drinks cause the room's volcanoes to erupt or a storm to brew! Trader Sam's is

also known for its excellent tacos. After 8pm, Trader Sam's is 21 and older only.

2. TEPPAN EDO – Epcot World Showcase, Japan
Theme: Teppanyaki grill with live chefs
Price: $$$ / **Disney Dining Plan:** Yes
Why We Recommend It: Very similar to Benihana. Watch talented Japanese chefs make your choice of course right before your eyes! They are like ninjas with their knives and create delicious masterpieces on a hot grill. If you've never been to a Teppanyaki-style restaurant, you can't miss this one!

3. VICTORIA & ALBERT'S – Grand Floridian Hotel
Theme: Elegant, Victorian-style fine dining
Price: $$$$ / **Dining Plan:** Yes
Why We Recommend It: A 5-Diamond culinary experience. If you're craving a perfectly prepared meal for a special occasion, look no further than Victoria and Albert's.
Dress Code: This restaurant is only open for dinner and has a strict dress code. It's required for men to wear dinner jackets, slacks, and shoes. Women must wear a dress, pant suit, or skirt and blouse.

4. KIMONOS – Swan Hotel
Theme: Freshly made sushi house
Price: $$ / **Dining Plan:** No
Why We Recommend It: The best sushi and sake in Orlando! At night, Kimonos offers karaoke and hosts a sake bar.

5. JIKO – Animal Kingdom Lodge
Theme: African cuisine
Price: $$$$ / **Dining Plan:** Yes
Why We Recommend It: Get a taste for Africa in a unique, wild setting. Try an African wine or specially marinated chicken or vegetables. When you're done eating, you can roam the Hotel and see some of the exotic animals on site.
Dress Code: This restaurant is only open for dinner and has a dress code, though it's not as strict as Victoria & Albert's. It's requested that men wear collared shirts, slacks or jeans, and close-toed shoes. Women may wear a dress, jeans or capris, dress shorts or skirts. Dinner jackets are not required. Hats, tank tops, swimming gear, and cut-off clothing are not permitted.

6. ROSE & CROWN DINING ROOM – Epcot World Showcase, United Kingdom

Theme: British Pub
Price: $$$ / **Dining Plan:** Yes, but not for alcohol
Why We Recommend It: A cool environment with great beer, cocktails, and tasty fish and chips. Book a reservation to see the Epcot fireworks from the patio.

7. LA CAVA DEL TEQUILA – Epcot World Showcase, Mexico
Theme: Tequila cellar with authentic Mexican flare
Price: $$ / **Dining Plan:** No
Why We Recommend It: Dim lighting, air conditioning, and delicious margaritas! Need we say more?

8. ENZO'S HIDEAWAY – Disney Springs
Theme: Prohibition-Era Speakeasy
Price: $$ / **Dining Plan:** Yes
Why We Recommend It: Head underground for this surprising, rustic bar. It's a lot of fun "discovering" Enzo's Hideaway before you dine on lite bites and drink cocktails.

9. RIVER ROOST – Port Orleans Riverside
Theme: Southern-style lounge
Price: $$ / **Dining Plan:** No
Why We Recommend It: If you're craving some zany performances with a Southern feel, this is the place to be! Yehaa Bob performs a wacky, high-energy show here, twice a night, Wednesday through Saturday (8:30pm and 10:30pm).

10. YACHTSMAN STEAKHOUSE – Yacht Club Resort
Theme: New England steakhouse
Price: $$$$ / **Dining Plan:** Yes
Why We Recommend It: Savory steaks and wines made better here than anywhere else in the WDW Resort.
DRESS CODE: This restaurant is only open for dinner and has a "business casual" dress code.

11. TERRITORY LOUNGE – Wilderness Lodge
Theme: A rustic, woodland bar with an array of craft beers, wine, and specialty drink choices
Price: $$ / **Dining Plan:** No
Why We Recommend It: A very calm, underrated bar to relax. If you're hungry, try one of their savory flatbreads.

12. JELLYROLLS – Boardwalk Resort
Theme: Boardwalk-style dueling piano bar for those 21+

Price: $$ / **Dining Plan:** No
Why We Recommend It: If you are into loud, fun piano music, this is the place to be. Everyone laughs and sings along to the performers.

UNIQUE FINE DINING

HIGHWAY IN THE SKY DINE AROUND
Theme: Unique monorail dining experience for adults 21+
Price: $170 per person / **Disney Dining Plan:** No
Why We Recommend It: If you're craving something different, adventurous, romantic, and unforgettable, look no further than Highway in the Sky! Check at in the Contemporary hotel and hop aboard Disney's monorail system to start your tasting journey. You'll be served 5 courses in several different locations like the Grand Floridian and Polynesian. The menu varies but is filled with American and fusion cuisine and alcoholic beverages to please the most discerning tastebuds!
Reservations Required: disneyworld.disney.go.com/dining/contemporary-resort/highway-in-the-sky-dine-around/

AVOIDING CHILDREN

It's impossible to absolutely avoid *all* children at the WDW Resort. But you can avoid being around the bulk of them. We've listed some great tips on how to stay clear of families with small children at the Resort.

RESORTS WITH THE FEWEST CHILDREN

1. **Disney's Grand Floridian Resort** – It's expensive, so many families won't want to spend their budget on this.
2. **Disney Contemporary Resort Bay Lake Tower** – The modern edge of this tower and its simple pool appears to deter children.
3. **Coronado Springs** – Not our favorite hotel, but on a budget, this is a great choice to avoid kids.

MORE TIPS

1. **The Right Place, the Right Time** – No one under 21 is allowed in Trader Sam's after 8PM. Jelly Rolls is also 21+ only.
2. **Stick to Epcot's World Showcase** – You'll have plenty of adult activities that will simply bore children.
3. **Avoid the Water Parks** – These are often wall-to-wall with families with kids.
4. **Stay Away from Pools with Water Slides** – Even at night the children play in these. The simple pools without water slides have by far the fewest children.
5. **Avoid "Kids Lands"** – Fantasyland in the Magic Kingdom Park, Toy Story Land in Hollywood Studios, and Rafiki's Planet Watch in Animal Kingdom are all spots filled with kid attractions. Avoid them.
6. **Ride the Thrills** – Attractions with height requirements will weed out the littlest ones.
7. **Go at Night** – The Parks are often open late during the peak seasons of Summer and Winter. They may stay open as late as 2AM with Extra Magic Hours. It'll be less common to see children at those times.
8. **Avoid Parades and Shows** – These attractions are like magnets for small children. You've been warned! Instead, plan to ride attractions during the shows and parades to avoid the families with children.
9. **Dine at a Bar** – Pick from one of the places we've mention in the previous section of this chapter.
10. **Forget the Characters** – You might be *dying* to meet Ariel from *The Little Mermaid*, but if you're looking to avoid the kids, you'll have to make some sacrifices. Bye, Ariel!

ADULT EXPERIENCES

1. **Get a Massage** – Traveling can be stressful. Navigating around the parks can be stressful. Dealing with your kids... well, you get it. Take some time for yourself and schedule a message with your Resort Hotel. They are world-class and unforgettable:
   - Animal Kingdom Lodge – Zahanati Massage & Fitness Center

- Boardwalk Villas – Muscles & Bustles Health Club
- Contemporary Resort – Olympiad Fitness Center
- Coronado Springs – La Vida Health Club
- Dolphin Hotel – Mandara Spa
- Saratoga Springs – Senses
- Wilderness Lodge Villas – Sturdy Branches
- Yacht Club – Ship Shape Massage Salon

Mandara Spa Reservations: (407) 934-4772
Reservations for all other Spas: (407) 939-7727

2. **See a Concert –** The House of Blues in Disney Springs offers a wide variety of live music shows. We always recommend pre-booking tickets for these events in case they sell out.
http://www.houseofblues.com/orlando

3. **Catch a Movie –** AMC Disney Springs 24 offers a wide selection of movies. They also have an amazing Dine-In experience where you can sit and eat while you watch a movie.   Visit **www.amctheatres.com** for show times.

4. **Experience The VOID –** Star Wars comes to life in this unique virtual reality experience! Reserve your group for some action-packed fun! Visit: **www.thevoid.com/dimensions/starwars/secretsoftheempire**

5. **Golf** – Walt Disney World has some world-class golfing!

6. **Go Shopping** – Pick up a bag at Kate Spade or a polo at Lacoste.

7. **Hit the Gym** – If fitness is your thing, here are the locations:
   - Animal Kingdom Lodge – Zahanati Massage & Fitness Center
   - Animal Kingdom Villas – Survival of the Fittest Fitness Center
   - Boardwalk Villas – Muscles & Bustles Health Club
   - Contemporary Resort – Olympiad Fitness Center
   - Coronado Springs – La Vida Health Club
   - Grand Floridian – Senses
   - Old Key West – Old Key West Exercise Room
   - Saratoga Springs – Senses
   - Wilderness Lodge Villas – Sturdy Branches
   - Yacht Club – Ship Shape Massage Salon

CHAPTER SEVENTEEN

NON-RIDER GUIDE

INTRODUCTION

Typically, the first thing that comes to mind when people think about Walt Disney World is Mickey Mouse. The second thought is usually the rides that fill the Resort's Parks. But what if you or your guest don't enjoy the drops, turns, and twists? Are there things for you to do? Would you enjoy yourself? Would it be worth the money to plan a vacation around a set of theme parks? In short, is the Walt Disney World Resort for you?

The answer is *yes*! There are about 150 attractions all around the WDW Resort—and the best part for non-riders is that most of them aren't rides. These attractions are found in every Park, whether you'd like to see exotic tigers in Disney's Animal Kingdom, watch a stunning fireworks display at the Magic Kingdom, see a Broadway-style musical at Disney's Hollywood Studios, sunbathe at the water parks, or sample an array of worldly cuisine at Epcot.

In this chapter, we explore the dozens of options in each park and give non-riders the opportunity to discover the best that Walt Disney World has to offer without the craze of the heart-racing rides.

TOP RECOMMENDATIONS

1. Photograph the Sights – The Walt Disney World Resort is truly a feast for the eyes. The Parks offer intricate architecture, well-planned lands, and lush, meticulously manicured foliage. There are unlimited things to take photos of!
2. Try Gourmet Food – Dazzle your senses with savory meals and sweet treats all around the Parks, Hotels, and Disney Springs. Epcot offers some of the best samplings from all over the globe!
3. Meet Famous Characters – Take a photo with your favorite Disney character.
4. See a Music Group – Watch one of the many musical bands playing around the park. We recommend seeing the barbershop quartet, the Dapper Dans, on Main Street in the Magic Kingdom Park.
5. Ride a Slow-Moving Attraction – Some rides don't have drops or move fast, many of them can be perfect for your speed as you experience the magnificent stories these rides have to offer. Epcot has over a dozen slow-moving boat rides perfect for everyone.
6. See Stunning Shows – The WDW Resort is known for magnificent shows. Every park has a huge list of attractions.

MOST RECOMMENDED SHOWS (in order):

1. Festival of the Lion King (Animal Kingdom)
2. *Finding Nemo* –The Musical (Animal Kingdom)
3. Happily Ever After Fireworks (Magic Kingdom)
4. Fantasmic! (Hollywood Studios)
5. Hoop-Dee-Doo Musical Revue (Fort Wilderness)
6. Indiana Jones Stunt Spectacular! (Hollywood Studios)

BEST SLOW RIDES AND OTHER ATTRACTIONS (not in order):

- **Epcot** – This theme park is *filled* with slow-moving rides. Journey into Imagination with Figment is a great start, especially for kids.
- **Jungle Cruise** (Magic Kingdom) – A humorous tour guide takes you on a riverboat through the Amazon and Africa.
- **Peter Pan's Flight** (Magic Kingdom) – See the story of *Peter Pan* while flying in a slow-moving pirate ship.

- **The Little Mermaid – Ariel's Undersea Adventure** (Magic Kingdom) – a slow-moving "dark ride" that explores the story of Disney's *The Little Mermaid*.
- **Haunted Mansion** (Magic Kingdom) – A slow-moving dark ride through a haunted house. Might be too scary for Young Kids.
- **"it's a small world"** (Magic Kingdom) – The classic, slow-paced boat ride around the world.
- **Tomorrowland Transit Authority PeopleMover** (Magic Kingdom) – Another classic WDW attraction that travels slowly through Tomorrowland. It's also a great way to beat the heat!
- **The Walt Disney World Railroad** (Magic Kingdom)
- **Go Shopping** – There are stores on every corner of the resort. Disney Springs is loaded with stores for yourself or to bring back souvenirs. We've spent *hours* looking at the unique items in the World of Disney store!
- **Get a Princess Makeover at the Bibbidi Bobbidi Boutique** – Perfect for kids who want to dress as their favorite Disney Princess. The Boutiques are located in Disney Springs, the Magic Kingdom Park, and the Grand Floridian Resort.
- **People Watch** – This will either sound fun or creepy to you, but WDW has some unique visitors in creative outfits and style. Or just sit by a ride like Splash Mountain in the Magic Kingdom Park and watch them plummet!
- **Look for Hidden Mickeys!** – We have a list of elusive, Mickey Mouse-shaped hidden marks found all over the resort. Read the Hidden Mickey chapter later in this guide.

MORE TO DO

The ESPN Wide World of Sports Complex – Get your game on in this massive 220-acre hub for athletics located in the Walt Disney World Resort, close to Disney's All-Star Resorts. There are baseball fields, softball diamonds, basketball courts, cross country courses, track and field, and so much more. The base fee for entry is $17.50 for Adults and $12.50 for Children ages 3-9.
For more information, visit: https://www.espnwwos.com

Disney Mini Golf – The WDW Resort is home to a few fantastic, Disney-themed mini golf courses. Not only are these inexpensive, but they are stunning. The price is $14.00 for Adults and $12.00 for Children ages 3-9. The golf courses include the magical Fantasia

Gardens by the Walt Disney Swan Hotel and the snowy Winter Summerland near Blizzard Beach.

Disney Golf – Disney has enormous golf courses located just outside the Magic Kingdom near the Grand Floridian and Disney's Polynesian Resort Village. These lush courses include up to 36 par courses. There are strict dress codes and reservations are a must.
For more information, visit: **http://golfwdw.com**

EVEN MORE

Most of the hotels will come with volleyball, tennis, or basketball courts to play games. Many of the Resorts based on water have fishing and boat rentals for extra fun. Always check out the Times Guide brochure when arriving to your hotel.

FINDING CHARACTERS

Disney is known for its iconic, heartwarming, and even villainous characters. That is why they bring them to life inside the Walt Disney World Resort. You can meet most of your favorite Disney characters throughout the Parks and hotel. They are always happy to sign autographs, interact, and take a photo with guests. Aren't sure if you should meet a character? We recommend it! After getting a hug from Mickey, Goofy, or a Disney Princess, people of all ages will get a smile that won't go away! Sadly, not every character comes out each day. Here, we offer some invaluable tips to easily finding your favorite characters.

HOW TO EASILY FIND CHARACTERS

1. **Get the App** – Download the Walt Disney World App on your mobile device to track the characters! Simply search by park or character name to find them.
2. **Grab a Map** – Many of the characters have "show times" in certain locations. Be sure to check the character times on the Park maps early in the day.

3. **Book a Character Dining Buffet** – The Resort Parks and Hotels have many characters who will interact with you while you eat. Sometimes you can meet 6 or more in one meal!

4. **Pick the Perfect Dining Spot** – If you are looking to meet several Disney princesses, get a reservation at the Akershus Royal Banquet Hall in Epcot.

5. **Keep Your Eyes Peeled** – You may also see Disney characters unexpectedly walking around the Parks, and in the shows and parades.

6. **Book a FastPass+** – If meeting the characters is high on your list, consider using a FastPass+ selection to book a meeting time and avoid the long lines

MORE TIPS

1. Kids will love the character autograph books sold on Main Street.

2. During the holidays, characters are often dressed in seasonal outfits (Halloween, Christmas, and other special days).

3. The Princess Fantasy Faire is the best way to take a photo with a Disney Princess.

4. If you love villains, come during Halloween (mid-August through October 31st) to see more of them roaming the parks. You can also take photos with them in several character meeting spots!

5. Sadly, not every character comes out each day—though one of your favorites is sure to be there!

> **· Magic Tips ·**
> If you're dying to meet an unlisted Disney character, Hollywood Studios may be the place! An unlisted event known as "Character Palooza" happens almost daily at the park. This is where characters from the shows meet around Hollywood Studios to take photos with guests! Since this event is unofficial, we recommend checking social media in the late afternoon for the hashtag, #characterpalooza to see where this pops up! However, the characters only stay out for about 20 minutes, so be ready with your camera to catch them!

CHAPTER EIGHTEEN

FASTPASS+ TIPS & HACKS

INTRODUCTION

One of the best features about the Walt Disney World Resort is that you can pre-book a place in line on your favorite rides. This is done through their FastPass+ system up to 60 days before the first date of your purchased reservation. FastPass+ reserved times give you an hour window to visit the ride and effectively cut the line to board faster than anyone else. WDW has this system down with separate FP+ lines that empty into the same ride at the end. Typically, you'll wait about 10-20 minutes from the FastPass line. Sometimes, on less popular rides, the line is virtually a walk-on for FP+ holders.

The FP+ works with your MagicBand or Park ticket to allow easy scanning by Cast Members at the FastPass+ lines. The amazing thing about FP+ is that it's so easy to book time slots to your favorite rides that even kids could do it. Choosing your FP+ selections can be tricky. If you're not extremely familiar with the popularity of certain rides (or when you'll want to ride them), you might not pick the appropriate FP+ selection.

Typically, you'll be allowed to choose three FastPass+ selections a day, one park at a time (whether or not you have a Park Hopper option). The four main parks have FP+ (Magic Kingdom, Epcot, Hollywood Studios, and Epcot) while the water parks do not. FastPass+ usually deals with rides, but many of the more popular shows will have reserved seating or standing for FP+ as well. Truthfully, you may not always get to pick each ride you'd like. Some of the more popular rides like Frozen Ever After in Epcot can run out of reservations weeks ahead of your visit. For these, we recommend booking as soon as possible to ensure you get your desired time slot. In this chapter, we explore the FastPass+ selection process and our recommendations on which to book and which aren't necessary. Planning with the best options will save you hours and hours of time waiting in lines.

HOW TO BOOK FASTPASS+

1. Purchase Park tickets.
2. Wait until it's 60 days before your Resort reservation or from the date of your ticket purchase (30 days if you aren't staying at a WDW Resort Hotel).
3. Visit **https://disneyworld.disney.go.com/plan** and log in to begin on your computer, phone, or tablet. If you haven't set up an account, you'll need to on the WDW website. If you've purchased tickets via a 3rd party site, visit the link we provided and you'll be able to "Link Your Tickets.

Note: The easiest way to create, update, and cancel FastPass+ reservations is through the Disney World mobile application. If you need assistance with booking, call Disney at (407) 939-4357.

FASTPASS+ HACKS

1. **Book Early** – We can't stress this enough. 60 days before your trip the FP+ selections become available to you. If you buy a 5-day pass, you will be allowed 5 days of selections during your stay.
2. **Reserve Early Time Slots** – We recommend booking all of your FP+ times before noon. Once you've completed all of your reservations, you can book additional selections one at a time. If you are planning on park hopping, WDW now allows you to

book the additional FastPasses (after you've used your first 3), at other Parks around the Resort.

3. **You Can Change Your Mind** – If you've decided to switch Park days or times, you can do so as long as there is availability. The website and app are quick and easy ways to make these changes.

4. **Arrive at Opening** – The best way to enjoy the attractions that you've missed on FP+ is to arrive early at the opening of the Park. Experience this attraction first as to avoid the long lines that form later. Sometimes you can get 3-4 rides done in the first hour!

5. **Early and Late Arrivals** – If you arrive too early to the FastPass queue, you won't be allowed to use your pass. The Cast Member will tell you how much more time you have and instruct you to wait. If you arrive late, you often have a 15-minute window. Of course, this can change on busier days, but Disney knows that sometimes traffic buildup and other factors can lead to late arrivals, so they allow you to show up a few minutes afterward.

6. **Always Ask** – If for some reason you show up after or too early, you can always ask special permission from the Cast Member to use your Pass out of turn. They aren't obligated to assist you on this, but often times they are able to work something in your favor. Just be polite and you'll get far with Disney employees.

7. **FastPass Adds** – Disney doesn't release all of its FastPass+ selections at once. We're not entirely sure why this happens, but several selections for previous "sold out" rides may suddenly become available on a later date.

8. **Keep Checking the App** – When someone changes or cancels a FastPass+ selection, it becomes available to other guests. If you weren't able to book all of your top choices, they might become available at these seemingly random times. Keep checking the Walt Disney World app throughout the day to see if you can find the attraction or time slot you're looking for.

FASTPASS+ KIOSKS

In the event that your phone dies or you don't have data service, there are several FastPass+ kiosks throughout the Parks. These allow you to change your reservations and add additional ones with ease on a touch screen. Often, a Cast Member will be available to assist you.

MAGIC KINGDOM PARK
Adventureland – near Jungle Cruise
Fantasyland – near Mickey's PhilharMagic
Fantasyland – near Pete's Silly Sideshow
Liberty Square – near The Diamond Horseshoe
Tomorrowland – near Buzz Lightyear Space Ranger Spin
Tomorrowland – near the Tomorrowland entrance bridge

EPCOT
Future World – near Innoventions
World Showcase – near the International Gateway, between France and the United Kingdom pavilions

HOLLYWOOD STUDIOS
Entrance – at the corner of Hollywood Boulevard and Sunset Boulevard
Sunset Boulevard – at the End of Sunset Boulevard
Toy Story Land – Toy Story Land entrance

ANIMAL KINGDOM
Discovery Island – near Island Mercantile
Africa – near Harambe Market
Asia – near Dawa Bar

· **Magic Tips** ·
Disney usually adds FastPass+ selections throughout the day. We've noticed a 3PM "drop" where several highly coveted selections become available.

FP+ RECOMMENDATIONS
We've listed the FastPass+ reservations by their demand and wait time length. High and Very High attractions book the quickest while Low and Very Low attractions may not need FastPass+ selections at all:

MAGIC KINGDOM

Barnstormer	Very Low
Big Thunder Mountain Railroad	Medium

Buzz Lightyear's Space Ranger Spin	Medium
Dumbo the Flying Elephant	Low
Enchanted Tales with Bell	Medium
Haunted Mansion	Medium
"it's a small world"	Low
Jungle Cruise	Medium
Mad Tea Party	Low
The Magic Carpets of Aladdin	Low
The Many Adventures of Winnie the Pooh	Low
Meet Ariel at Her Grotto	Medium
Mickey's PhilharMagic	Low
Monsters, Inc. Laugh Floor	Very Low
Peter Pan's Flight	High
Pirates of the Caribbean	Medium
Princess Fairytale Hall (Character Meet)	Medium
Seven Dwarfs Mine Train	Very High
Space Mountain	Very High
Splash Mountain	Medium*
Tomorrowland Speedway	Medium
Town Square Theater (Character Meet) High	
Under the Sea – Journey of The Little Mermaid	Low

During spring and summer, this attraction books quickly in the middle of the day. Morning and evening rides are easier to book.

EPCOT

Epcot has 2 different categories for FastPass+ selections. Unfortunately, you can only choose 1 from Group A and 2 from Group B:

GROUP A

Frozen Ever After	High
Epcot Forever	High
Meet Disney Pals	Medium
Soarin'	High
Test Track	Very High

GROUP B

Disney & Pixar Short Film Festival	Very Low
Journey Into Imagination With Figment	Very Low
Living with the Land	Low
Mission: SPACE	Medium
The Seas with Nemo & Friends	Low

Spaceship Earth   Low
Turtle Talk With Crush   Low

DISNEY'S HOLLYWOOD STUDIOS

Hollywood Studios has 2 different categories for FastPass+ selections. Unfortunately, you can only choose 1 from Group A and 2 from Group B—or you can choose 3 from Group B. We expect FastPass+ tiers for Hollywood Studios to change in 2020 and incorporate Mickey and Minnie's Runaway Railway and Star Wars: Galaxy's Edge attractions.

GROUP A
Alien Swirling Saucers   Medium
Slinky Dog Dash   Very High
Toy Story Mania!   Medium
The Twilight Zone Tower of Terror   High
Rock 'n' Roller Coaster   High

GROUP B
Beauty and the Beast – Live on Stage   Low
Disney Junior Dance Party!   Medium
Fantasmic!   Medium
Frozen Sing-Along   Medium
Muppet*Vision 3D   Very Low
Indiana Jones Stunt Spectacular   Very Low
Star Tours – The Adventures Continue   Medium
Voyage of the Little Mermaid   Low

DISNEY'S ANIMAL KINGDOM

Animal Kingdom's FastPass+ selections are only limited by the Pandora—World of Avatar attractions. You may only book one of your FP+ selection for the Pandora rides, Avatar Flight of Passage or the Na'vi River Journey. Your other selections may be used elsewhere in the park. You also do not have to book an Avatar attraction, but we highly recommend it since these attractions are very popular.

GROUP A
Avatar Flight of Passage   Very High
Na'vi River Journey   Medium

GROUP B

The Animation Experience at Conservation Station	Low
Adventures Outpost (Character Meet)	Medium
DINOSAUR	Medium
Expedition Everest	Medium
Festival of the Lion King	Low
Finding Nemo – The Musical	Medium
It's Tough to be a Bug!	Very Low
Kali River Rapids	Low
Kilimanjaro Safaris	High
Primeval Whirl	Medium
Rivers of Light: We Are One	Medium
Up! A Great Bird Adventure	Medium

· **Magic Tips** ·

See our FastPass+ recommendations by interest and age group in our Pre-Planned Attraction Lists chapter.

KID RETURN "FASTPASS"

At times, kids will just barely miss the height requirement to ride an attraction. This can cause a lot of tears. To mend this, Disney Cast Members often carry around a "come back when you're taller" pass. This unique printed card isn't a guaranteed handout (and it's not available for every attraction), but if gifted, the child can return in the future and present the pass for their entire party to use as as FastPass!

GETTING EXTRA FASTPASSES

Guests staying in club level rooms and select 2 and 3-bedroom suites have access to purchase an additional 3 FastPass+ selections per day. Each day is $50 per guest with a minimum of 3 days. These FastPass+ selections are available for all attractions 90 days before your visit. There are no tier restrictions and you may book for multiple parks at once! Purchase these when booking your trip to maximize the benefit.

CHAPTER NINETEEN

HIDDEN MICKEY LOCATIONS

INTRODUCTION

You know that famous logo of the Mickey ears? It's just three circles, a large one for the face and two smaller ones for the ears. Well, these show up *everywhere* from the bubbles while Cinderella scrubbed the floors during her labors to a quick scene where Jasmine's pet tiger, Raja, changes briefly into a Mickey-like head. Even *Frozen* has a Mickey doll in a bookcase in one of the scenes.

But like we said, Mickey doesn't just show up in the films—he's also all over the parks. These often hard-to-spot images of him are called "Hidden Mickeys" because, well, they're hidden! Who does this? Is it on purpose? It's hard to say because Disney rarely confirms any, but our sources point to the Imagineers. Disney Imagineers are the people responsible for the creation of the rides and attractions inside and outside of the Parks. Since they make every detail from the structure to the paint, they often ensure that the Mouse leaves his mark.

But why? Think of Hidden Mickeys as a nod to Walt, the spirit of the Parks, and as a special treat for the guests. Finding Hidden Mickeys is a fun way to pass the time while waiting in the decorated queues. Discovering the Mickeys is fun for everyone of all ages—especially tweens and teens. Even if you know where one is, it's always exciting when you see one for the first time. As we've discovered, once you find one, you start seeing them everywhere! In this exciting chapter, we reveal dozens of Hidden Mickeys from the Parks to the Resort Hotels and Disney Springs!

THE MAGIC KINGDOM

1. Adventureland – Look for the Jungle Cruise sign. There are some bumps on the wood below the curve of the "J" that reveal a small Hidden Mickey.
2. Adventureland – Look for a wooden tiki near the entrance. The paint reveals a mousy shape.
3. Fantasyland – The Be Our Guest Restaurant has a few Hidden Mickeys. The first are along the walls where the corner craftwork twists together to form a Mickey Mouse head (this may be easier to spot in back of the knight armor).
4. Fantasyland – Still in the Be Our Best Restaurant, this Hidden Mickey is located at the top where the axes point between silk banners. Check out the steel on one of the axes to see a shape punctured through the middle of the blade.
5. Fantasyland – Still in the Be Our Best Restaurant, the soap suds of the Mrs. Potts and Chip mural reveal a Mickey!
6. Fantasyland – Naturally, the Cinderella Castle has a Hidden Mickey, but it's hard to see. Look near the roof canopy to see a Mickey Mouse head (it's right above a vent-looking piece).
7. Fantasyland – In the pond with the ducks and frogs during The Little Mermaid–Ariel's Undersea Adventure, look for three lily pads in the shape of Mickey's head.
8. Frontierland – Look inside of the Mercantile store to see the shapes of the ropes on the cashier wall.
9. Frontierland – In the grass near the station in Big Thunder Mountain are three gears covered in rust. They come together to make a Hidden Mickey.
10. Frontierland – Splash Mountain has a clever Hidden Mickey that's very rewarding once you find it. Look for Brer Frog and his fishing pole. The red and white bobber is an unmistakable shape.
11. Liberty Square – Check out the shape of the three charts on a wall in the Harbour House.
12. Liberty Square – Enter the Hall of Presidents to spot George Washington holding a gold sword. You might have to squint for this one, but the Hidden Mickey is located at the tip of his sword.
13. Liberty Square – There's a fancy, rustic Hidden Mickey on the hinges of the Haunted Mansion gates.
14. Main Street, U.S.A – One of our favorite Hidden Mickeys is also one of the loveliest of all. Located in Tony's Town Square restaurant, there's a bouquet of flowers near some book on a high shelf. Three red roses make the shape of a Hidden Mickey.
15. Tomorrowland – Buzz Lightyear's Space Ranger Spin ride has a couple of great Hidden Mickeys. The first is a bit hard to spot. Right after loading

onto the ride, look on the glowing wall paint to see a pile of batteries. On the left side is a Mickey Mouse-shaped head with a blue face and orange ears.

16. Tomorrowland – Another great Buzz Lightyear Space Ranger Spin Mickey is in the gift shop where the exit is. One of the monitors in the mural with the aliens has a Mickey.

17. Tomorrowland – This one is a little hard to spot. Look for a sign for the Recreational Rocket Vehicle Show on a dark blue wall. There's a moon on the sign with craters that make a Hidden Mickey.

18. Tomorrowland – The Mickey's Star Traders store naturally has a row of Hidden Mickeys. They are side-by-side, lining the walls with characters inside their portholes.

19. Tomorrowland – Stay inside Mickey's Star Traders to see the murals on the walls. One is an expressway filled with cars. The tracks make up a hidden Mickey.

20. Tomorrowland – There's another one in the same mural! Look at the satellite tower windows!

21. Tomorrowland – Yet another Hidden Mickey in Mickey's Star Traders! Look above to the front of the train painting. You'll see the sideways shape of Mickey's head in the chrome.

EPCOT

22. Canada Pavilion – Look for a spotted wooden trout in the décor of the Northwest Mercantile store. Some of its spots form a very familiar shape!

23. China Pavilion – The white posts at the entrance to China have Mickey heads carved into them.

24. France Pavilion – The painting of Vincent Van Gogh has a Hidden Mickey in the sky near his left shoulder (his left, not yours).

25. Germany Pavilion – When roaming this section, look for the clock tower in the Biergarten. There is a bell held onto the stone wall with an iron hoist. Look at the shape of the iron to reveal a Hidden Mickey.

26. Mexico Pavilion – Look for the erupting volcano in the back of the pyramid. The smoke is in a cloudy, familiar shape.
27. Morocco Pavilion – The Moroccan Souk has metal plates on the red store door. Three of them come together for that famous shape.
28. United Kingdom Pavilion – The Sportsman's Shoppe sign just outside of the door has several sports items that make a peculiar shape.
29. United States Pavilion – There's a painting called "Building a Future Together" where construction workers do their job high in the sky. The man in the center is standing on a crane. The metal hooks at his feet appear to make a Mickey Head.
30. Future World – Imagination! the ride has a small, glittery Hidden Mickey just below the dragon's mouth as he blows air. It's hard to spot as it's printed in one of the pink clouds.
31. Future World – Test Track has a couple of cool Mickeys. The first is in the queue where a few bolts on the table of tools from the shape.
32. Future World – The second Test Track Hidden Mickey we've seen is also in the queue. Look for the depiction of the artist drawing on the wall with a dry erase pen. He's recently outlined a small Mickey Head.
33. Future World – Living with the Land has one in the last fish tank on the right. It's made of mesh.
34. Future World – Living with the Land has a second Mickey in the green house. Look for the chocolate vine curling around the familiar shape.
35. Future World – The Land's Soarin' Around the World has a great Hidden Mickey that you'll never miss once you see it. During the ride there is a fireworks display right behind Epcot's Spaceship Earth. Two bursts of light come behind the globe to reveal a massive Hidden Mickey.
36. Future World – There's yet another Hidden Mickey in Soarin' Around the World. Look for three hot air balloons that come together to make a Hidden Mickey.

HOLLYWOOD STUDIOS

37. Echo Lake – Look for a Mickey Mouse-shaped piece under the lightsaber builder of the Star Tours gift shop. It's a bit hard to find, but there are black markings to make the ears look like they might have been made by laser blasts.
38. Grand Avenue – During the Muppet*Vision 3D ride, look for the 3D character changing into Mickey Mouse.
39. Grand Avenue – In the waiting area, look for a set of pressure gauges in the shape of a Mickey head.
40. Grand Avenue – On the fountain with Ms. Piggy as Lady Liberty, look for a Muppet standing on a rubber ducky with a Mickey-shaped head.
41. Grand Avenue – This is one of the trickiest to find. In the Company Store, look up to see cables on the lighting fixtures that form a Hidden Mickey with looped wire ears.
42. Sunset Boulevard – The Rock 'n' Roller Coaster Starring Aerosmith has a couple of Hidden Mickeys. The first is lead singer Steven Tyler's blouse which is covered in Mickey print.

43. Sunset Boulevard – The second from the Rock 'n' Roller Coaster is in the groovy-looking carpet. The warped swirls make out Mickey heads.

44. Sunset Boulevard – The Hollywood Tower of Terror has one located in the cobweb-covered office at the ride's exit. Look for a drawer with a Hidden Mickey popping out of it.

45. Toy Story Land – In the queue for Toy Story Mania! look for a red sign that reads "Circus Fun!" The dot of the exclamation point is a Hidden Mickey!

46. Toy Story Land – While in the queue for Alien Swirling Saucers, look at the Space Ranger control panel mural. Three buttons make a Hidden Mickey!

47. Toy Story Land – While boarding the Slink Dog Dash coaster, look for Andy's hand-drawn mural. You'll notice that one of the clouds looks very familiar.

48. Star Wars: Galaxy's Edge – The back of Docking Bay 7 Food & Cargo has a Hidden Mickey blasted into the wall. Look for three laser hits in the shape of the famous mouse!

49. Star Wars: Galaxy's Edge – In the queue for the Millennium Falcon: Smugglers Run ride, look for a monitor with Hondo Onaka giving you flight instructions. On the side of the monitor are bolts in the shape in a Hidden Mickey!

50. Star Wars: Galaxy's Edge – In the Millennium Falcon: Smugglers Run ride, look at the top of the cockpit in the center of the space to see a Hidden Mickey!

51. Star Wars: Galaxy's Edge – In Oga's Cantina, look directly at DJ R-3X's face and you'll see that his mouth and eyes look like Hidden Mickey!

ANIMAL KINGDOM

52. Africa – The flamingo island on the Kilimanjaro Safari is made to look like a Mickey head.

53. Asia – There are three very cool Hidden Mickeys around Expedition Everest. The first is in the queue for the ride where a Mickey-shaped head is behind some wires in the initial supply area.

54. Asia – Expedition Everest's second Hidden Mickey is a rustic Mickey head at the top of the pillars in the queue.

55. Asia – The third from Expedition Everest is hard to find and located near the restrooms. The posts have metal wires that look near the top to form a Mickey.

56. DinoLand U.S.A. – A few of the scales on the triceratops head on TriceraTop Spin appear to make a Hidden Mickey.

57. DinoLand U.S.A. – Look for the asteroid on Primeval Whirl (below the "The End Is Near" sign). There's a Hidden Mickey made of craters.

58. DinoLand U.S.A. – There's a blue dinosaur on the left side of Chester & Hester's Dino-Rama! sign. Look on his arm and you'll see a Hidden Mickey made up of his scales.

59. Pandora – Look at the ground in front of Windtraders to see a familiar shape in the rust.
60. Pandora – When you exit the Flight of Passage ride and head toward Windtraders, look in the tree to see a fruit in the shaped like Mickey's head!

WDW RESORT HOTELS

61. Disney's All-Star Sports Resort – Look for a Mickey head made of a baseball in the gift shop.
62. Disney's Animal Kingdom Lodge – In the grand center of the lodge, look for a Mickey in the many pieces of art. One depicts a monkey with orange and red swirls.
63. Disney's Animal Kingdom Lodge – The Jiko restaurant has carpet with cheetah spots—some that look like Mickey heads.
64. Disney's Animal Kingdom Lodge – In fact, most of the spotted flooring has Mickey heads, even in the hallways leading to the rooms and on the rugs.
65. Disney's Art of Animation – They are everywhere here! Look for one in the spots of the fish outside of the Finding Nemo building.
66. Disney's Boardwalk Inn – Mickeys decoratively appear in the wooden carvings on the TV stands in the rooms.
67. Disney's Boardwalk Inn – The lobby has a Hidden Mickey located on the floral rug.
68. Disney's Coronado Springs – In the Gran Destino Tower, look for Hidden Mickeys in the light-up pillars around the lobby.
69. Disney's Grand Floridian Resort & Spa – Look for an entire Mickey Mouse (and Minnie) in the tile work in the grand lobby.
70. Disney's Grand Floridian Resort & Spa – The M. Mouse Mercantile has a Hidden Mickey on its sign.
71. Disney's Port Orleans Resort – Look for Hidden Mickeys on the chair designs in the rooms.
72. Disney's Polynesian Village Resort – In the gift shop, look for netting filled with certain round items that make a Mickey head.
73. Disney's Yacht Club Resort – In the rooms, look for Hidden Mickeys made of knotted ropes between the boats.

DISNEY SPRINGS

74. Pin Traders – There's a large Hidden Mickey (maybe it's not-so hidden) located in the concrete just outside of this store.
75. Once Upon a Toy – Check out the build your own Mr. Potato Head section. The sandals have little Hidden Mickeys on them (there's also a Mickey Mouse hat he can wear).
76. T-Rex Café – Look for the truck in front of the sign. Inside of the truck, there is a lot of dirt—except in one area. Look closely and you'll see that the missing dirt is in fact a Hidden Mickey.

77. Tren-D – Look for a mannequin with short blonde hair. Under her left eye is a very familiar black design.

DID YOU FIND THEM ALL?

Now keep your eyes peeled around the Parks, stores, and Resort Hotels for Mickey Mouse's iconic look. There are hundreds (maybe thousands) of more Hidden Mickeys to find around the parks!

CHAPTER TWENTY

WALT DISNEY WORLD SECRETS

INTRODUCTION

We've uncovered hundreds of tips, tricks, and other insider insights to help plan your Walt Disney World vacation. In this chapter, we reveal some of the Resort's hidden secrets and history in order to expand your knowledge of the parks. These are some of Disney's best-kept secrets, so we hope you enjoy!

MAGIC KINGDOM

1. **Above All Things** – The Magic Kingdom is actually built above a secret building. Beneath the theme park are tunnels between for costumed characters and Cast Members to roam!

2. **Opening Day Tickets** – The Magic Kingdom opened on October 1st, 1971. Admission for an adult was $3.50 (for those 18 and older), $2.50 for juniors (those ages 12-17), and only $1 for a child (ages 3-11)!

3. **What's in This?** – Guests can visit City Hall on Main Street and ask for recipes and ingredients to meals served at the Magic Kingdom!

4. **Is This Code for Something?** – Visit the Main Street Railroad Station and keep your senses alert. You can hear the beeping of Morse code, but not just any code. It's the actual translated speech that Walt Disney gave when he opened Disneyland in 1955!

5. **Romantic Dinner for Two** – Also outside of Tony's Town Square Restaurant, you'll find paw prints of a couple of spaghetti-loving dogs—Lady and the Tramp!

6. **A Timely Tower** – Cinderella Castle only took about a year and a half to construct!

7. **The Golden Touch** – The dazzling spires on the castle were made with real gold!

8. **Make Her Royal** – There's a fountain behind the castle with Cinderella placed perfectly in the center. Notice the pink backdrop with a gold crown. If you position yourself just right, the crown will look placed on Cinderella's head!

9. **Watch Yer Step** – After riding Pirates of the Caribbean, look for yellow footprints as you exit the attraction. You'll see a peg-legged stamp from a pirate missing a foot!

10. **Eight-Legged Creature** – In the queue of the *Jungle Cruise*, you'll see a tarantula in a cage. If you get too close, though, you might rattle him!

11. **Stinky Streets** – The brown-colored concrete walkway through Liberty Square is designed after the colonial method for the disposing sewage. Yuck!

12. **Mr. Memory** – When the classic *Mr. Toad's Wild Ride* closed in 1998, Mr. Toad's tombstone was placed in the lawn of the *Haunted Mansion*.

13. **The Death Count** – The *Haunted Mansion* is said to be haunted by 999 ghosts—spooky!

14. **Stretching Out** – Both Disneyland and the Magic Kingdom's versions of the *Haunted Mansion* feature a stretching room. The

biggest difference is that in the Magic Kingdom, the walls pull up, and at Disneyland, the guests are lowered like an elevator.

15. **You Dropped Something** – When waiting in the queue for the *Haunted Mansion*, look for a wedding ring stuck in the pavement. It belongs to the corpse bride who haunts the mansion!

16. **Lucky 13** – The 13 Lanterns hanging from the Liberty Tree represent the 13 original colonies of the United States.

17. **Out Dated** – The numbers at the top of the buildings in Frontierland aren't street addresses. They represent a time period in which they were modeled after!

18. **Legacy Bears** – The *Country Bear Jamboree* was one of the final attractions developed by Walt Disney before he passed away.

19. **Five-Story Splash** – The total drop of *Splash Mountain* is 50 feet —or five stories!

20. **Wait for Longer** – *Splash Mountain's* line grows longer in the heat, but it's worth the wait. At nearly 11-minutes in length, Splash Mountain is one of Walt Disney World's longest attractions (*Space Mountain* runs only 2.5 minutes)!

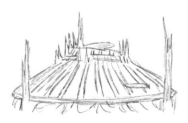

21. **Experimental Prototype PeopleMover of Tomorrow** – The *PeopleMover* was originally designed by Disney to fit in Epcot. This, of course, was during the days when Epcot also had a real neighborhood where residents could use the *PeopleMover* to go

everywhere from the theme parks to the grocery store and back home!

22. **Million Mover** – About half of the people who visit the Magic Kingdom ride the *PeopleMover* attraction!

EPCOT

23. **Home Is Where the Golf Ball Is** – Walt Disney's original concept for Epcot was an actual town where thousands of people could live. They would shop, work, and also travel by monorail and the *PeopleMover*!

24. **When It Rains...** – To keep the giant orb dry, *Spaceship Earth* was built with a special drainage system. Therefore when it rains, the water funnels through the system and eventually runs into the lagoon!

25. **Twin Parks** – Future World and World Showcase act as two different theme parks—though you only need one admission ticket to access both! Future World has an entrance near Spaceship Earth and World Showcase's entrance is between the France and United Kingdom pavilions. Both sides of Epcot often open and close at different times with Future World available in the early morning and World Showcase in the later morning.Guests staying at the Walt Disney World Resort will also notice Extra Magic Hours that are different for Future World and World Showcase!

26. **Now That's a Lot of Fish!** – *The Aquarium of the Seas* is the second largest aquarium in the United States!

27. **Ride-Sized** – With its 5.7 million gallons of water, *The Aquarium of the Seas* is big enough to hold all of *Spaceship Earth*!

28. **A Popular Innovation** – After opening in 1999, *Test Track* was so popular that it became one of Disney's first attractions to be issued a Single Rider Line! *Test Track* is an ideal attraction for single riders since its odd number of seats per rows (three with a total of six riders per car) would otherwise not be fully filled!

29. **Free Drink!** – Walking around Epcot might work up a thirst! To quench this, head over to Club Cool where Coca Cola beverages from around the world are available to sample for free!

30. **Rush Hour** – The walkways in the China pavilion were designed close together so that crowds cluster like in Beijing!

31. **Northern Influence** – The huge troll statue in The Puffin's Roost store in the Norway Pavilion was inspired by the statues found in Voss, Norway!

32. **The Next Chapter** – Instead of a retelling of the *Frozen* film, Imagineers decided to tell a continuation story involving beloved characters like Elsa, Anna, and Olaf. In *Frozen Ever After's* storyline, Elsa uses her magic to bring a snow day during summer!

33. **Get It Strait** – Between the France and Morocco pavilions, there is a section of pavement that becomes gradually darker. This area represents the Strait of Gibraltar, a body of water that separates Europe from Africa!

34. **United Nations** – What are some of the countries that may be added? Spain, Israel, and Equatorial Africa were announced to join, but never came to be. Brazil has been rumored to be Epcot's next added country!

HOLLYWOOD

35. **Mickey to the Rescue!** – The Crossroads of the World tower at the park's entrance has a metal Mickey Mouse on top that works as a lightning rod—just in case!

36. **Good Boy (and Girl)** – There are two foo dog statues outside of the Chinese Theater (these look like small lions). The right is a male dog and the left is a female. How do we know? Well, the female dog has a pup under her paw while the male has an orb!

37. **Inside Was Out** – The *Rock 'n' Roller Coaster* was first built outside before having the building constructed around it! Some guests also have photos of the former outdoor coaster before the walls went up!

38. **Second Choice** – Though Aerosmith received a big welcome for their placement on the *Rock 'n' Roller Coaster*, Disney originally wanted U2. Eventually the band declined and so Aerosmith was asked—we prefer Aerosmith anyway!

39. **Plates of Vanity** – The cars for the *Rock 'n' Roller Coaster* are shaped like limos. Check out the funny sayings on their license plates before you ride!

40. **Matching Plates** – The car you get chooses the song. For instance, the limo coaster with the "2FAST4U" plays "Sweet Emotion" and "UGOBABE" plays "Walk This Way" and "Love in an Elevator."

41. **The Same Scream** – From below the Tower of Terror, you'll hear guests screaming as they plummet. Much of the sound that you're hearing is actually "canned," meaning Disney uses pre-recorded sound effects to make your hair stand on end.

42. **Stay Tuned!** – When designing the Hollywood Tower Hotel, Imagineers watched over 150 episodes of "The Twilight Zone" to get ideas for the attraction.

43. **Always Halloween** – In true "Twilight Zone" fashion, the Hollywood Tower Hotel ride dates October 31st, 1939!

44. **A Dubbing Recast** – Since Rod Serling passed away in 1975, nearly 20 years before the ride opened, voice actor Mark Silverman dubbed over the clips. Rod Serling's widow, Carol Serling, was heavily involved in the casting process for her husband's iconic voice.

45. **Icon-neck** – Echo Lake's famous prehistoric resident, Gertie the Dinosaur, is based on the world's first keyframe animation. The cartoon clip was first released in 1914!

46. **Star Traders** – Like in the *Star Wars* films, Jawas will trade you for interesting objects! When you meet one, offer it a pen or a Disney pin and get something cool in return!

47. **Mouseketeer in Here** – In the waiting area for Muppet*Vision 3D, look for a hanging net with Jell-O cubes. This is a nod to the late Annette Funicello from the Mickey Mouse Club (a net full of Jell-O)!

48. **Muppet in Training** – Sweetums comes to life during the Muppet*Vision 3D show. The Cast Members playing him go through a lot of schooling from muppeteers to get the movements just right!

49. **LEGO-Foot** – Toy Story Land has over 400 toy blocks scattered around it!

50. **The Forbidden Instrument** – Andy's crayons line the walkways of *Toy Story Mania*. Most of them have dull or partly dull heads. Only one goes unused—pink!

51. **Robots Say What?** – While Star Wars: Galaxy's Edge takes place on the fictional planet of Batuu, the trading outpost is known as Black Spire Outpost. This name was first mentioned in the Star Wars film, Solo, by Lando's robot, L3.

52. **Mini-lennium Falcon** – There's a smaller version of the Millennium Falcon built into the actual ship. It's a bit hard to describe its exact location, but it's on the bottom of the cockpit beneath an oil-greased bar. Can you spot it?

53. **Crash Site** – At the Toy Story Land entrance to Galaxy's Edge, look for a crater with some spaceship parts. While many people believe that this is the crash site of Oga Cantina's DJ R-3X, it's actually one of a probe droid (which can be found in a net near the restrooms in back of Droid Depot).

ANIMAL KINGDOM

54. **Mickey to the Rescue!** – The Crossroads of the World tower at the park's entrance has a metal Mickey Mouse on top that works as a lightning rod—just in case!

55. **Moldy Steps** – To create an authentic feel of Asia, Africa, and also the ancient past, Disney's Imagineers made molds of actual

ground in foreign countries. They then used these molds to print the pavement all over Animal Kingdom!

56. **Plant Planet** – Animal Kingdom is home to over 4 million species of plants from all around the world!

57. **A Mountain of Stone** – Animal Kingdom's natural look goes beyond plants and animals. The rocks give the park the rough and wild edge of the wilderness. There's more than double the stone in Animal Kingdom than in all of Mount Rushmore sculptures!

58. **Lion King Is Cool** – To get the lions to hangout on Pride Rock (and in public view), the rock has air conditioning to keep the cats cool.

59. **Memories Above** – While the Forbidden Mountain is the most striking landmark in Animal Kingdom's Asia, the many colorful square flags easily catch the eye. You'll notice them strung from above and even on the *Expedition Everest* roller coaster—but what are they? These are prayer flags, based on the Himalayan culture in India. Each waving flag is said to bring good fortune as the wind blows. The flags in Animal Kingdom are printed with animals and other designs that don't have as much meaning.

60. **What's in a Name?** – The *Dinosaur* ride was originally named, *Countdown to Extinction*. However, after initial tests, the ride was deemed too scary. Instead, Disney re-themed it to *Dinosaur* after the kid-friendly CGI film of the same name.

61. **Eastern Influence** – Imagineers used the Wulingyuan historical site in China as inspiration for Pandora. The green-topped mountains in Wulingyuan appear to float when dense fog crawls between them!

Want more secrets? Check out our Walt Disney World Secrets book, filled with over 650 secrets, facts, and hidden knowledge!
www.magicguidebooks.com/secrets

CHAPTER TWENTY-ONE

UNIVERSAL STUDIOS
ORLANDO

INTRODUCTION

If you're planning an extended stay at the Walt Disney World Resort, we highly recommend visiting the Universal Studios Orlando Resort. With three world-class theme parks, Universal Studios Florida, Universal's Islands of Adventure, and the new water park, Volcano Bay, there is plenty to do. Even if you just have one extra day to spend at Universal, we highly recommend

getting a park-to-park ticket to see the Harry Potter attractions at both parks. In other words, there is plenty of magic to experience outside of Disney!

In this chapter, we review Universal Studios Orlando from the rides to the shows and also our choice dining spots!

TRAVELING TO UNIVERSAL

There are many ways to visit Universal Orlando from the Walt Disney World Resort or anywhere else in Orlando. While WDW doesn't offer transport to Universal, many other hotels do.

Shuttle – Staying outside of the WDW? Check with your hotel about their shuttle services that might take you for free to Universal for the day!

Ride Share – We prefer using Lyft to get to Universal Orlando. This way, we can go and return as we choose fairly inexpensively. Rides start around $20 each way for a standard car and it takes about 30 minutes to drive there.

Rental or Your Own Car – You can also drive to Universal Studios yourself and pay $25 for the entire day to park.

WHICH PARK SHOULD I VISIT?

If you can't decide which park to visit, we *highly* recommend both— especially if you are only visiting for one day! The Harry Potter attractions are in both parks (Hogsmeade Village is in Islands of Adventure and Diagon Alley is in Universal Studios Florida) and you can only ride the Hogwarts Express if you have a park-to-park ticket, which connects the two theme parks by a gentle and fun Harry Potter-themed train! Though Hogsmeade is stunning and home to many more rides, Diagon Alley is somehow even more breathtaking. You'll magically enter the area—we won't tell you how, as it's a surprise for when you get there—and visit shops, dark back alleys, and Gringotts bank. The centerpiece of Diagon Alley is a life-size fire-breathing dragon. Yes, *real* fire!

Universal Studios Florida uses a lot of motion simulation for its rides while Islands of Adventure sticks mostly to immersive dark rides and roller coasters. If you get motion sickness from motion simulation rides like Star Tours, you might want to skip Universal Studios and just to Islands of Adventure. Overall, we believe that Islands of Adventure is one of the best Theme Parks is the world. The immersive lands and unique rides will impress any theme park fan!

UNIVERSAL STUDIOS FLORIDA

In 1986, after the success of Universal Studios Hollywood and Walt Disney World, Universal broke ground on a new world-class theme park. Utilizing Florida's warm, tropical weather and abundance of land, the movie studio, along with co-founder, Steven Spielberg, began designing attractions for a new set of tourists. While its Hollywood sister park brought guests inside actual film studios, Universal Studios Florida would focus on "riding the movies." The park feels like you're stepping into a Hollywood studio backlot before you plunge into worlds like Springfield from the Simpsons and the super-popular Diagon Alley from Harry Potter.

RIDES

DESPICABLE ME MINION MAYHEM
Description: A motion simulation ride with moving seats that follows characters of the Despicable Me film series.
Type: Motion Simulation Ride
Perfect for: Kids, Tweens, Family
Height Restriction: 40"
Review: This ride is a lot of fun with its comedy and large screen surprises. Even if you're not a fan of Despicable Me, put this zany attraction on your list.

SHREK 4-D
Description: A 4D theater show starring the characters from the Shrek franchise.
Type: 3D Theater Show (with "4D" effects)
Perfect for: Kids, Tweens, Family
Height Restriction: None
Review: Children 12 and under will likely enjoy this attraction very much. Filled with hilarious characters and 3D effects, Shrek gives lots of enjoyment. Adults and Teens may find the attraction a little too silly and wish for more. However, the 4D effects like water spritzes and moving seats keep everyone on their toes.

Note: Non-moving seats are available on Shrek 4-D.

HOLLYWOOD RIP RIDE ROCKIT
Description: A high-speed steel roller coaster set to your choice of music.
Perfect for: Thrill Riders
Height Restriction: 51" minimum and 79" maximum
Review: The Rip Ride Rockit has a very cool feature of selecting your own soundtrack. Pick from around 30 different songs from pop and rock to country and dance before you ride. Then you'll soar over 16 stories in the sky before dropping nearly straight down at up to 65 miles per hour.

TRANSFORMERS: THE RIDE-3D
Description: An explosive, 3D motion simulation ride starring the robots from Transformers.
Perfect for: Kids, Tweens, Teens, Adults, Thrill Riders
Height Restriction: 40"
Review: Battle the Decepticons in a city as you ride along with the Autobots. The ride is very similar to The Amazing Adventures of Spider-Man ride at Islands of Adventure. Though Transformers has much crisper and newer special effects and action sequences.

REVENGE OF THE MUMMY
Description: An Egyptian-themed indoor roller coaster.
Perfect for: Tweens, Teens, Adults, Thrill Riders
Height Restriction: 48"
Review: Face everything from darkness to pyrotechnic effects as you face the wrath of an ancient mummy. This lengthy roller coaster moves through several rooms before reaching 45 miles per hour just before the climax.

FAST AND FURIOUS: SUPERCHARGED
Description: A 3D high-speed race simulator starring the characters from the Fast and Furious franchise.

Perfect for: Kids, Tweens, Teens, Adults, Thrill Riders
Height Restriction: TBA
Review: This action-packed ride includes concept cars, an original storyline from Fast and the Furious, and 3D motion simulation and additional "4D" effects.

RACE THROUGH NEW YORK STARRING JIMMY FALLON
Description: 3-D Motion Simulator
Perfect for: Kids, Tweens, Teens, Adults
Height Restriction: 40"
Review: Enter a façade of NBC's New York building and race through New York City along with Tonight Show host, Jimmy Fallon. The ride is set up theatre style with a large screen in front. It's a little bit cheesy with the jokes, but tweens and fans of Jimmy Fallon will enjoy this ride the most.

MEN IN BLACK: ALIEN ATTACK
Description: A laser-guided shooting ride.
Perfect for: Young Kids, Kids, Tweens, Teens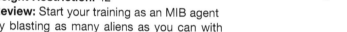
Height Restriction: 42"
Review: Start your training as an MIB agent by blasting as many aliens as you can with your laser gun.

THE SIMPSONS RIDE
Description: Motion simulation ride starring characters from The Simpsons.
Perfect for: Tweens, Teens, Adults
Height Restriction: 40"
Review: One of the funniest rides ever, The Simpsons delivers edgy, top-quality amusement. Join Homer, Bart, Marge, Lisa, Maggie, Grampa, and the rest of Springfield as Sideshow Bob threatens to destroy Krustyland.

KANG AND KODOS' TWIRL' 'N' HURL
Description: A spinning kids' ride starring aliens from The Simpsons.
Perfect for: Young Kids and Kids
Height Restriction: None
Review: The Simpsons meets Dumbo the Flying Elephant ride in this classic spin-around kiddie attraction. Despite the ride's name, this attraction is rather slow-paced and aimed at families with young kids.

E.T. ADVENTURE

Description: Ride flying bikes to help save E. T. and his home planet.
Perfect for: Families
Height Restriction: None
Review: The magic of E. T. is brought to life with animatronics and also sends you soaring on a flying bicycle. If you've experienced Peter Pan's Flight at Disney, it's a bit like that. While we enjoy E.T., you'll either love the nostalgia of the ride or wish that Universal will tear E.T. down to make room for an updated attraction.

WOODY WOODPECKER NUTHOUSE COASTER

Description: An outdoor "junior coaster" designed for families with kids.
Perfect for: Families
Height Restriction: None
Review: Ride around on Woody Woodpecker's train coaster. It's slow-paced and a lot of fun for kids looking for something thrilling for them to experience.

SHOWS

FEAR FACTOR LIVE

Description: An audience interactive stunt show
Perfect for: Thrill Riders who want to participate
Length: 20 min
Review: Fear Factor Live allows visitors to audition for various stunts like jumping over cars and reaching into a tank of live eels. While it may be fun for participants to watch, audience members are often bored and unamused by the flat jokes and dull stunts. When a winner is crowned, everyone is ready for the show to be over already.

ANIMAL ACTORS ON LOCATION!

Description: A stage show starring talented animals
Perfect for: Families
Length: 20 Minutes
Review: Live animals take over a stage and show audiences their natural talents. There are tons of laughs for families with kids. Watch birds soar, dogs perform tricks, and maybe also hear a pig snort. At the end of the show, the animal trainers may allow audience members to pet some of the animals.

A DAY IN THE PARK WITH BARNEY

Description: A stage show starring Barney the purple dinosaur
Perfect for: Young Kids
Length: 30 Minutes
Review: Barney and his friends sing songs and play games in a stage designed like a happy park. Young kids will love singing along and the silly fun. After the show, kids can play with Barney on an outdoor playground.

UNIVERSAL ORLANDO'S CINEMATIC CELEBRATION

Description: A fantastic nighttime water show with special effects and characters from *Jurassic World*, *Harry Potter*, *Despicable Me* and more.
Perfect for: Everyone
Review: This stunning, 20-minute water show brings movies alive with music and projections on water fountains in the center lagoon. Scenes from popular film franchises are projected onto the water with music and colors. This effect looks a bit like the Bellagio Fountains in Las Vegas or the World of Color show at the Disneyland Resort in California. Cinematic Celebration brings to life the best experiences in the parks with thrilling *Harry Potter* sequences, hilarious *Despicable Me* vignettes, and a roaring *Jurassic Park* segment. We highly recommend planning this show as a conclusion to your day.

> **· Magic Tips ·**
>
> Showtimes vary throughout the year and depend on park hours and sunset times. We recommend showing up at least 40 minutes before showtime for a better view of the water features. The key is to sit back far enough in the seating section to see all of the projections around the theme park, but close enough for the best view of the water features. The best viewings are in the center of the tiered seating area, but the show can be viewed from anywhere around the lagoon.

MORE ATTRACTIONS

FIEVEL'S PLAYLAND

Shrink down to enjoy massive scenery and water fun designed by the *An American Tail* and *Fievel Goes West* animated films. Kids might not know the stories, but they'll love the water slide!

CURIOUS GEORGE GOES TO TOWN

A brightly colored playground straight out of the Curious George book series. It's famous for splash areas and things to climb. Perfect for parents who need a break and kids who have a lot of energy.

HORROR MAKE-UP SHOW

Horror movies come to life in this unique Hollywood make-up show. Where there are more laughs than screams, audience members will love the informative make-up effects and creepy monsters that arise from them. It may be too scary for young kids.

DIAGON ALLEY
THE WIZARDING WORLD OF HARRY POTTER

RIDES

HARRY POTTER & THE ESCAPE FROM GRINGOTTS

Description: A 3-D steel roller coaster starring characters from the Harry Potter film series
Perfect for: Kids, Tweens, Teens, Adults, Thrill Riders
Height Restriction: 42"
Review: Enter the cavernous vaults of Gringotts bank and ride an enchanted mine cart as you face Lord Voldemort and his Death Eaters. The visuals are stunning from the elevator that takes your deep into the depths of the bank to the cave-like start of the coaster. 3D glasses add to the magic as magical creatures and dark wizards attack, unleashing fury until Harry Potter arrives to save the day! Escape from Gringotts is a great first ride, even from the details in the queue. While Thrill Riders will wish the coaster was a bit more intense, families with children will find the speed just right.

HOGWARTS EXPRESS

Description: A steam engine train that takes visitors from Universal Orlando to Islands of Adventure

Perfect for: Everyone

Required: A Park-to-Park admission ticket

Review: Zip through the wall of Platform 9 ¾ to board the Hogwarts Express. You'll see famous characters from Harry Potter outside the window and face danger in this slow moving, yet exciting attraction. We highly recommend this ride for every Harry Potter fan. Since the train links both parks, you will need a Park-to-Park admission in order to ride.

SHOWS

OLLIVANDERS

Description: A brief show where the wand chooses the wizard

Perfect for: Harry Potter fans of all ages

Review: Located next to the famous Ollivanders—where Harry Potter gets his wand—this show isn't to be missed by any Wizarding World fan. Garrick Ollivander, or one of his assistants, chooses one lucky person to discover their wand. Sadly, you don't get to keep the wands, but they are available for purchase in the next room.

> **· Magic Tips ·**
>
> There isn't a precise way to get chosen for Ollivanders, but from what we've noticed, participants usually near the front and to his right get chosen. Though there are always exceptions, he mostly chooses someone under the age of 21 and above the age of 8.

ISLANDS OF ADVENTURE

Universal Studios Florida continued its legacy of world-class entertainment when it broke ground in May 1999 with Islands of Adventure. The theme is a set of eight islands placed across a massive lagoon. All pulling from popular franchises like Harry Potter, Jurassic Park, Marvel Comics, and Dr. Seuss, every island is captivating. While Universal Studios makes you feel immersed in a Hollywood backlot, Islands of Adventure brings fictional worlds to life. Jurassic Park Island is filled with palm trees and dinos while Hogsmeade Village plunges guests into the magical, snow-covered world of Harry Potter.

RIDES

THE INCREDIBLE HULK
Description: A fast-launching steel roller coaster with loops.
Type: Roller Coaster
Perfect for: Thrill Riders
Height Restriction: 54"
Review: The Incredible Hulk roller coaster has been revamped in 2016 to include a new storyline and special effects. Prepare for 7 loops, high speeds, and a lot of thrilling fun! In our opinion, The Hulk Coaster is one of the best.

Note: The Incredible Hulk does not permit loose items such as hats, sunglasses, or cell phones in pockets. A metal detector scans guests before riding, so make sure you put these items in a free locker near the roller coaster before riding.

STORM FORCE ACCELATRON
Description: A spinning ride similar to Disney's tea cups.
Perfect for: Kids, Tweens
Height Restriction: None
Review: Battle Magneto alongside Storm from X-men. Designed like the spinning Tea Cups at The Magic Kingdom, Storm Force is dizzying fun for families with kids—and strong stomachs. The cups

spin as fast as you turn the wheel, so you're in control of how dizzy you want to feel.

THE AMAZING ADVENTURES OF SPIDER-MAN
Description: A 3-D motion simulation ride with a moving car.
Perfect for: Kids, Tweens, Teens, Adults, Thrill Riders
Height Restriction: 40"
Review: Grab your 3D glasses for this motion simulator based around the many of adventures of Spider-Man. Combat villains like Dr. Octopus and Hobgoblin as you race through New York City. This ride is great fun for everyone with its unique style of large screens and a moving vehicle—only the Transformers ride feels similar. Families will leave Spider-Man's ride with a smile.

DR. DOOM'S FALL
Description: An 18-story freefall ride.
Perfect for: Thrill Riders
Height Restriction: 52"
Review: Calm your nerves before facing Dr. Doom's revenge for you and The Fantastic Four. Smoke, lights, and a massive drop will make any heart race! At least while you're at the top, there's an amazing view of the park. But what goes up must come down. We only recommend this scary ride for Thrill Riders.

THE CAT IN THE HAT
Description: A slow-paced ride starring The Cat in the Hat.
Type: Dark Ride
Perfect for: Kids
Height Restriction: 36"
Review: Hop aboard a slow-moving car that takes you through the storyline of The Cat in the Hat. Families with kids under 10 will love the colorful scenes and crazy animatronics. Actually, any Dr. Seuss fan will find this ride completely charming.

THE HIGH IN THE SKY SEUESS TROLLEY TRAIN RIDE
Description: A slow-moving train that winds around Seuss Landing.
Perfect for: Families
Height Restriction: 40"

Review: Travel over the low buildings of Seuss Landing on this vivid train. It's a nice time if you'll looking for a break, as the lines are rarely long.

CARO-SEUSS-EL
Description: A Dr. Seuss-themed carousel
Perfect for: Young Kids
Height Restriction: None
Review: Hop on bobbing yaks, elephants, and other Seuss-drawn creatures. Another well-detailed ride designed for families with young kids.

ONE FISH, TWO FISH, RED FISH, BLUE FISH
Description: A fish-themed ride like Dumbo the Flying Elephant at Disneyland and the Magic Kingdom
Perfect for: Young Kids and Kids
Height Restriction: None
Review: Gently soar about the water on your choice of primary-colored fish. Control how high—or how low—your fish goes! Young kids will especially love this attraction.

POPEYE AND BLUTO'S BILGE-RAT BARGES
Description: A water rapids raft ride with the characters from Popeye cartoons
Type: River rapids raft ride
Perfect for: Kids, Tweens, Teens, Adults
Height Restriction: 42"
Car: 12 riders per raft with seats in pairs of 2
Review: Rush down a raging rapid on rafts as Popeye and Bluto battle for Olive Oyl's attention. This is one of the best rapid rides we've ever experienced with its comical humor and cartoon design. You will get wet and you may get soaked! Prepare for laughs and sopping clothes.

DUDLEY DO-RIGHT'S RIPSAW FALLS
Description: A log water ride starring characters from Rocky and Bullwinkle's Dudley Do-Right cartoon
Perfect for: Kids, Tweens, Teens, Adults
Height Restriction: 44"
Review: Journey through the wacky tale of Canada's cartoon Mountie on a log raft fit for 5. At the end, you'll plunge down a 7 story waterfall. We love Dudley Do-Right's Ripsaw Falls for the beautiful decorations, comedy, and excellently made water ride. This attraction is especially popular in the summer, so visit just before

noon to avoid the longer lines. You will get wet, but likely not nearly as soaked as Popeye and Bluto's Bilge-Rat Barges.

Note: If you're worried about your belongings getting soaked on the water rides, store them in a free locker near the queues.

SKULL INSLAND: REIGN OF KONG
Description: A 3D journey into the island ruled by the giant gorilla, King Kong
Type: 3D simulation ride
Perfect for: Tweens, Teens, and Adults
Height Restriction: 36"
Review: Step into a dark, forbidden temple that houses a fierce, massive gorilla. A safari truck takes you into Kong's world where dinosaurs and massive spiders might attack at any moment. The ride is divided into segments including a 360 3-D screen that domes over the caravan. In the queue, there are a few spooky surprises as well. At the end, prepare to face Kong himself. This ride may be too terrifying for young kids.

JURASSIC PARK RIVER ADVENTURE
Description: A water-based boat ride with dinosaurs and an 85-foot drop
Type: Boat ride
Perfect for: Thrill Riders
Height Restriction: 42"
Review: A ride that begins with gentle, animatronic giants ends up just like the movies with attacking carnivores. Drift calmly at first until the raptors and T-Rex show their teeth, then get ready for the big, 8-story fall! You'll likely get wet, but it'll be worth it because Jurassic Park River Adventure is one of the best rides in Islands of Adventure!

PTERANODON FLYERS
Description: High-flying kids' gliders on a track
Type: Glider coaster
Perfect for: Thrill Riders
Height Restriction: 36" minimum and 56" maximum. Since this attraction is designed for kids, adults must have a child between 36" and 48" with them to ride.
Review: Kids soar around Jurassic Park island on these high-up tracked gliders. This ride's loading system is a bit slow, so lines often back up. Luckily, Universal started a Virtual Line for this attraction. A

kiosk in front of the ride distributes return times so your kids can have fun in the playground instead of waiting in a long line!

SHOWS

POSEIDON'S FURY
Description: A special effects theatre show in a cave.
Perfect for: Kids, Tweens, and Teens
Length: 15 minutes
Review: The Olympian God, Poseidon, unleashes his aquatic wrath on all those who intrude his ruins. Hokey comedy and special effects make this show a cool first watch. Kids and tweens will likely love it and teens will find it fine.

RAPTOR ENCOUNTER
Description: Photo opportunity a Velociraptor.
Perfect for: Everyone
Length: 5 minutes
Review: Meet "Blue" the Velociraptor from the Jurassic World film series. This giant costumed character can be a bit intimidating for younger kids. Still, brave kids will love to take photos with her!

HOGSMEADE VILLAGE
THE WIZARDING WORLD OF HARRY POTTER

RIDES

HAGRID'S MAGICAL CREATURES MOTORBIKE ADVENTURE
Description: Wind through the Forbidden Forest on this story-based rollercoaster with cinematic scenes, animatronic magical creatures, and beautiful forested scenery.
Type: Roller coaster
Perfect for: Kids, Tweens, Teens, Adults, Thrill Riders
Height Restriction: 48" (122 cm)
Car: 2 riders per row with motorbike and sidecar seats
Single Rider Available
Review: Hagrid's Magical Creatures Motorbike Adventure is a nearly 3-minute long journey of fantastic Harry Potter storytelling. There are animatronics, stop-and-go zips, and also surprising drops! Riders sit

side by side on a motorbike-style coaster with side car or bike seat options. Each seat provides a different experience. The driver's seat has a thrilling motorbike feel while the sidecar is similar to a classic roller coaster (though larger riders will feel more comfortable with the less-cramped driver's seat). You may have to wait a while for this coaster, but it's well worth your time!

· **Magic Tips** ·

1,000 trees were planted to create the Forbidden Forest that surrounds Hagrid's Motorbike Adventure! There are also several Harry Potter-related surprises within the queue that you won't want to miss!

If the line for this coaster is too long, opt for the Single Rider entrance!

HARRY POTTER AND THE FORBIDDEN JOURNEY

Description: An adventure ride starring the characters of the Harry Potter films.

Type: Simulation dark ride

Perfect for: Kids, Tweens, Teens, and Adults

Height Restriction: 48"

Review: Enter the magnificent Hogwarts castle and meet Harry Potter characters in the various rooms. Look for enchanted portraits, magic spells, a winding garden, and stunning artwork. The queue is just as entertaining as the ride. You'll fly through Hogwarts to encounter a game of Quidditch, a run-away dragon, spitting spiders, and soul-sucking Dementors. Harry Potter and the Forbidden Journey is one of the most unique rides in the world, and not to be missed!

Note: If you're worried about your comfort on Harry Potter and the Forbidden Journey, a test seat is available before the queue. Also, those with motion sickness may feel it the most on this attraction.

FLIGHT OF THE HIPPOGRIFF
Description: An outdoor, family-friendly roller coaster.
Type: Junior Roller coaster
Perfect for: Young Kids, Kids, Tweens
Height Restriction: 36"
Review: A hippogriff is half eagle, half horse and very snappy. Hagrid, the groundskeeper at Hogwarts castle, once had a hippogriff named Buckbeak who befriends Harry Potter. This ride revolves around that creature. Flight of the Hippogriff is a perfectly gentle introductory roller coaster for kids who need a stepping stone to the bigger coasters. Though the ride is just over a minute in length and fun for the whole family. The seats on this ride are designed for kids, so taller and larger guests may not fit comfortably in the seats. Unfortunately, Flight of the Hippogriff does not offer a test seat.

VOLCANO BAY

Looking for another water park outside of Disney? Volcano Bay is the newest and greatest family-friendly aquatic theme park to hit Orlando! Based around a towering volcano, this tropical theme park offers everything from gentle pools to extreme water slides! Adults can ride with the kids or sip cocktails on lounge chairs. Meanwhile, kids of all ages will wear themselves out riding all of the popular slides throughout the park. Even better is Volcano Bay's "queue-less" line system. Guests receive a free water-proof wristband pager for the most popular

slides and only go when pinged. Then you can select another attraction from your wristband to try after you ride!

CHOICE CITYWALK DINING

Within walking distance of the parks is Universal CityWalk. Designed like a mall focused on entertainment and dining experiences, CityWalk delivers some tasty bites! In this section, discover our most-recommended dining locations for food and ambience.

ANTOJITOS AUTHENTIC MEXICAN FOOD
Price: $$ – $$$ / **Type:** Table Service / **Open:** Lunch and Dinner
Description: Mexican dining with live music.
Review: Antojitos is certainly one of the better restaurants in Universal Orlando. We love the south of the border ambiance with colorful décor, friendly staff, and mariachi music playing around the restaurant.
Menu Overview: chips and guacamole, nachos, beans, quesadillas, taco salad, enchiladas, fajitas, tacos, carnitas, burritos, chimichangas, tortilla soup, margaritas, tequila, cocktails, soda — *Kids:* tacos, quesadillas, empanadas, grilled chicken breast
Recommendations: Chimichanga, Fajitas, Margarita (21+)

BUBBA GUMP SHRIMP CO.
Price: $$ / **Type:** Table Service / **Open:** Lunch and Dinner
Description: Forest Gump themed seafood and American dining.
Review: This restaurant from *Forest Gump* comes to life with some very delicious fried seafood and American favorites! Prepare for your waiter to ask you Forest Gump trivia—it's a lot of fun, even if you haven't seen the movie in years.
Menu Overview: burger, shrimp, salad, clam chowder, sandwiches, fried chicken, cocktails, beer, wine, soda — *Kids:* hamburger, hot dog, chicken fingers
Recommendations: Shrimpers Heaven, Mama's Southern Fried

THE COWFISH
Price: $$–$$$ / **Type:** Table Service / **Open:** Lunch and Dinner
Description: A clever name! The Cow stands for burgers and the Fish stands for sushi. Grab either at this trendy dining joint.

Review: Cowfish is sort of genius because there's something for everyone. The sushi lovers will get their fill and those just craving a great burger will feel satisfied. Known for decent size portions in this multi-level building, you'll certainly get your fill. We love sushi and burgers, but their signature Burgushi—where the mix sushi and hamburgers—sounded strange. However, the rolls were extremely delicious and a must try. Even if you don't like sushi, the Burgushi's powerful blend will be tasty (and, don't worry, they skip the seaweed).

Menu Overview: Sushi, burgers, salads, calamari, edamame, sandwiches, cocktails, wine, beer, shakes, soda, desserts

Recommendations: The All-American Bacon Double Cheeseburgooshi

BIGFIRE

Price: $$$ / **Type:** Table Service / **Open:** Dinner

Description: American favorites cooked over a massive wood-burning fire.

Review: A fun concept for diners looking for something a little different. Get steaks, burgers, and more cooked over a giant "bigfire" grill in the restaurant. Each meal is placed on a piece of wood—cherry, pecan, and oak—to give added flavor to the dish being cooked. The menu is a bit like one you'd find at a steakhouse, but the theatrics of the big fire make it something much more fun.

Menu Overview: Steaks, seafood, fried chicken, burgers, fish, lamb chops, salads, desserts, wine, beer, sodas

Kids: chicken fingers, sliders, mac and cheese, steak, chicken and beef skewers, juice, chocolate milk, milk, root beer

Recommendation: steak, bison burger, s'mores (dessert), Smoked Smoked Maple (sweet Bourbon for 21+)

CHAPTER TWENTY-TWO

PRE-PLANNED ATTRACTION LISTS

INTRODUCTION

With so many choices of things to do in Walt Disney World, it's impossible to get everything done in one day without a plan. However, with our pre-made ride and attraction lists, you can enjoy the very best that WDW has to offer. These are proven to work using multiple tests, and we recommend following one of these in order to save yourself the hassle of hustling through enormous crowds. That's right, these pre-made lists work on even the busiest days!

TIME-SAVING TIPS

1. Choose one of our pre-made ride and attraction lists to follow.
2. Book any recommended FastPass+ selections (we recommend 60 days before). Make sure that these selections begin around 30-60 minutes after the Park opens. If the Park has earlier Extra Magic Hours, then you can book in the first time slots.
3. Pre-Book any dining reservations (up to 180 days in advance).
4. Get to the Park before it opens.
5. Grab a map at the entrance to help guide you around.
6. Prepare to take a break when you need to in between rides.
7. Your FastPass+ choice may not sync with our suggested time. You may have to switch a ride placement if this happens.
8. Don't rush. Keep calm, enjoy the sights, and take in the magical feelings on your unforgettable vacation!

MUST-SEE ATTRACTIONS

THE MAGIC KINGDOM
MUST-SEE ATTRACTIONS PLAN

FP : **Make these your FastPass+ Selections**

1. **Magic Kingdom Welcome Show** (Cinderella Castle)
2. **Peter Pan's Flight** (Fantasyland)
3. **"it's a small world"** (Fantasyland)
4. **The Haunted Mansion** (Liberty Square)
5. **Seven Dwarfs Mine Train** *FP* (Fantasyland)
6. **Mad Tea Party** (Fantasyland)
7. **Pirates of the Caribbean** *FP* (Adventureland)
8. **Swiss Family Treehouse** (Adventureland)
9. **Transit Authority PeopleMover** (Tomorrowland)
10. **Space Mountain** *FP* (Tomorrowland)

LUNCH: Be Our Guest Restaurant or Liberty Tree Tavern

11. **Under the Sea~Journey of the Little Mermaid** (Fantasyland)
12. **Walt Disney World Railroad** (Fantasyland to Frontierland)
13. **Big Thunder Mountain Railroad*** (Frontierland)
14. **Splash Mountain** (Frontierland)
15. **Jungle Cruise*** (Adventureland)
16. **Magic Kingdom Fireworks** (Main Street, U.S.A.)

BONUS (OR SUBSTITUTIONS)
17. **The Many Adventures of Winnie the Pooh** (Fantasyland)
18. **Dumbo the Flying Elephant** (Fantasyland)
19. **Buzz Lightyear's Space Ranger Spin** (Tomorrowland)
20. **The Barnstormer** (Fantasyland)

* Select these FastPass+ choices after you've used your first three.

EPCOT
MUST-SEE ATTRACTIONS PLAN

FP : **Make these your FastPass+ Selections**

1. **Test Track** (Future World East)
2. **Mission: SPACE** *FP* (Future World East)
3. **Spaceship Earth** (Future World East)
4. **The Seas with Nemo & Friends** *FP* (Future World West)
5. **SeaBase aquarium** (Future World West)
6. **Journey into Imagination with Figment** (Future World West)
7. **Frozen Ever After** *FP* (Norway)

LUNCH: Via Napoli (Italy) or Garden Grill (The Land)

8. **Gran Fiesta Tour** (Mexico)
9. **Soarin'*** (Future World West)
10. **Living with the Land** (Future World West)
11. **Epcot Forever**

BONUS (OR SUBSTITUTIONS)
12. **Disney & Pixar Short Film Festival** (Future World West)

* Select these FastPass+ choices after you've used your first three.

DISNEY'S HOLLYWOOD STUDIOS
MUST-SEE ATTRACTIONS PLAN

FP : **Make these your FastPass+ Selections**

1. **Star Wars: Rise of the Resistance** (Star Wars: Galaxy's Edge)
2. **Explore Star Wars: Galaxy's Edge**
3. **Muppet*Vision 3D** *FP* (Grand Avenue)
4. **Star Tours – The Adventures Continue** *FP* (Echo Lake)
5. **Mickey & Minnie's Runaway Railway** *FP* (Hollywood Boulevard)
6. **Indiana Jones Epic Stunt Spectacular!** (Echo Lake)

LUNCH: Sci-Fi Dine-In Theater Restaurant or Docking Bay 7

7. **Twilight Zone Tower of Terror*** (Sunset Boulevard)
8. **Lightning McQueen's Racing Academy** (Sunset Boulevard)
9. **Rock 'n' Roller Coaster*** (Sunset Boulevard)
10. **Toy Story Mania!*** (Toy Story Land)
11. **Slinky Dog Dash*** (Toy Story Land)
12. **Alien Swirling Saucers** (Toy Story Land)
13. **Millennium Falcon: Smugglers Run** (Star Wars: Galaxy's Edge)
14. **Fantasmic!** (Sunset Boulevard)

* *Select these FastPass+ choices after you've used your first three.*

Note: Disney's Hollywood Studios will likely change its FastPass+ selection process in 2020 to include Star Wars: Galaxy's Edge attractions.

DISNEY'S ANIMAL KINGDOM
MUST-SEE ATTRACTIONS PLAN

FP : **Make these your FastPass+ Selections**

1. **DINOSAUR** (DinoLand U.S.A.)
2. **Primeval Whirl** (DinoLand U.S.A.)
3. **Expedition Everest** *FP* (Asia)
4. **Maharajah Jungle Trek** (Asia)
5. **Kilimanjaro Safaris** *FP* (Africa)
6. **Gorilla Falls Exploration Trail** (Africa)
7. **Kali River Rapids** (Asia)
8. **AVATAR Flight of Passage** *FP* (Pandora)

LUNCH: Satu'li Canteen or Yak & Yeti Restaurant

9. **Na'vi River Journey*** (Pandora)
10. **Festival of the Lion King** (Asia)
11. **It's Tough to Be a Bug!** (Discovery Island)
12. **Finding Nemo–The Musical*** (DinoLand U.S.A.)
13. **Rivers of Light: We Are One** (Asia)

BONUS (OR SUBSTITUTIONS)
14. **Wildlife Express Train** (Africa)
15. **The Animation Experience** (Rafiki's Planet Watch)

* Select these FastPass+ choices after you've used your first three.

VISITING WITH KIDS

MAGIC KINGDOM
VISITING WITH KIDS PLAN

FP : **Make these your FastPass+ Selections**

1. **Magic Kingdom Welcome Show** △ (Cinderella Castle)
2. **Tomorrowland Speedway** (Tomorrowland)
3. **Peter Pan's Flight** *FP* △ (Fantasyland)
4. **"it's a small world"** △ (Fantasyland)
5. **Seven Dwarfs Mine Train** *FP* (Fantasyland)
6. **Swiss Family Treehouse** (Adventureland)
7. **Pirates of the Caribbean** *FP* (Adventureland)

LUNCH: Be Our Guest Restaurant

8. **Under the Sea~Journey of the Little Mermaid** △ (Fantasyland)
9. **Princess Fairytale Hall*** △ (Fantasyland)
10. **Festival of Fantasy Parade** △ (Fantasyland)
11. **Dumbo the Flying Elephant** △ (Fantasyland)
12. **Mad Tea Party** (Fantasyland)
13. **The Many Adventures of Winnie the Pooh** △ (Fantasyland)
14. **Mickey's PhilharMagic** (Fantasyland)
15. **Jungle Cruise*** (Adventureland)
16. **Magic Kingdom Fireworks** (Main Street, U.S.A.)

BONUS (OR SUBSTITUTIONS)
17. **Walt Disney World Railroad** (Fantasyland to Frontierland)
18. **Buzz Lightyear's Space Ranger Spin** (Tomorrowland)
19. **The Barnstormer (junior roller coaster)** * (Fantasyland)

* Select these FastPass+ choices after you've used your first three.
△ Attractions recommended for Ages 3-5.

EPCOT
VISITING WITH KIDS PLAN

FP : **Make these your FastPass+ Selections**

1. **Test Track** Ø (Future World East)
2. **Spaceship Earth** *FP* (Future World East)
3. **The Seas with Nemo & Friends** *FP* △ (Future World West)
4. **SeaBase aquarium** △ (Future World West)
5. **Journey into Imagination with Figment** (Future World West)
6. **Frozen Ever After** *FP* △ (Norway)

LUNCH: Via Napoli (Italy) or Garden Grill (The Land)

7. **Gran Fiesta Tour** △ (Mexico)
8. **Soarin'*** (Future World West)
9. **Living with the Land** (Future World West)
10. **Epcot Forever**

BONUS (OR SUBSTITUTIONS)
11. ***Disney & Pixar Short Film Festival*** (Future World West)

* Select these FastPass+ choices after you've used your first three.
△ Attractions recommended for Ages 3-5.
Ø <u>Not</u> for ages 3-5.

DISNEY'S HOLLYWOOD STUDIOS
VISITING WITH KIDS PLAN

FP : Make these your FastPass+ Selections

1. **Star Wars: Rise of the Resistance** Ø (Star Wars: Galaxy's Edge)
2. **Explore Star Wars: Galaxy's Edge**
3. **Muppet*Vision 3D** *FP* (Grand Avenue)
4. **Star Tours – The Adventures Continue** *FP* (Echo Lake)
5. **For the First Time in Forever: A Frozen Sing-Along Celebration** △ (Echo Lake)
6. **Lightning McQueen's Racing Academy** (Sunset Boulevard)

LUNCH: Sci-Fi Dine-In Theater Restaurant or Woody's Lunch Box

7. **Mickey & Minnie's Runaway Railway** *FP* (Hollywood Boulevard)
8. **Toy Story Mania!*** (Toy Story Land)
9. **Slinky Dog Dash*** (Toy Story Land)
10. **Alien Swirling Saucers** (Toy Story Land)
11. **Millennium Falcon: Smugglers Run** Ø (Star Wars: Galaxy's Edge)
12. **Fantasmic!** (Sunset Boulevard)

 * *Select these FastPass+ choices after you've used your first three.*
△ *Attractions recommended for Ages 3-5.*
Ø *Not recommended for Ages 3-5.*

DISNEY'S ANIMAL KINGDOM
VISITING WITH KIDS PLAN

FP : **Make these your FastPass+ Selections**

1. **Na'vi River Journey** *FP* △ (Pandora)
2. **It's Tough to Be a Bug!** △ (Discovery Island)
3. **Kilimanjaro Safaris** *FP* △ (Africa)
4. **Gorilla Falls Exploration Trail** (Africa)
5. **Wildlife Express Train** (Africa)
6. **Conservation Station** (Rafiki's Planet Watch)
7. **Habitat Habit!** (Rafiki's Planet Watch)

LUNCH: Rainforest Cafe or Satu'li Canteen

8. **Maharajah Jungle Trek** (Asia)
9. **UP! A Great Bird Adventure** △ (Asia)
10. **DINOSAUR** ∅ (DinoLand U.S.A.)
11. **Finding Nemo–The Musical** *FP* △ (DinoLand U.S.A.)
12. **Kali River Rapids*** ∅ (Asia)
13. **Rivers of Light: We Are One** (Asia)

BONUS (OR SUBSTITUTIONS)
14. **AVATAR Flight of Passage** (Pandora)

* *Select these FastPass+ choices after you've used your first three.*
△ *Attractions recommended for Ages 3-5.*
∅ <u>*Not*</u> *recommended for Ages 3-5.*

THRILL RIDES

MAGIC KINGDOM
THRILL RIDE ATTRACTION PLAN

FP : **Make these your FastPass+ Selections**

1. **Magic Kingdom Welcome Show** (Cinderella Castle)
2. **Pirates of the Caribbean** (Adventureland)
3. **The Haunted Mansion** (Liberty Square)
4. **Seven Dwarfs Mine Train** *FP* (Fantasyland)
5. **The Barnstormer** (Fantasyland)
6. **Space Mountain** *FP* (Tomorrowland)
7. **Big Thunder Mountain Railroad** *FP* (Frontierland)

LUNCH: Be Our Guest Restaurant or Liberty Tree Tavern

8. **Splash Mountain*** (Frontierland)
9. **Mad Tea Party** (Fantasyland)
10. **Jungle Cruise*** (Adventureland)
11. **Magic Kingdom Fireworks** (Main Street, U.S.A.)

BONUS:
12. **Peter Pan's Flight** (Fantasyland)
13. **Transit Authority PeopleMover** (Tomorrowland)

* Select these FastPass+ choices after you've used your first three.

EPCOT & HOLLYWOOD STUDIOS
THRILL RIDE ATTRACTION PLAN

Note: If you're only looking to experience thrill rides, we recommend purchasing a Park Hopper for Epcot and Hollywood Studios. There aren't enough thrill rides to fill a day, so combining them works best.

FP : **Make these your FastPass+ Selections**

Start at Disney's Hollywood Studios
1. **Star Wars: Rise of the Resistance** (Star Wars: Galaxy's Edge)
2. **Millennium Falcon: Smugglers Run** (Star Wars: Galaxy's Edge)
3. **Indiana Jones Epic Stunt Spectacular!** *FP* (Echo Lake)
4. **Star Tours – The Adventures Continue** *FP* (Echo Lake)
5. **Twilight Zone Tower of Terror** *FP* (Sunset Boulevard)
6. **Slinky Dog Dash** (Toy Story Land)
7. **Rock 'n' Roller Coaster** (Sunset Boulevard)

LUNCH: Star Wars Cantina or Sci-Fi Dine-In Theater Restaurant

Head to Epcot
8. **Test Track*** ◊ (Future World)
9. **Mission: SPACE** (Future World)
10. **Frozen Ever After*** (World Showcase - Norway)
11. **Soarin'*** (Future World - The Land)
12. **Epcot Forever**

BONUS (OR SUBSTITUTIONS)
13. **Alien Swirling Saucers** (Toy Story Land)
14. **Toy Story Mania!** (Toy Story Land)

* *Select these FastPass+ choices after you've used your first three.*
◊ *If you are unable to get a FastPass, consider the Single Rider Line*

DISNEY'S ANIMAL KINGDOM
THRILL RIDE ATTRACTION PLAN

Note: Since Animal Kingdom is more than just rides, we've also included some jungle treks to this plan. The exotic animals, after all, are one of the main reasons for visiting this theme park. Thrill riders usually attempt to experience Expedition Everest and Avatar Flight of Passage more than once during a day to Animal Kingdom.

FP : **Make these your FastPass+ Selections**

1. **AVATAR Flight of Passage** *FP* (Pandora)
2. **DINOSAUR** (DinoLand U.S.A.)
3. **Expedition Everest** *FP* (Asia)
4. **Maharajah Jungle Trek** (Asia)
5. **Kilimanjaro Safaris** *FP* (Africa)
6. **Gorilla Falls Exploration Trail** (Africa)
7. **Kali River Rapids** (Asia)
8. **Na'vi River Journey*** (Pandora)
9. **Primeval Whirl*** (DinoLand U.S.A.)

* Select these FastPass+ choices after you've used your first three.

CUSTOM RIDE LIST

Theme Park: _____

Names: _____   _____

          _____   _____

          _____   _____

1. _____
2. _____
3. _____
4. _____
5. _____
6. _____
7. _____
8. _____
9. _____
10. _____
11. _____
12. _____
13. _____
14. _____
15. _____
16. _____
17. _____
18. _____
19. _____
20. _____
21. _____
22. _____
23. _____
24. _____

CUSTOM RIDE LIST

Theme Park: _____

Names: _____   _____

_____   _____

_____   _____

1. _____
2. _____
3. _____
4. _____
5. _____
6. _____
7. _____
8. _____
9. _____
10. _____
11. _____
12. _____
13. _____
14. _____
15. _____
16. _____
17. _____
18. _____
19. _____
20. _____
21. _____
22. _____
23. _____
24. _____

CUSTOM RIDE LIST

Theme Park: _____

Names: _____   _____

_____   _____

_____   _____

1. _____
2. _____
3. _____
4. _____
5. _____
6. _____
7. _____
8. _____
9. _____
10. _____
11. _____
12. _____
13. _____
14. _____
15. _____
16. _____
17. _____
18. _____
19. _____
20. _____
21. _____
22. _____
23. _____
24. _____

CUSTOM RIDE LIST

Theme Park: _____

Names: _____   _____

_____   _____

_____   _____

1. _____
2. _____
3. _____
4. _____
5. _____
6. _____
7. _____
8. _____
9. _____
10. _____
11. _____
12. _____
13. _____
14. _____
15. _____
16. _____
17. _____
18. _____
19. _____
20. _____
21. _____
22. _____
23. _____
24. _____

VACATION CHECKLIST

- ❏ Park Tickets
- ❏ Ride List
- ❏ ID
- ❏ Credit Card / Cash
- ❏ Hotel Address
- ❏ Phone (and charging cable)
- ❏ Sunscreen
- ❏ Toiletries: toothbrush, toothpaste, etc.
- ❏ Swimsuit
- ❏ Jacket
- ❏ Comfortable Shoes
- ❏ Plastic bag for cellphone (water rides)
- ❏ Snacks
- ❏ Water bottles (if you aren't flying)
- ❏ Backpack or bag
- ❏ Restaurant Reservations
- ❏ Walt Disney World 2020 by Magic Guidebooks
- ❏ _____
- ❏ _____
- ❏ _____
- ❏ _____
- ❏ _____
- ❏ _____
- ❏ _____
- ❏ _____
- ❏ _____
- ❏ _____

CONCLUSION
AND THE FUTURE OF THE
WALT DISNEY WORLD RESORT

The Walt Disney World Resort is always changing and so will this guide throughout the years. As noted at the beginning, we are Walt Disney World fans and we've created this book from our firsthand knowledge and research. We sincerely hope that our tips have been a valuable resource for your vacation.

With Walt Disney World's 50th anniversary arriving in 2021, several new and exciting attractions are on their way. The Magic Kingdom will open a *Tron*-themed roller coaster and Epcot will undergo the largest theme park reimagining in Disney history! A Guardians of the Galaxy: Cosmic Rewind indoor roller coaster, a reimagined Spaceship Earth, a Moana attraction, and a Mary Poppins-themed area are all headed to Epcot in the coming years.

We're often asked what we'd like from the Walt Disney World Resort and our answer is always: more! Disney is committed to bringing its beloved franchises to its theme parks, including Star Wars, Marvel, and Pixar. So keep an eye out for even more changes!

To conclude, we'd like to invite you to stay connected with us. Our website, **magicguidebooks.com**, is packed with new information and details about Walt Disney World, Disneyland, and the Universal Studios theme parks! Small parts of this book may need updating due to WDW's constant changes, however, we keep you up to speed to improve your vacation experience.

Happy and safe travels!
Magic Guidebooks

INDEX

C

D

E

F

G

J

K

L

M

N

O

P

Q

R

T

U

DINING NOTE: We did not index most restaurants as they are available in alphabetical order by resort area in the Dining Guide chapter.

GET UPDATES!
Walt Disney World 2020

Sign up for our FREE e-mail list!

www.magicguidebooks.com/signup
(We will never spam your information)

Wishing you a magical vacation!
Magic Guidebooks

Was this book helpful?

If so, can you please leave us a quick review on
Amazon.com?

Your reviews GREATLY help us out!
THANK YOU!

Wishing you a magical vacation!
Magic Guidebooks

Printed in Great Britain
by Amazon